General Sports English
体育通识英语

1

主　编：刘振忠　荣　晶

分册主编：李　雷　陈丽江　王　芳　冯　政

分册副主编：周　栋　于宝英　刘　明　曹　阳

编　者（按姓氏音序排列）：

艾险峰	白毅鸿	陈玉玲	杜思民	关景军	贾　京
金兴玉	兰　洁	李　晖	李继东	李丽辉	李文静
李晓玲	刘占辉	吕红梅	马国义	马敏卿	潘　浪
乔李平	任　峰	苏如峰	孙　斌	汤印超	田国立
徐美云	杨　勇	张国杰	张文钰	赵春丽	郑　辉
钟圆成	周　静				

清华大学出版社

北　京

内 容 简 介

《体育通识英语》系列教材按体育运动项目和体育基础知识两大板块编写，共三册。本书为第一册，主题内容涵盖田径运动、体操、球类运动、舞蹈、武术及其他传统体育项目，共29课，每课包括听说、阅读、练习、规则与概念、拓展阅读五个板块。教材视角多元，涵盖与体育项目和赛事相关的各个领域；活动设计贴近专业实践，切合体育专业学生学习需求。教材以语言学习、专业学习与通识教育三者融合为编写理念，具有广泛性、通识性、实用性的特点。

本书可作为体育类专业大学英语拓展课程教材，也适用于体育外事专业、英语专业（体育英语方向）的基础阶段体育英语教学。

图书在版编目（CIP）数据

体育通识英语. 1 / 刘振忠，荣晶主编；李雷等分册主编. —北京：清华大学
出版社，2016（2019.9重印）
　ISBN 978-7-302-45610-0

Ⅰ. ①体… Ⅱ. ①刘… ②荣… ③李… Ⅲ. ①体育–英语–高等学校–教材
Ⅳ. ①G807.4

中国版本图书馆CIP数据核字（2016）第270219号

责任编辑：曹诗悦
封面设计：平　原
责任校对：王凤芝
责任印制：杨　艳

出版发行：清华大学出版社
　　　网　　　址：http:// www.tup.com.cn，http:// www.wqbook.com
　　　地　　　址：北京清华大学学研大厦A座　　　邮　　编：100084
　　　社 总 机：010-62770175　　　邮　　购：010-62786544
　　　投稿与读者服务：010-62776969，c-service@tup.tsinghua.edu.cn
　　　质量反馈：010-62772015，zhiliang@tup.tsinghua.edu.cn
印 装 者：三河市铭诚印务有限公司
经　　销：全国新华书店
开　　本：185mm×260mm　　　印　　张：20　　　字　　数：324千字
版　　次：2016年10月第1版　　　印　　次：2019年9月第7次印刷
定　　价：69.00元

产品编号：070235-03

前言

一、教材编写背景

英语作为全球目前使用最广泛的语言，在世界舞台上扮演着重要角色。进入 21 世纪以来，随着体育竞赛、体育科技与文化交流活动的日趋国际化，体育英语日渐呈现出其特有的地位与作用。为适应体育全球化的发展趋势，我们迫切需要加强体育英语教育，让更多的人掌握一些体育通识英语知识，这是摆在我们面前的重要教育任务。

培养学生的英语应用能力，使之能够在今后的工作和社会交往中有效使用英语进行口头和书面语言交流，同时具备一定的专业学术英语能力，这是目前我国高校大学英语教育的改革趋势与必然要求。体育院校作为体育人才培养的重要阵地，长期以来遵循以基础英语教育为主的教学模式，缺乏渗透体育元素的专业英语教育熏陶。转变教学观念，优化教学内容，构建融合型的英语教学体系势在必行。在确保提高学生英语水平的基础上，融入一些体育英语知识，将对提高英语教育教学质量、培养高素质应用型体育人才起到积极的促进作用。

基于体育领域的人才需求以及体育院校大学英语教学的需要，遵循语言学习规律，结合体育专业学生特点、认知风格和学习策略，本书编写组历经三年多的策划、调研、编写与试用修改，现正式出版《体育通识英语》。

二、教材编写依据

教材以体育专业学生为教学对象，考虑到体育院校学生的英语基础、认知水平、学习策略和教学需要，依据"因材施教、学以致用"的教学理念，确定了"易学、易懂、易用"的编写思路。在选篇收集过程中，编者从国内外体育类书报杂志与网站的众多文章中精心筛选出了鲜活生动、富含体育元素、满足学生专业兴趣诉求的素材。选文题材广泛，涵盖与体育相关的各个领域，包括体育运动的起源与发展、体育项目现状、竞赛方式与相关规则、体育组织与机构、运动场地与设备、体育运动常识、人体科学知识、体育产业与管理、明星成长与培养等方面的知识与信息，让学习者提高英语交流能力与学术水平，同时感受体育魅力。

教材以即将颁布的《大学英语教学指南》中的基础目标与提高目标为指导，以提高学生体育英语能力为目标，借助丰富多样的素材、灵活实用的教学资源，让学生了解体育英语的语言特点，掌握体育项目技战术和体育赛事的专业术语及相关表达。在此基础上，使学生能听懂有关体育项目的一般对话，能够在对外体育文化活动与国际赛事上使用英语进行一般的交流，能够在国内外体育机构从事一般性的口译工作；使学生能读懂一般性题材的体育资料，承担基本的体育信息与资料的翻译工作；使学生能完成一般性写作，承担体育赛事的新闻采访、编稿与简要解说工作；使学生能够顺利通过裁判员等级英语考试，并能够在体育产业相关领域从事翻译、服务、组织和管理工作。

教材采取以语言学习、专业学习与通识教育三者并重的教育理念。以英语语言知识传授为导引，设有听说与阅读板块，配有写作和翻译练习，全面提高学生英语语言能力；以语言技能训练为基础，每单元设有与主题相关的情景对话和交互性任务，切合专业学习特点；以学习体育英语知识带动英语学习，任务活动包括口头、书面与亲身实践等形式，满足课堂内外的语言实践。

综上，本教材将语言学习、专业学习和通识教育有机结合，使学生在提升语言能力的同时拓展专业视野，提升人文素养，以适应未来职业发展的需要。

三、教材特色

《体育通识英语》系列教程是一套理念新颖、视野开阔、内容丰富、以专业内容为依托的新型教材，具有广泛性、通识性、易懂性、实用性等特点。编者结合体育专业英语教学与学习的需求以及体育专业的特性，对每一个话题进行了仔细讨论、推敲，在知识体系、主题内容、练习活动、授课讲解、结构设计、适用范围等方面呈现出以下特色。

知识体系：从体育专业英语教学实际出发，教材将体育文化、体育历史、体育科技、赛事规则、场馆器材、运动科学、体育产业等知识与语言材料相结合，各单元设计了听说、情景对话、讨论、阅读、词汇、写作和拓展练习等活动，并配有详细的参考译文，构成完整的知识体系。知识分布点面结合，难度适中，贴近实际，让学习者所学的知识和技能在实际工作、学习、生活中得到应用。

主题内容：教材内容丰富多彩，综合了体育学科下各专业的特点。素材视角多元，贴近专业教学需要，切合学生知识需求。材料涉及体育文化、赛事组织、体育机构、体育项目发展、竞赛规则和体育明星等，覆盖体育教育、运动训练、社会体育、运动人体科学、民族传统武术、体育艺术等体育本科专业以及运动人体科学、运动康复、体育管理、体育新闻等体育相关专业。

练习活动：教材将英语学习与体育知识相结合，练习多样，突出实践性。对话贴近实际，选取课堂、训练、赛场、治疗、旅途等场景，使学生亲身参与，创新思考，学以致用。此外，练习内容还包括体育解说词编写、赛事服务实践报告、体育信息与资料整理、赛事采访提纲撰写等写作训练，有效检测学生的知识运用能力。

授课讲解：根据课程计划安排、学生英语水平和专业特点，教师可灵活选取不同单元作为教学材料，采取多样的教学方法，激发学生体育英语学习的兴趣。教师可运用现代多媒体手段，有趣地、系统地传授体育英语知识，发挥教材特色，实现因材施教、寓教于乐，以培养学生英语应用能力、自主学习能力和体育文化素养。根据实际需要，教师可以选择三册同时进行教学，也可分册进行，其中有些内容可作为学生课外阅读材料。

结构设计：教材框架、体例、结构设计新颖，具有一定的独特性。设计充分考虑到体育项目所涵盖的知识面，每一单元涉及的知识点既相辅相成，又相对独立，符合体育专业学生的知识需求、学习习惯与审美情趣。教材内容与艺术设计有机结合，创设了轻松的学习环境，更能激发学生的学习兴趣。

适用范围：教材适用于英语专业（体育英语方向）、体育外事专业基础阶段的体育英语教学，可作为体育类专业以及体育院校的新闻、管理、心理、体育人文等学科的大学英语教材，以拓宽学生知识面，培养学生语言能力、学习能力与思维能力；也可作为大学英语课程的拓展训练材料以及体育类专业英语选修课程教材，以开阔学生视野，培养学生跨文化体育英语交流能力；同时也可作为具有一定英语水平的教练员、运动员、体育工作者和体育爱好者的参考读物。

四、教材结构

《体育通识英语》按体育运动项目和体育基础知识两大板块编写，共三册。第一、二册主题为各类体育运动项目，涉及奥运比赛项目与非奥运项目共 50 个。第一册分为田径运动、体操、球类运动、舞蹈、武术及其他传统体育项目五个章节，共 29 课；第二册分为水上运动、冰上运动、雪上运动、重竞技及其他项目、户外与休闲文体活动，五个章节，共 23 课；第三册主题为体育基础知识，分为体育基本形态、体育组织与管理、运动场地与设备、运动生物科学基础、体育产业与管理，五个章节，共 17 课。

每课的基本结构为：

第一部分：听说（Listening and Speaking）。根据单元主题设计一段情景对话，配有录音 *。此外，还配有相关的词汇和短语列表及交互性口语活动。

第二部分：阅读（Reading）。包括两篇短文，内容为与单元主题相关的体育运动项目、体育知识、体育赛事或组织机构的介绍。每篇文章后均配有相关的词汇和短语列表、体育专业词汇表，以及相应的思考题，引导学生加深对赛事项目的了解。

第三部分：练习（Exercises）。任务形式灵活，突出实践性，形式包括观赛讨论、赛事策划、资料翻译等口笔头活动，帮助学生巩固本单元所学内容。

第四部分：概念与常识（Rules and Concepts）/ 概念与常识（Definitions and General Knowledge）。简要介绍各项比赛的竞技规则或体育运动中涉及的相关概念，供学习者了解和参考。

第五部分：拓展阅读（Further Reading）。介绍与单元主题相关的体育名人、历史事件等，帮助学习者完善知识结构，提高学习兴趣。

五、编写团队

《体育通识英语》教程由河北体育学院张绰庵策划、刘振忠组织编写，由全国 22 所院校的教师共同参与完成。编写小组由英语教师和具有国内外大赛裁判、体育教学训练经历且理论功底深厚的体育教师组成，确保了英文编写和中文参考译文两方面的准确性、语言地道性和任务真实性，保证了教材质量。

---

*　与本教程配套的音频，可从清华大学出版社的资源库里免费下载。请学习者访问 ftp://ftp.tup.tsinghua.edu.cn/，进入"外语分社"目录下，选择所需的音频文件。

　　《体育通识英语》教程在策划和编写过程中还得到了国内兄弟院校老师们的指导和帮助，教材中凝聚了他们的经验和智慧。国内英语专家以及外籍教师 Carl Malcolm Ramsey（英）、Brin Kerr（美）、Jason Robert Cormier（加）、Coleman Javier Dixon（美）对教材的英文部分进行了详细、认真地审阅，并提出了许多建设性建议。在此一并表示衷心感谢！

　　《体育通识英语》系列教程涉及体育项目多，内容覆盖面广，编写难度较大，由于编写时间紧迫，加之编者水平有限，书中不当之处在所难免，敬请各位专家、学者和读者批评指正，以便再版更正。

《体育通识英语》编写组

2016 年 1 月

Contents

Contents

1

Chapter

Athletics

Lesson 1

Athletics

Activity 1

🎧 Listen to the following conversation, and then work in pairs to act it out.

(The theme of today's P.E. theory class is athletics. After explaining why athletics is the mother of sports, Mr. Zhang answered some questions from John.)

A: Why is track and field called the mother of sports?

B: Because it serves as the basis for other sports through its training methods. These methods are widely used to develop physique. Track and field can also improve one's quality of training.

A: OK. So, what are the categories of track and field?

B: As you might expect, there are just three: field events, track events and all-round events.

A: Got it. I'm also curious about its history. Can you tell me about the earliest track and field competition?

B: Sure. It was the straight sprint, which was held at the first ancient Olympic Games in the Olympic Village of Greece in 776 B.C.

A: Oh, I see.

Words and Expressions

athletics /æθˈletɪks/ *n.* 田径运动

track and field 田径

basis /ˈbeɪsɪs/ *n.* 基础

physique /fɪˈziːk/ *n.* 体格；身体素质

category /ˈkætəgərɪ/ *n.* 分类，种类

field event 田赛项目

track event 径赛项目

all-round event 全能项目

2

Activity 2

👤 Work in pairs and answer the following questions.

> Question 1: Why is track and field an important index of a country's sports
> level?
>
> Question 2: What are the distinct characteristics of track and field?

Part Two Reading

Passage 1

Directions: Read the passage about track and field events in the world and discuss the following questions with your partner.

Track and Field Events in the World

Olympic track and field events are the earliest track and field events in the world. Men's events started at the first modern Olympic Games in 1896, while women were first allowed to compete in track and field in the 9th Olympics in 1928. Track and field events are the basis of the Olympic Games and can fully embody the Olympic motto of "faster, higher, stronger". The Olympic Games which are held every four years urge better records and eminent athletes.

The IAAF World Championships in Athletics were first held in Helsinki, Finland in 1983. From then on they were held every four years, the year before Olympic Games and then every two years after the third one in 1991. It comprised track and field competitions plus the marathon and race walking competitions. In effect, the IAAF World Championships in Athletics serve as an inspection of the Olympic Games. The IAAF World Indoor Championships in Athletics have been held every two years since 1985 and they are the only world championship that consist of solely track and field events.

The marathon is a long-distance running event with an official distance of 42.195 kilometers. Having been highly supported by Pierre de Coubertin, it has been listed as an Olympic event since 1896. The women's marathon was not introduced into the Olympics until the 1984 Los Angeles Olympic Games. It is usually run as a road race, with either a round-trip of the starting point and terminal point at the same place, or

with a one-way route of the starting and the terminal point at different places. There is no world record with the marathon, which only announces the best result. Nowadays, more than 500 marathons are held throughout the world each year, with the vast majority of competitors being recreational athletes as larger marathons can have tens of thousands of participants.

Words and Expressions

embody /ɪmˈbɒdɪ/ v. 体现，使具体化

motto /ˈmɒtəʊ/ n. 格言，座右铭

urge /ɜːdʒ/ v. 驱策，推进，力促

eminent /ˈemɪnənt/ adj. 杰出的

comprise /kəmˈpraɪz/ v. 包含，由……组成

inspection /ɪnˈspekʃn/ n. 视察，检查

round-trip adj. 双程的，往返的

terminal /ˈtɜːmɪnl/ n. 终点

route /ruːt/ n. 路线

announce /əˈnaʊns/ v. 宣告，宣布

Sports Terms

faster, higher, stronger 更快、更高、更强

IAAF World Championships in Athletics 世界田径锦标赛

marathon /ˈmærəθən/ n. 马拉松赛

race walking 竞走

IAAF World Indoor Championships in Athletics 世界室内田径锦标赛

road race 公路赛

Questions:

1. When were track and field events listed as Olympic events?

2. What's the purpose of the IAAF World Championships in Athletics?

3. How long is the whole journey of a marathon?

Passage 2

Directions: Read the passage about the International Association of Athletics Federations and discuss the following questions with your partner.

International Association of Athletics Federations

The International Association of Athletics Federations (IAAF) was founded as the worldwide governing body for the sport of track and field on 17 July, 1912 in Stockholm, Sweden. Since October 1993, it has been headquartered in Monaco. The IAAF's current president is Sebastian Coe of the United Kindom. It has a total of 215 member federations divided into six area associations in Europe, Asia, Africa, Central and North America, South America and Oceania. English, French, Russian, German and Spanish are the working languages. There are five professional committees, namely, the Technology Committee, Women Committee, Walking Committee, Cross-country Race Committee and Medical Committee. The Chinese Athletic Association (CAA) joined the IAAF in 1978.

The IAAF organizes many major athletics competitions worldwide. Track and field contests make up the majority of events in the Olympics, which occur every four years. Other major international competitions for track and field include the IAAF World Championships in Athletics, the IAAF World Cup, the IAAF World Junior Championships in Athletics, the IAAF World Youth Championships in Athletics, the IAAF World Indoor Championships in Athletics, the IAAF Golden League, the International Association of Athletics Finals, the IAAF Super Grand Prix, the IAAF Grand Prix and the IAAF Grand Prix Final.

Words and Expressions

Oceania /ˌəʊsɪˈɑːnɪə/ n. 大洋洲	majority /məˈdʒɒrətɪ/ n. 多数，大多数

Sports Terms

International Association of Athletics Federations (IAAF) 国际田径联合会（国际田联）

Chinese Athletic Association (CAA) 中国田径协会（中国田联）

IAAF World Junior Championships in Athletics 世界青年田径锦标赛

IAAF World Youth Championships in Athletics 世界少年田径锦标赛

IAAF Golden League 国际田联黄金联赛

International Association of Athletics Finals 国际田径协会决赛

IAAF Super Grand Prix 国际田联超级大奖赛

IAAF Grand Prix 国际田联大奖赛

IAAF Grand Prix Final 国际田联大奖赛总决赛

Questions:

1. Where is the IAAF's headquarters? Who is the current president?
2. What are the working languages of the IAAF?
3. What competitions does the IAAF mainly organize?

Part Three Exercises

Directions: Do the following exercises.

1. Give a brief account of the development of track and field in China from the perspective of the National Games.
2. Talk about your favorite track and field event, and give your reasons.

Part Four Rules and Concepts

1. Track and field is a sport which combines sprints, middle- and long-distance events, hurdling, relay races, steeplechase, marathon, high jump, pole vault, long jump, triple jump, shot put, discus, hammer, javelin, race walking, and all-round events.

2. The events of track and field include the following:

Men's
- Running
  100, 200, 400, 800, 1500, 5000, and 10,000 meters
  3000 meters steeplechase
  marathon
  4×100 meters and 4×400 meters relays
  110 meters hurdles and 400 meters hurdles
  20 km and 50 km race walk
- Jumping
  high jump
  long jump
  pole vault
  triple jump

- Throwing
  javelin
  shot put
  hammer
  discus
- Decathlon

Women's

- Running
  100, 200, 400, 800, 1500, and 3000 meters
  marathon
  4×100 meters and 4×400 meters relays
  100 meters hurdles and 400 meters hurdles
- Jumping
  high jump
  long jump
- Throwing
  javelin
  shot put
  discus
- Heptathlon

3. Every athlete shall be provided with two bibs which, during the competition, shall be worn visibly on the breast and back, except in the high jump and pole vault, where one bib may be worn on the breast or back only. The bib shall correspond with the number allocated to the athlete on the start list or in the program.

4. If an athlete is disqualified in an event for an infringement of any rule, reference shall be made in the official results to the rule which has been infringed. Such disqualification from an event shall not prevent an athlete from taking part in any further event in that competition.

5. Disqualification from an event for unsportsmanlike or improper behavior shall render the athlete liable to disqualification by the referee from participation in all further events.

6. In a match where the result is to be determined by the scoring of points, the method of scoring shall be agreed upon by all the competing countries before the start of the match.

7. All races shall be started by the report of the starter's gun fired upwards after he has ascertained that athletes are steady and in the correct starting position.

8. In a relay race, the baton shall be carried by hand throughout the race. Athletes are not permitted to wear gloves or to place substances on their hands in order to obtain a better grip of the baton.

9. In all relay races, the baton shall be passed within the take-over zone. Passing of the baton outside of the take-over zone shall result in disqualification.

10. Each athlete may have practice trials at the competition area before the beginning of the event. In the case of throwing events, the practice trials will be in draw order and always under the supervision of the judges.

Part Five Further Reading

Usain Bolt

Usain Bolt, a Jamaican sprinter, is an Olympic gold medalist. He is the first man to hold both the 100 meters and 200 meters world records since fully automatic time became mandatory and also holds the world record as a part of the 4×100 meters relay. Bolt is the most successful sprinter in history.

Bolt turned professional in 2004, beginning with the CARIFTA Games in Bermuda. He became the first junior sprinter to run the 200 meters in under twenty seconds, taking the world junior record outright with a time of 19.93 s. On 31 May 2008, Bolt set a new 100-meter world record at the Reebok Grand Prix held in New York City with a time of 9.72 s, and this was his first world record.

At the 2008 Beijing Olympics, Bolt gained worldwide popularity for his double sprint victory in world record times. In the Olympic 100-meter final, Bolt broke new ground, winning in 9.69 s. This was an improvement upon his own world record. Then in the 200-meter final, he set a new world and Olympic record of 19.30 s. In the 4×100 meters relay, his team claimed the championship by breaking the world record with a time of 37.10 s. The feat made him the first sprinter to win 100 meters, 200 meters and 4×100 meters relay and break world records simultaneously at the same Olympics. At the 2012 London Olympics, he successfully defended the gold medal in 100 meters, 200 meters and 4×100 meters relay. At the 2016 Rio Olympics, Bolt yet again won consecutive gold medals in 100 meters, 200 meters and 4×100 meters relay. With that, Bolt obtained the "triple-triple", three sprinting gold medals in three consecutive Olympics.

A nine-time Olympic gold medalist and an eleven-time world champion, his achievements in sprinting have earned him the nickname "Lightning Bolt". His awards include the IAAF World Athlete of the Year, Track & Field Athlete of the Year, and Laureus World Sportsman of the Year (three times). Bolt has stated that he intends to retire from athletics after the 2017 World Championships.

Lesson 2 Running

Part One Listening and Speaking

Activity 1

🎧 Listen to the following conversation, and then work in pairs to act it out.

(In a P.E. class, Mr. Zhang is answering the questions from John about running.)

A: Mr. Zhang, what is track?

B: Track is a running sport that involves calculating grades by time.

A: How many track events are there?

B: Quite a few. There's sprint, middle- and long-distance race, steeplechase, hurdling, relay, and marathon.

A: What does short distance running refer to?

B: Generally it includes 50 meters, 100 meters, 200 meters, 400 meters, 4×100 meters and 4×400 meters relay.

A: I see. And what about jogging? Is it considered an aerobic exercise program?

B: Yes, absolutely. Frequent jogging can efficiently improve your body's functions. It's especially good for building endurance.

A: Really? That's great! I like jogging, so I will get up early tomorrow morning to jog.

B: Very good!

Words and Expressions

track /træk/ *n.* 跑道；小径；径赛	**jogging** /'dʒɒgɪŋ/ *n.* 慢跑
calculate /'kælkjuleɪt/ *v.* 计算	**aerobic** /eə'rəʊbɪk/ *adj.* 有氧的
sprint /sprɪnt/ *n. & v.* 短跑	**efficiently** /ɪ'fɪʃntlɪ/ *adv.* 有效地，高效地
steeplechase /'stiːpltʃeɪs/ *n.* 障碍赛跑	
hurdling /'hɜːdlɪŋ/ *n.* 跨栏赛跑	**endurance** /ɪn'djʊərəns/ *n.* 耐力；忍耐
relay /'riːleɪ/ *n.* 接力	

Activity 2

👤 Work in pairs and answer the following questions.

Question 1: A sprinter injured his right foot during his training and fell down. How should he deal with the pain?

Question 2: Do you know the world records of the men's and women's 100 meters race?

Part Two Reading

Passage 1

Directions: Read the passage about running and discuss the following questions with your partner.

Running

In ancient times, ancestors in the struggle with nature and wild animals developed all sorts of survival skills such as running and jumping while crossing swamps, plains, streams and other obstacles in order to survive. With the development of human beings and society, the original track and field sports formed. Running competitions have probably existed for most of the human history and were a key part of the ancient Olympic Games as well as the modern Olympics. Nowadays, competitive running events make up the core of the sport of athletics.

Running is characterized by the contact of one foot with the ground or both feet off the ground alternatively, and involves repetitive scissors action of two legs. Running races, or track events, are contests to determine which of the competitors is able to run a certain distance in the shortest time. It is split into events divided by distance and sometimes includes permutations such as the obstacles in steeplechase and hurdles. Events are usually grouped into several classes, each requiring substantially different athletic strengths and involving different tactics, training methods, and types of competitors.

Sprint methodology involves start, acceleration, steady running and bursting for the tape. Runners' performance is measured by the start response speed, accelerative ability, the distance at the fastest speed and the quality of accomplishing maneuvers. Middle- and long-distance events and marathon are aimed at developing one's endurance. In running, runners will likely feel chest tightness and shortness of breath due to the lag-behind oxygen supply to the needs of the muscle activity, which is called "extremes". So middle- and long-distance trainers should notice it and adopt the step-by-step approach.

Words and Expressions

survival /sə'vaɪvl/ *n.* 生存，幸存

obstacle /'ɒbstəkl/ *n.* 障碍（物）

survive /sə'vaɪv/ *v.* 生存

core /kɔː(r)/ *n.* 核心

alternatively /ɔːl'tɜːnətɪvlɪ/ *adv.* 二者择一地；交替地

repetitive /rɪ'petətɪv/ *adj.* 重复的

split /splɪt/ *v.* 劈开，分裂

substantially /səb'stænʃəlɪ/ *adv.* 实质上；大体上

tactic /'tæktɪk/ *n.* 策略，技巧

acceleration /əkˌselə'reɪʃn/ *n.* 加速，提速

burst /bɜːst/ *v.* 爆发

tape /teɪp/ *n.* 终点线；磁带

maneuver /mə'nuːvə(r)/ *n.* 控制

chest /tʃest/ *n.* 胸部

oxygen /'ɒksɪdʒən/ *n.* 氧气

Questions:

1. How does running come into being?

2. How are running events divided?

3. What is the "extreme" in middle- and long-distance running?

Passage 2

Directions: Read the passage about hurdling and discuss the following questions with your partner.

Hurdling

Hurdling, originating in England, developed from a game in which goatherds stepped over the sheepfold. It is an act of running and jumping over an obstacle at speed. In the sport of athletics, hurdling forms the basis of a number of track and field events which are highly specialized forms of obstacle racing. In these events, a series of barriers known as hurdles are set at precisely measured heights and distances which each athlete must pass by running over.

The most prominent hurdling events are the 110 meters hurdles for men, 100 meters hurdles for women, and 400 meters hurdles (both sexes)—these three distances are all contested at the Summer Olympics and the World Championships in Athletics. The two shorter distances take place on the straight of a running track, while the 400-meter version covers one whole lap of a standard oval track. Hurdling races are also part of all-round events contests, including the decathlon and heptathlon.

In track races, hurdles are normally between 68 cm and 107 cm in height, and vary depending on the age and gender of the hurdler. In international competitions, men compete for high hurdles with a height of 106.7 cm, while women compete for low hurdles with a height of 83.8 cm. The number of hurdles is ten, which is the same in men's and women's races.

Words and Expressions

at speed 迅速地，高速地

barrier /ˈbærɪə(r)/ n. 障碍

prominent /ˈprɒmɪnənt/ adj. 突出的；卓越的

contest /kənˈtest/ v. 争夺；竞赛

n. 比赛，竞赛

lap /læp/ n. 一圈

standard /ˈstændəd/ adj. 标准的

oval /ˈəʊvl/ adj. 椭圆的

hurdler /ˈhɜːdlə(r)/ n. 跨栏选手

Sports Terms

110 meters hurdles for men 男子 110 米栏

100 meters hurdles for women 女子 100 米栏

400 meters hurdles 400 米栏

decathlon /dɪˈkæθlən/ n. 十项全能

heptathlon /hepˈtæθlən/ n. 七项全能

Questions:

1. Do you know the origin of hurdling?

2. What are the most prominent hurdling events?

3. What are the differences between men's and women's hurdling events?

Part Three Exercises

Directions: Do the following exercises.

1. Make a morning running plan for a middle school student.

2. Attend or watch a marathon and write an essay in no less than 250 words.

Part Four Rules and Concepts

1. A standardized track event takes place on one length of a 400-meter track.

2. The passwords for short-distance running are "On your marks", "Set" and "Fire", while passwords for middle- and long-distance running are "On your marks" and "Fire".

3. "On your marks" should be prolonged. "Set" should be smooth and short.

4. A recall starter sounds if the offending athlete is guilty of a false start.

5. The finish judge determines the order of competitors in a sprint race and is responsible for recording the order of athletes on each lane at the finish line. A middle- and long-distance judge records the number of cycles each competitor has run to judge places in a competition.

6. The checking judge is responsible for checking the site and equipment before the competition and the violation of the rules during the competition, i.e., whether an athlete remains in the same lane from start to finish in a short-distance competition, whether an athlete is pushed or forced out by another person in a middle- and long-distance competition, or whether the hurdle is knocked over by hand or foot.

7. Any competing athlete who jostles or obstructs another athlete, so as to impede his progress, shall be liable to disqualification from that event.

8. An athlete, after voluntarily leaving the track, shall not be allowed to continue in the race.

9. In any race decided on the basis of the distance covered in a fixed period of time, the starter shall fire the gun exactly one minute before the end of the race to warn athletes and judges that the race is nearing its end.

10. An athlete shall be disqualified, if he doesn't jump each hurdle, or he trails his foot or leg below the horizontal plane of the top of any hurdle at the instance of clearance; or in the opinion of the referee deliberately knocked down any hurdle.

Part Five Further Reading

Liu Xiang

Liu Xiang is a retired Chinese 110 meter hurdler. He is an Olympic gold medalist and world champion. His 2004 Olympic gold medal was the first in a men's track and field event for China.

Liu is one of China's most successful athletes and has emerged as a cultural icon. He is the only male athlete in history to have achieved the "triple crown" in the 110-meter hurdles event: world record holder, world champion and Olympic champion.

At the 2004 Athens Olympics, he won the Olympic final to take the gold medal in a world record-equaling time of 12.91 s, matching the feat of Colin Jackson. In 2006, Liu set a new world record in the 110 meters hurdles at the Super Grand Prix in Lausanne, Switzerland, with a time of 12.88 s. He was the favorite to win another gold in the 110 meters hurdles at the Beijing Olympics, but he had to withdraw from competition at the last moment after a false start and aggravating a previously unrevealed injury. Again a gold medal favourite in the 110 meters hurdles at the London Olympics, he pulled his Achilles tendon attempting to clear the first hurdle in the heats and thus ended his journey in London empty-handed.

On 7 April, 2015, he made a retirement announcement on his Sina Weibo officially ending his sports career.

Lesson 3 Jumping

Part One Listening and Speaking

Activity 1

🎧 Listen to the following conversation, and then work in pairs to act it out.

(In a P.E. theory lesson, Mr. Zhang is answering some questions about jumping events from his students.)

A: Mr. Zhang, what is a field event?

B: As you may have guessed, it's a sport that takes place on a field. It's measured by height and distance, and generally it includes jumping and throwing events.

A: What are all the jumping events?

B: Long jump and high jump. But more concretely, long jump, triple jump, high jump and pole vault.

A: What are the most commonly used techniques for high jumpers?

B: The back style, or fosbury flop, is most common.

A: Do you know any famous Chinese jumpers?

B: The first one that comes to my mind is Zhu Jianhua. He was once a world record holder.

A: Really? What was his personal best?

B: 2.39 meters.

A: Wow. Such a great height!

Words and Expressions

measure /'meʒə(r)/ *v.* 衡量

concretely /'kɒnkriːtlɪ/ *adv.* 具体地

triple /'trɪpl/ *adj.* 三倍的

triple jump 三级跳远

long jump 跳远

high jump 跳高

pole vault 撑竿跳高

personal best 个人最好成绩

Activity 2

👤 Work in pairs and answer the following questions.

Question 1: Do you like jumping events? What is your favorite jumping event?

Question 2: Are you going to participate in the long jump or high jump at your school's sports meeting? Why or why not?

Part Two Reading

Passage 1

Direction: Read the passage about jumping and discuss the following questions with your partner.

Jumping

Jumping is an event where the objective is to clear both vertical and horizontal obstacles, and hence is relevant to height and distance. Jumping events in the Olympic Games include the long jump, triple jump, high jump and pole vault.

The high jump and long jump are subject to the same motion law, but also have respective characteristics in kinetics and dynamics. The long jump techniques include approach, take-off, action in the air and landing. The air postures include the squat, swan style and stride-in-air flight. The triple jump with the approach as its start, is a field event in which athletes take three horizontal jumps in one continuous sequence, referred to as hop, skip and jump. This event requires good physical quality and high technique to ensure the excellent performance.

The bar-clearing techniques of the high jump include scissors, roll, straddle and fosbury flop, of which the fosbury flop is the most representative one, containing approach, take-off, clearing the bar and landing. Compared with those mentioned above, the pole vault is unique in kinetics and techniques, which can be divided into the following phases: grip approach, plant, swing up, extension, turn, stretch and clearing the bar.

Words and Expressions

vertical /'vɜːtɪkl/ *adj.* 垂直的

horizontal /ˌhɒrɪ'zɒntl/ *adj.* 水平的

relevant /'reləvənt/ *adj.* 相关的

subject /'sʌbdʒɪkt/ *v.* 使……经历，遭受

motion law 运动定律

kinetics /kɪ'netɪks/ *n.* 运动学

dynamics /daɪ'næmɪks/ *n.* 动力学

continuous /kən'tɪnjuəs/ *adj.* 连续的

sequence /'siːkwəns/ *n.* 顺序，次序

representative /ˌreprɪ'zentətɪv/ *adj.* 代表性的

Sports Terms

approach /ə'prəʊtʃ/ *n.* 助跑

take-off /teɪk-ɒf/ *n.* 起跳

landing /'lændɪŋ/ *n.* 落地

air posture 空中姿势

squat /skwɒt/ *n.* 蹲踞式

swan style 挺身式

stride-in-air flight 走步式

hop /hɒp/ *n.* 单足跳

skip /skɪp/ *n.* 跨步跳

bar-clearing 过杆

scissors /'sɪzəz/ *n.* 剪式

roll /rəʊl/ *n.* 滚式

straddle /'strædl/ *n.* 俯卧式

fosbury flop 背越式

grip approach 持竿助跑

plant /plɑːnt/ *n.* 插竿准备与插竿

swing up 上摆

extension /ɪk'stenʃn/ *n.* 拉引

turn /tɜːn/ *n.* 转体

stretch /stretʃ/ *n.* 蹬伸

Questions:

1. What are the four phrases of long jump techniques?

2. What is the triple jump?

3. What do bar-clearing techniques of the high jump include?

Passage 2

Direction: Read the passage about pole vault and discuss the following questions with your partner.

Pole Vault

The pole vault is a field event for men and women. Vaulting with poles was originally a practical method for crossing natural obstacles such as ditches and marshes. The men's pole vault has been a medal event at every modern Olympics, while the women's competition was first held in Sydney in 2000.

In this event, competitors sprint along a runway of 40 meters to 50 meters carrying a long, flexible pole which they plant in a box and use to lever themselves over a crossbar suspended above the ground between two uprights. The height of the crossbar is raised after every round and athletes are eliminated from the competition if they fail three consecutive jump attempts. Officials are on hand to oversee the contest and adjust the height of the crossbar.

An opening bar height and a sequence of incremental heights is decided by an official, and vaulters choose the height at which they wish to enter the competition. Athletes take turns to vault. If two or more of them cleared the bar, the height would be increased by the agreed distance, typically 5 cm or 15 cm. Vaulters may decline to jump at a certain height and wait to try at a higher one. If at the end of the competition there is a tie, the number of failures is taken into consideration. If two or more vaulters have the same number of misses, there may be a sudden-death jump-off.

Words and Expressions

pole /pəʊl/ *n.* 杆，竿

runway /'rʌnweɪ/ *n.* 跑道

lever /levə/ *v.* 用杠杆撬

suspend /sə'spend/ *v.* 悬浮，悬置

eliminate /ɪ'lɪmɪneɪt/ *v.* 除名；排除

consecutive /kən'sekjətɪv/ *adj.* 连续的

oversee /ˌəʊvə'siː/ *v.* 监督，审查

adjust /ə'dʒʌst/ *v.* 调节，调整

incremental /ˌɪŋkrə'mentl/ *adj.* 增加的

decline /dɪ'klaɪn/ *v.* 谢绝，婉拒

tie /taɪ/ *n.* 打成平手，平局

sudden-death *adj.* 决赛中一分或一球定胜负的

vault /vɔːlt/ v. （用手或竿支撑）跳跃   **upright** /'ʌpraɪt/ n. 支柱，跳高架

crossbar /'krɒsbɑː(r)/ n. 横杆   **vaulter** /vɔːltə/ n. 撑竿跳高运动员

Questions:

1. When was the pole vault event first held at the Olympic Games?

2. What's the height that the crossbar will be raised if two or more vaulters clear the bar in a pole vault event?

3. What should be done if there is a tie at the end of a pole vault event?

Part Three Exercises

Directions: Do the following exercises.

1. Write a dialogue between the athletes and the referees in a triple jump event with 20 competitors participating.

2. Which jumping event do you like to engage in? Discuss your reasons.

Part Four Rules and Concepts

1. The athletes compete in the designated field site, and jump according to the displayed number. A white flag is raised following a successful attempt; otherwise, a red one is raised.

2. At the end of a high jump or pole vault competition, the eliminated jumpers have to leave the field guided by the referee.

3. Each athlete in the long jump and triple jump has three attempts, while the top eight have another three attempts in a reverse order. If the athletes are fewer than eight in number, each will have to jump six times.

4. A preliminary round shall be held in field events in which the number of athletes is too large to allow the competition to be conducted satisfactorily in a single round (final).

5. When a preliminary round is held, all athletes shall compete in, and qualify through that round. The accomplished performance in a preliminary round shall not be considered as part of the final.

6. If, for any reason, an athlete is hampered in a trial, the referee shall have the authority to award him a substitute trial.

7. Each athlete shall be credited with the best result of all his trial.

8. Before the competition begins, the chief judge shall announce to the athletes the starting height and the subsequent heights to which the bar will be raised at the end of each trial.

9. All measurements shall be made in whole centimeters, perpendicularly from the ground to the lowest part of the upper side of the bar.

10. Athletes must jump at every height until a decision is reached or until all of the athletes concerned decide not to jump further.

Part Five Further Reading

Javier Sotomayor

Javier Sotomayor is a Cuban former track and field athlete, who specialized in the high jump and is the current world record holder. The 1992 Olympic champion, he was the dominant high jumper of the 1990s; his personal best of 2.45 m (8.04 ft) makes him the only person ever to have cleared eight feet.

He was a two-time gold medalist at the IAAF World Championships in Athletics and also won two silver medals at the competition. At the IAAF World Indoor Championships he won four gold medals between 1989 and 1999. In addition, he won three straight titles at the Pan American Games from 1987 to 1995. He is regarded as the best high jumper of all time.

Cuban boycotts the Olympics in 1984 and 1988 and an injury in 1996 cost him chances at additional Olympic medals, but he returned to win the silver medal at the 2000 Olympics in Sydney. Sotomayor retired in 2001.

Lesson 4

Throwing

Listening and Speaking

Activity 1

🎧 Listen to the following conversation, and then work in pairs to act it out.

(In a throwing lesson, Mr. Zhang answered some questions from John about the classification of throwing and the skills of shot put.)

A: Mr. Zhang, would you mind giving me some more details about throwing? For example, what events does it include?

B: Hey, John. Sure. There are just four: shot put, discus, javelin and hammer.

A: OK. So, how about shot put? What techniques can be used in official competitions?

B: Currently, two putting styles are often used by shot put competitors: the glide and the spin.

A: Oh. How big is the throwing circle?

B: Competitors take their throw from inside a marked circle of 2.135 meters in diameter.

A: Do you know how much the apparatus weighs?

B: Men's shot weighs 7.26 kg and the women's 4 kg.

A: I see, thank you very much!

B: No problem.

Words and Expressions

throwing /ˈθrəʊɪŋ/ *n.* 投掷运动

shot put 铅球

discus /ˈdɪskəs/ *n.* 铁饼

javelin /ˈdʒævlɪn/ *n.* 标枪

hammer /ˈhæmə(r)/ *n.* 链球

glide /glaɪd/ *n.* 背向滑步式

spin /spɪn/ *n.* 旋转式

diameter /daɪˈæmɪtə(r)/ *n.* 直径

apparatus /ˌæpəˈreɪtəs/ *n.* 器械；装置，器具

weigh /weɪ/ *v.* 称重

Activity 2

Work in pairs and answer the following questions.

Question 1: Why do female shot putters prefer the glide style to the spin style?

Question 2: Do you think that the discus throw and the hammer throw are dangerous events? Why or why not?

Part Two Reading

Passage 1

Direction: Read the passage about hammer throw and discuss the following questions with your partner.

Hammer Throw

The hammer throw is one of the four throwing events in regular track and field competitions, along with the discus throw, shot put and javelin. It originates in Scotland. The handle of a hammer was once made of wood, but now it is of steel chain to allow for handy throwing. The hammer throw is one of the oldest competitions at the Olympic Games, first included at the 1900 Games in Paris, France. Its history since the late 1960s and legacy prior to inclusion in the Olympics have been dominated by European and Eastern European influence, which has affected interest in the event in other parts of the world.

While the men's hammer throw has been part of the Olympics since 1900, the International Association of Athletics Federations did not start ratifying women's marks until 1995. The women's hammer throw was first included in the Olympics at the 2000 Summer Games in Sydney, Australia, after having been included in the World Championships a year earlier. The men's hammer world record is held by Yuriy Sedykh, who threw 86.74 meters at the 1986 European Athletics Championships in Stuttgart. The world record for the women's hammer throw is held by Anita Włodarczyk, who threw 82.98 meters.

Although commonly thought of as a strength event, technical advancements in the last thirty years have evolved the hammer throw competition to a point where more focus is on speed in order to achieve a maximum distance. The throwing motion involves about two swings from a stationary position, then three, four or very rarely five rotations of the body in a circular motion using a complicated heel-toe movement of the foot. The ball moves in a circular path, gradually increasing in velocity with each turn with the high point of the hammer ball toward the target sector and the low point at the back of the circle. The thrower finally releases the ball from the front of the circle.

Words and Expressions

handle /ˈhændl/ n. 手柄

steel chain 钢链

handy /ˈhændɪ/ adj. 便利的；容易取得的

legacy /ˈlegəsɪ/ n. 遗产

prior to 在……之前，优先

dominate /ˈdɒmɪneɪt/ v. 控制，支配

ratify /ˈrætɪfaɪ/ v. 认可，许可

evolve /ɪˈvɒlv/ v. 进化，发展

swing /swɪŋ/ n. 摇摆，摆动

stationary /ˈsteɪʃənrɪ/ adj. 固定的，静止的

rotation /rəʊˈteɪʃn/ n. 旋转

circular /ˈsɜːkjələ(r)/ adj. 圆形的，环形的

heel /hiːl/ n. 脚后跟

toe /təʊ/ n. 脚趾

velocity /vəˈlɒsətɪ/ n. 速度

target /ˈtaːgɪt/ n. 目标；靶子

release /rɪˈliːs/ v. 发射；释放

Questions:

1. When was the hammer throw event first held at the Olympics?

2. Who are the holders of the men's and women's hammer throw world record respectively?

3. Can you explain the throwing motion of a hammer?

Direction: Read the passage about discus throw and discuss the following questions with your partner.

Discus Throw

The discus throw is a track and field event in which an athlete throws a heavy disc—called a discus—in an attempt to mark a farther distance than his competitors. It is an ancient sport, as demonstrated by the fifth-century-B.C. Myron statue, *Discobolus*. Originally part of the pentathlon in the ancient Olympics, the discus throw now stands alone as a field event in its own right. The men's competition has been a part of the modern Summer Olympic Games since the first Olympiad in 1896. The women's competition was added to the Olympic program in the 1928 Games.

The rules of the competition for discus are virtually identical to those of shot put, except that the circle is larger, a stop board is not used and there are no formal rules concerning how the discus is to be thrown. There are mainly four technical links of handling, ready position, initial movement in the circle, final force and balance of the body after the throwing. The technique of discus throwing is quite difficult to master and requires a lot of experience to get right, thus most top throwers are 30 years of age or older.

To make a throw, the competitor starts in a circle of 2.5 m in diameter, which is recessed in a concrete pad by 20 mm. The thrower typically takes an initial stance facing away from the direction of the throw. He then spins anticlockwise (for right-handers) around one and a half times through the circle to build momentum, then releases his throw. The discus must land within a 34.92-degree sector. The distance from the front edge of the circle to where the discus has landed is measured, and distances are rounded down to the nearest centimeter. The competitor's best throw from the allocated number of throws, typically three to six, is recorded, and the competitor who legally throws the discus the farthest is declared the winner. Ties are broken by determining which thrower has the longer second-best throw.

Words and Expressions

disc /dɪsk/ n. 圆盘

demonstrate /'demənstreɪt/ v. 证明

statue /'stætʃuː/ n. 雕塑，雕像

virtually /'vɜːtʃuəlɪ/ adv. 事实上，几乎

identical /aɪ'dentɪkl/ adj. 一致的，一模一样的

pad /pæd/ n. 垫

stance /stæns/ n. 姿势；位置

face away from 把脸转向别处

anticlockwise /ˌæntɪ'klɒkwaɪz/ adj. & adv. 逆时针的 / 地

momentum /mə'mentəm/ n. 动力，势头

sector /'sektə(r)/ n. 扇形；区域

edge /edʒ/ n. 边缘，边界

round down to 四舍五入到，精确到

allocated /'æləkeɪtɪd/ adj. 分配的，指派的

Sports Terms

stop board 抵趾板

handing /'hændɪŋ/ n. 握法

ready position 预备姿势

initial movement in the circle 预摆旋转

final force 最后用力

balance of the body 身体平衡

Questions:

1. How far does the discus throw date back to?

2. When was the discus throw first listed in the Olympic Games?

3. How is the distance measured in discus throw events?

Part Three Exercises

Directions: Do the following exercises.

1. Write a press release entitled "Gliding Javelin" in no less than 250 words.

2. Write an inspirational story about a shot-putter that you like.

Part Four Rules and Concepts

1. The Olympic throwing event is made up of six rounds. Javelin is the only one that is permitted in the run-up.

2. Each event just reports the best record. After the first three rounds, the top eight reach the following three rounds of the final; the order of appearance is according to the reverse order of the first three rounds. If there is a draw, the second best grades can be referred to. If there is still a tie, then in the same way, the third best grades can be consulted on, and so on and so forth.

3. Athletes must finish their throws in one minute.

4. Athletes can also give up halfway and start over on the condition that throwing doesn't occur or that the athlete's feet haven't stepped out of the throwing circle or track.

5. The diameter of the throwing circle for shot put and hammer events is 2.135 meters, while that for discus is 2.5 meters. There is a runway in the field of javelin with two boundary lines, at the end of which a curve is equipped with metal or wood. The athlete must throw the javelin behind the back of the curve.

6. There is a touch-down zone for the four throwing events which is a flat area with marks by cinder or lawn.

7. The shot is usually made of iron or brass, and must have a smooth surface with a diameter between 110 mm and 130 mm in the men's event and 95 mm and 110 mm in the women's event.

8. The discus, made by metal or wood, is a heavy lenticular disc with a weight of 2 kg and a diameter of 219 mm for the men's event, and a weight of 1 kg and a diameter of 180 mm for the women's program.

9. In international competitions, men throw a javelin between 2.6 m and 2.7 m in length and 800 g in weight, and women throw a javelin between 2.2 m and 2.3 m in length and 600 g in weight.

10. The hammer consists of a ball, a steel wire, and a roughly triangular-shaped handle. The men's hammer weighs 7.26 kg and measures 121.3 cm in length. The women's hammer weighs 4 kg and is 119.4 cm in length.

Part Five Further Reading

Li Meisu

Li Meisu is a famous female shot put athlete, the champion of the Asian Games and the Asian Championships.

She joined the Hebei Track and Field Team in 1976. Thanks to strict systematic training, her achievements gradually increased in scale. She won the championship and broke the record of women's shot put at the 9th Asian Games in 1982. She set new historical records six times and came in the fifth place with a result of 17.96 meters at the Los Angeles Olympic Games in 1984. She came in the second place at the Asian Athletics Championships in 1985. She broke Asian records twice and won a gold medal at the 6th National Games and was ranked the seventh place in the world in 1987. She again set a new Asian record in 1988, which she achieved with a result of 21.76 meters, and won a bronze medal at the 24th Olympic Games with the record of 21.06 meters, fulfilling the zero breakthrough in winning medals in a throwing event. This was the one and only medal won by Asian athletes in track and field events at that Olympic Games.

Lesson 5

All-round Events

Activity 1

🎧 Listen to the following conversation, and then work in pairs to act it out.

(In a P.E. theory class, Mr. Zhang explained what all-round events are and he also answered some questions from his student John.)

A: Mr. Zhang, what are all-round events?

B: That refers to a collection of track and field events. So, as you would expect, it's made up of runs, jumps and throws, and it calculates results by scoring.

A: How many all-round events are there in the Olympic Games?

B: There are just two, including men's decathlon and women's heptathlon.

A: What are the disciplines of men's decathlon?

B: "Deca-" means ten, so the event consists of ten different track and field competitions: 100-, 400-, and 1500-meter runs, 110-meter hurdles, javelin, discus throws, shot put, pole vault, high jump, and long jump.

A: What are the disciplines of women's heptathlon?

B: "Hepta-" means seven, so there are seven competitions: the long jump, high jump, 200- and 800-meter runs, 100-meter hurdles, shot put and javelin.

A: I got it. Thank you, sir!

Words and Expressions

scoring /ˈskɔː(r)ɪŋ/ *n.* 评分

discipline /ˈdɪsɪplɪn/ *n.* 项目

Activity 2

👤 Work in pairs and answer the following questions.

> Question 1: Can extensional motion after training help clear up lactic acid accumulation and relieve fatigue?
>
> Question 2: The pentathlon was admitted into the fifth modern Olympic Games, but was canceled later on. Do you know these five events included in the pentathlon? What are they?

Part Two Reading

Passage 1

Direction: Read the passage about men's decathlon and discuss the following questions with your partner.

Men's Decathlon

The decathlon is an all-event in athletics consisting of ten track and field events. It is contested mainly by male athletes, while female athletes typically compete in the heptathlon.

The event developed from the ancient pentathlon. Pentathlon competitions were held at the ancient Greek Olympics. It involved five disciplines—long jump, discus throw, javelin throw, sprint and a wrestling match. Introduced in Olympia in 708 BC, the competition was extremely popular for many centuries. By the sixth century BC, pentathlons had also become part of religious games. A ten-event competition known as the "all-around" or "all-round" championship, similar to the modern decathlon, was first contested at the United States Amateur Championships in 1884 and reached a consistent form by 1890. An all-around event was held at the 1904 Summer Olympics, though whether it was an official Olympic event has been disputed. The modern decathlon first appeared at the fifth Olympic Games held in Stockholm, Sweden in 1912.

Traditionally, the title of "World's Greatest Athlete" has been given to the person who wins the Olympic decathlon. This began when King Gustav V of Sweden told Jim Thorpe, "You, Sir, are the world's greatest athlete" after Thorpe won the decathlon at the Stockholm Olympics in 1912.

Events are held over two consecutive days and the winners are determined by their combined performance in all events. Decathlon consists of four track events, three jumps and three throw events, which are held in the order below.

Day 1	**Day 2**
• 100 meters	• 110 meters hurdles
• Long jump	• Discus throw
• Shot put	• Pole vault
• High jump	• Javelin throw
• 400 meters	• 1500 meters

Words and Expressions

consistent /kən'sɪstənt/ *adj.* 始终如一的，一致的

dispute /dɪ'spjuːt/ *v.* 争论；怀疑

Sports Terms

pentathlon /pen'tæθlən/ *n.* 五项全能

Questions:

1. When did the modern decathlon first appear in the Olympic Games?

2. What physical abilities are required by the decathletes?

3. What events does the decathlon include? Can you list them in order?

Passage 2

Direction: Read the passage about women's heptathlon and discuss the following questions with your partner.

Women's Heptathlon

A heptathlon is a track and field combined events made up of seven disciplines.

There are two heptathlons—the women's heptathlon and the men's—composed of different disciplines. The men's heptathlon is older and is held indoors, while the women's is held outdoors and was introduced in the 1980s.

Started in Russia in 1923 and approved by the IAAF in 1948, the women's pentathlon first occurred at the 1964 Olympic Games and was changed into heptathlon in 1984, which is held in the order below.

Day 1	Day 2
• 100 meters hurdles	• Long jump
• High jump	• Javelin
• Shot put	• 800 meters
• 200 meters	

The women's heptathlon is a contest of superior difficulty. Only those athletes who highlight their strengths on the basis of all-round improvement with long-time systematic training can achieve excellent results.

In recent years, some women's decathlon competitions have been conducted, consisting of the same events as the men's competition in a slightly different order, and the IAAF has begun keeping records for it, but the heptathlon remains the only championship-level combined event for women.

Words and Expressions

be made up of 由……组成，由……构成

compose /kəm'pəʊz/ v. 组成

superior /suː'pɪərɪə(r)/ adj. 优秀的，出众的；上层的；高级的

highlight /'haɪlaɪt/ v. 突出，彰显

strength /streŋθ/ n. 能力；力量

systematic /ˌsɪstə'mætɪk/ adj. 系统的

excellent /'eksələnt/ adj. 杰出的，极好的

conduct /kən'dʌkt/ v. 进行，实施

consist of 由……组成

slightly /'slaɪtlɪ/ adv. 稍微地，轻微地

championship-level 世锦赛级别的

Questions:

1. When did the women's heptathlon first appear in the Olympic Games?

2. When was the women's pentathlon approved by the IAAF?

3. What events does the heptathlon include? Can you list them in order?

Part Three Exercises

Directions: Do the following exercises.

1. Which do you like best in the all-round events? Explain your reasons.
2. Why are the winners of all-round events so highly regarded?

Part Four Rules and Concepts

1. Winners of the decathlon and pentathlon are determined by their combined performance in all events. Performance is judged based on a scoring system in each event.
2. There is a complex scoring system to ensure that the athlete who does well in all events can gain the highest score. Scores of each event are decided by an evaluation standard which is set by the Olympic Games. A table is fixed according to world records for the calculation of results. The total points are summations of results in each round.
3. There are special provisions for all-round competitions besides individual rules.
4. False starts are allowed no more than three times in track events. Athletes will be disqualified from the match but they can still take part in other events.
5. The total points and place in the competition are cancelled for those who give up in any event.
6. Records are admitted when the wind speed is under 4 m/s. If the wind speed is above 4 m/s, all-round records are unofficial.
7. Electric and manual timing are both allowed in all-round track competitions, but mixed use is forbidden.
8. In each competing team, there should be four or more than four contestants. Fewer than three is not permitted.
9. At the end of each competition, the referee will lead the athletes to have a rest in the prescribed lounge.
10. The order of the five events which comprise the modern pentathlon is fencing, swimming, shooting, cross-country running and riding.

Part Five Further Reading

Ashton Eaton

Ashton James Eaton is an American decathlete and two-time Olympic champion, who holds the world record in both the decathlon and indoor heptathlon events, and is the second decathlete (after Roman Šebrle) to break the 9000-point barrier, with 9039 points. On 29 August, 2015, he beat his own world record with a score of 9045 points.

In 2011, Eaton won the first international medal of his career, a silver, in the decathlon at the 2011 World Championships. The following year, Eaton broke his own world record in the heptathlon with a result of 6645 points at the 2012 World Indoor Championships held in Turkey, and then broke the world record in the decathlon at the Olympic Trials with a total of 9039 points. After setting the world record, Eaton won the gold medal at the 2012 Summer Olympics in London with absolute advantage. He successfully defended his Olympic title in Rio 2016 by winning the decathlon gold medal and tying the Olympic record.

Race Walking

Part One Listening and Speaking

Activity 1

🎧 Listen to the following conversation, and then work in pairs to act it out.

(While John was exercising on the playground, a group of walkers passing by him were practicing their techniques. Out of curiosity, John walked up to Mr. Zhang and asked him some questions about race walking.)

A: Mr. Zhang, can you tell me about race walking?

B: Race walking is a progression of steps taken, where the walker makes contact with the ground using one foot or two feet.

A: Oh. I've watched it before, and it almost looks like running. What's the main difference between race walking and running?

B: In race walking, one foot should always appear to be in contact with the ground. Both feet off the ground is not allowed, whereas in running it is permitted.

A: Are there different types of race walking?

B: The only major difference is the location. It can take place over fields or roads.

A: How are they classified by distance?

B: Men's 20 km and 50 km road walks, and women's 20 km road walks, and 5 km and 10 km field walks.

A: I see, thanks.

B: My pleasure. If you want to try it out, let me know and I'll give you more info.

Words and Expressions

curiosity /ˌkjʊərɪ'ɒsətɪ/ *n.* 好奇	take place 发生
progression /prə'greʃn/ *n.* 前进；连续	road walk 公路竞走
off the ground 腾空	field walk 场地竞走

Activity 2

👥 Work in pairs and answer the following questions.

Question 1: What is the difference between race walking and ordinary walking? Discuss with your partner based on your knowledge of the motion law of race walking.

Question 2: In race walking training, how should one increase the flexibility of the hip?

Part Two Reading

Passage 1

Direction: Read the passage about race walking events and discuss the following questions with your partner.

Race Walking Events

Race walking, known as a long-distance athletic event, takes place on fields and roads.

There are two race walking distances contested at the Summer Olympics: the 20 kilometers race walk (men and women) and 50 kilometers race walk (men only). Both are held as road events. The biennial IAAF World Championships in Athletics also features the same three events. The IAAF World Race Walking Cup, first held in 1961, is a stand-alone global competition for the discipline and it has 10 kilometers race walks for junior athletes, in addition to the Olympic-standard events. The IAAF World Indoor Championships featured 5000 meters and 3000 meters race walk variations, but these were discontinued after 1993. Top level athletics championships and games typically feature 20 kilometers race walking events.

In race walking competitions, athletes are governed by two rules. Firstly, it is regulated that the athlete's back toe cannot leave the ground until the heel of the front foot has touched. Violation of this rule is known as "loss of contact". Secondly, it is required that the supporting leg must straighten from the point of contact with the ground and remain straightened until the body passes directly over it. These rules are judged by the unaided human eye. Athletes regularly lose contact for a few milliseconds per stride, which can be caught on film, but such a short flight phase is said to be undetectable to the human eye.

Words and Expressions

biennial /baɪ'enɪəl/ *adj.* 两年一次的

feature /'fiːtʃə(r)/ *v.* 以……为特色

stand-alone *adj.* 独立的

Olympic-standard 奥林匹克标准的

variation /ˌveərɪ'eɪʃn/ *n.* 变体

violation /ˌvaɪə'leɪʃn/ *n.* 违反，违背

straighten /'streɪtn/ *v.* 蹬直，伸直

millisecond /'mɪlɪsekənd/ *n.* 毫秒

stride /straɪd/ *n.* 大步；跨一步；（距离）步幅

undetectable /ˌʌndɪ'tektəbl/ *adj.* 无法察觉的，发现不了的

Sports Terms

IAAF World Race Walking Cup 国际田联竞走世界杯

loss of contact 离地

flight phase 腾空阶段

Questions:

1. What are the international competitions for race walking?

2. What do Olympic-standard race walking events include?

3. What are the two rules that govern race walking?

Passage 2

Direction: Read the passage about the origin of race walking and discuss the following questions with your partner.

The Origin of Race Walking

Originating in the United Kingdom, race walking (road walk) is a track and field sporting event based on traveling.

The sport emerged from a British culture of long-distance competitive walking in the 19th century, known as pedestrianism. In 1866, Britain organized the first English Amateur Walking Championships, the distance being 7 miles (11.26 kilometers), which was won by John Chambers. In 1880, the first Championships Meeting was held by the Amateur Athletics Association in England, which symbolized the birth of modern athletics.

By the end of the 19th century, intercity walking was popular in Europe, and it soon spread to countries in North America, Oceania and other regions later on. At the beginning, race walking took an ordinary or arbitrary form, without strict technical rules. In 1906, race walking was introduced at the intercalated Olympics in Greece.

Race walking differs from ordinary walking in its features such as: quick stride frequency, big length of stride, powerful swing of arm, strong sense of rhythm, and heel-first contact with the ground. Advanced race walking technique should minimize the time spent supporting one leg or two legs, so as not to affect the length of step, and speed up shearing action of the legs. These are helpful in improving a competitor's race performance.

Words and Expressions

pedestrianism /pəˈdestrɪənɪzm/ *n.* 步行，徒步旅行

amateur /ˈæmətə(r)/ *adj.* 业余的

symbolize /ˈsɪmbəlaɪz/ *v.* 象征

intercity /ˌɪntəˈsɪtɪ/ *adj.* 城市间的

ordinary /ˈɔːdɪnərɪ/ *adj.* 普通的

arbitrary /ˈɑːbɪtrərɪ/ *adj.* 任意的

frequency /ˈfriːkwənsɪ/ *n.* 频率

minimize /ˈmɪnɪmaɪz/ *v.* 使最小

speed up 加速

Questions:

1. Where did race walking originate?

2. What was the first race walking competition? When and where was it held?

3. What are the features of race walking?

Part Three Exercises

Directions: Do the following exercises.

1. Watch a walking race on TV and then discuss it with your classmates.
2. Lay out a morning walking plan for yourself and propose concrete requirements.

Part Four Rules and Concepts

1. According to competition rules, race walking can be carried out on the road or on a 400 m track field.

2. In race walking over 20 km, a beverage supply station is set up every 5 km. Beverages consist of orange juice and strong tea with sugar, glucose and a little salt added.

3. In race walking, one foot should always appear to be in contact with the ground. The foreleg must be straightened for at least one moment when in the vertical upright position, not bent at the knee.

4. There shall be six to nine judges. According to the rules, the judging decisions are made through the human eye, without the help of any equipment.

5. Any judge may caution competitors violating rules by their yellow card and submit the record to the Chief Judge at the conclusion to the event.

6. When in the opinion of a judge, a competitor fails to comply with the definition of race walking, the judge should approach the competitor to caution him with a white card and record.

7. The red card is to be used if the competitor violates the rules twice. The infraction will be marked on the red card. When three red cards are issued to one competitor, he will be announced as disqualified.

8. Any judge shall notice in particular that competitors are in danger of violating rules during the start, transcension and final sprint.

Part Five Further Reading

Wang Zhen

Wang Zhen is a Chinese race walker who specializes in the 10 km and 20 km race walk. He holds the Asian record for the 20 km, and is also the Asian, Chinese and junior world record holder over 10 km.

In 2010, he was chosen to train with the national team for the first time. In April, 2012, he was the champion in the Olympic Trials and broke the Asian record. In May that year, he won his first world championship in the men's 20 km race walk at the IAAF World Race Walking Cup. At the London Olympic Games, he was chosen for the Chinese Olympic team and went on to secure the bronze medal in the 20 km walk. Finishing behind Chen Ding, he shared the honor of winning China's first ever Olympic medals in the event. In 2013, Wang claimed the crown of the men's 20 km race walk at the 12th China National Games. In the 2014 Incheon Asian Games, he set a new Asian record and won the gold medal. On 18 July, 2016, he went to Rio with the Chinese team for the Olympics. On 13 August, he won the men's 20 km race walk and became the third Chinese male gold medalist in track and field events after Liu Xiang and Chen Ding.

2
Chapter

Gymnastics

Gymnastics

Part One Listening and Speaking

Activity 1

🎧 Listen to the following conversation, and then work in pairs to act it out.

(Eric is a young gymnast. He always makes an unsteady landing when doing a forward somersault, which has made him feel worried. Now his coach is giving him some technical guidance.)

A: Sir, could I ask you about something that's been worrying me?

B: Please, feel free.

A: I always make an awkward landing when doing a forward somersault.

B: It probably has something to do with your technique. Are you keeping your legs fully tucked in close to your chest in the air?

A: I think so.

B: How do you feel about your take-off height? Is it sufficient?

A: I'm not sure, actually. Could you check my performance now?

B : OK.

(A minute later...)

B: That's most likely the issue. You have been doing the somersault well, but your take-off hasn't been high enough.

A: I see. Thanks for your help!

Words and Expressions

gymnast /'dʒɪmnæst/ *n.* 体操运动员

unsteady /ʌn'stedɪ/ *adj.* 不平稳的

somersault /'sʌməsɔːlt/ *n.* 筋斗，前（后）
空翻

guidance /'gaɪdns/ *n.* （对职业、学业
等的）指导

technical guidance 技术指导

awkward /'ɔːkwəd/ *adj.* 不雅观的；
使人尴尬的

have something to do with 和……有
关系

sufficient /sə'fɪʃnt/ *adj.* 足够的，充
足的；充分的

Activity 2

Work in pairs and make conversations according to the given situations.

Situation 1: A gymnast injured his right ankle badly when he lost his center of body weight and fell down during the floor exercise.

Situation 2: You have been so exhausted in recent days that you long to ask your coach for a leave.

Part Two Reading

Passage 1

Directions: Read the passage about modern gymnastics and discuss the following questions with your partners.

Modern Gymnastics

Gymnastics is a sporting event generally involving the performance of various physical exercises with bare hands or apparatus. Modern gymnastics can be traced back to the 18th and 19th century when its main schools emerged gradually in Germany, Sweden, Denmark and other countries, which not only promoted its development but also laid the solid foundation for modern gymnastics.

Modern gymnastics is divided into two kinds in terms of its aim and task: basic gymnastics and competitive gymnastics. The former means that routines and techniques are relatively simple including the exercises (which are set to radio music) and the workout, and it aims at building up one's body and improving the overall health. The latter means competing for achievements and medals in some major competitions such as competitive gymnastics, rhythmic gymnastics, aerobics, acrobatic gymnastics, and trampolining. It is worth mentioning that the competitive events set for male and female athletes are quite different. Men's contain the floor exercise, pommel horse, still rings, vaulting table, parallel bars and horizontal bar while women's involve vault, uneven bars, balance beam and the floor exercise which is performed to music.

Modern gymnastics was introduced to China after 1840, when it lagged behind so much that there were no gymnastic activities on a large scale in public. However, China has developed modern gymnastics so rapidly since 1949 that it has become one of the events that best captures the gold medal for the country. For example, Chinese gymnasts won 9 gold medals and 14 other medals at the 2008 Beijing Olympics and won 4 gold medals and 3 silver medals at the 2012 London Olympics. It is also worth mentioning that China's women's gymnastics team captured the gold for the first time in the team competition at the 2008 Beijing Olympics.

Words and Expressions

performance /pə'fɔːməns/ n. 表演

various /'veərɪəs/ adj. 各种各样的

emerge /ɪ'mɜːdʒ/ v. 涌现，出现

foundation /faʊn'deɪʃn/ n. 基础

routine /ruː'tiːn/ n. 套路；（舞蹈等

表演的）成套动作；常规；例行公事

workout /'wɜːkaʊt/ n. 体育锻炼，体育训练

contain /kən'teɪn/ v. 包含；阻止，遏制

capture /'kæptʃə(r)/ v. 获得，夺得

Sports Terms

competitive gymnastics 竞技体操

rhythmic gymnastics 艺术体操

aerobics /eə'rəʊbɪks/ n. 健美操

acrobatic gymnastics 特技体操，技巧运动

trampolining /'træmpəliːnɪŋ/ n. 蹦床

floor exercise 自由体操

pommel horse 鞍马

still rings 吊环

vaulting table （男子）跳马

parallel bars 双杠

horizontal bar 单杠

vault /vɔːlt/ n. （女子）跳马

uneven bars 高低杠

balance beam 平衡木

Questions:

1. What are the differences between the basic gymnastics and competitive gymnastics?
2. Do you remember those competitive events for both male and female athletes?
3. How many medals do Chinese gymnasts win totally in the Beijing Olympic Games?

Passage 2

Directions: Read the passage about the International Gymnastics Federation and discuss the following questions with your partners.

International Gymnastics Federation

The International Gymnastics Federation (FIG) was established in 1881. It is headquartered in Lausanne, Switzerland and currently consists of 142 members. The current president is an Italian—Bruno Grandi. Its official languages are French, English, German, Russian and Spanish.

The main duties of the FIG are: to appeal to the public to participate in its various gymnastic activities; to research gymnastic theory and practice; to issue its written documents and determine the gymnastics routines and competition regulations; to provide technical assistance for its members; and to hold the major events and strengthen friendly exchanges among athletes from different countries.

There are five major disciplines regulated by the FIG, including competitive gymnastics, aerobic gymnastics, acrobatic gymnastics, trampolining and rhythmic gymnastics. Its major events in the world typically involve gymnastics at the Summer Olympics held once every four years, the World Championships held once every two years (the odd-numbered year), the World Cup held once every year, the World Rhythmic Gymnastics Championships held once every year and the various continental championships and festivals where the demonstration performances of all gymnasts of all ages are viewed.

The Chinese Gymnastics Association, namely CGA, was founded in the year of 1954 and it is headquartered in Beijing. In October 1978, the CGA joined the FIG.

Words and Expressions

currently /'kʌrəntlɪ/ *adv.* 现时，当前

appeal to 呼吁，吁请

regulation /ˌregjuˈleɪʃn/ *n.* 规则

assistance /əˈsɪstəns/ *n.* 帮助，支持

aerobic /eəˈrəʊbɪk/ *adj.* 健美的

acrobatic /ˌækrəˈbætɪk/ *adj.* 特技的，杂技的

rhythmic /ˈrɪðmɪk/ *adj.* 韵律的

demonstration /ˌdemənˈstreɪʃn/ *n.* 示范表演；示范

Sports Terms

International Gymnastics Federation (FIG) 国际体操联合会

World Rhythmic Gymnastics Championships 世界艺术体操锦标赛

Chinese Gymnastics Association (CGA) 中国体操协会

Questions:

1. What gymnastics disciplines are governed by the FIG?

2. What competitions are governed by the FIG?

3. What are the main duties of the FIG?

Part Three Exercises

Directions: Do the following exercises.

1. Give a brief account of the special committees in the International Gymnastics Federation (FIG).

2. Write an article under the title "A Happy Gymnastic Lesson" in no less than 250 words.

Part Four Rules and Concepts

1. According to "Gymnastics Technical Regulation" of the International Gymnastics Federation, the competitions of the gymnastics are divided into four kinds: qualifying team and individual competitions, all-around final, apparatus final and team final.

2. During the matches, the sequences of performance on apparatus competitions are the following: Men: floor exercise, pommel horse, still rings, vaulting table, parallel bars, horizontal bar; Women: vault, uneven bars, balance beam, floor exercise.

3. For all the official FIG competitions (World Championships, Olympic Games, World Cup Finals), the apparatus jury will consist of a D-jury, an E-jury, supplementary judges and assistants.

4. Two separate scores, "D" and "E", will be calculated on all apparatus. The D-jury establishes the "D" score, the content of an exercise, and the E-jury establishes the "E" score, i.e. the exercise presentation related to compositional requirements, technique and body position.

5. The "D" score includes difficulty points, connection points, and element group points.

6. The "E" score will start from 10 points and will take away points for errors in form, artistry, execution, technique and routine composition.

7. The final score of an exercise will be established by the addition of the "D" and final "E" scores.

8. A floor exercise is composed predominantly of acrobatic elements combined with other gymnastic elements such as strength and balance parts, elements of flexibility, handstands, and choreographic combinations all forming an harmonious rhythmic exercise which is performed utilizing the entire floor exercise area.

9. A contemporary pommel horse exercise is characterized by different types of circular swings with legs apart and together in a variety of supporting positions on all parts of the horse, single leg swings and/or scissors. Swings through the handstand position, with or without turns, are permitted. All elements must be executed with swing and without the slightest interruption of the exercise. Strength and hold elements are not permitted.

10. An exercise on the still rings is composed of swing, strength and hold parts in approximately equal portions. These parts and combinations are executed in a hang position, to or through a support position, or to or through the handstand position, and execution with straight arms should be predominant.

Part Five Further Reading

Li Xiaopeng

Li Xiaopeng is a Chinese gymnast who specializes in parallel bars and vault. He currently holds 16 world titles, more than any other gymnasts in China. On 29 August, 2009, he was the torch bearer for the torch relay of the East Asian Games in Hong Kong.

He began gymnastics training at Changsha Spare-time Sports School in Hunan province at the age of 6, and became a member of the Hunan Provincial Team at 12. Li's diligence and skill soon set him apart from his peers, which was proven by his several provincial titles. At the age of 15, he was selected for the national team. At 16, Li Xiaopeng became China's youngest world (team) gymnastics champion ever when he and his teammates won the men's team final at the 1997 Lausanne World Championships. At the same event, Li also received a silver medal for parallel bars, just second to his teammate Zhang Jingjing, and a bronze for floor exercise. At the 2000 Sydney Olympic Games, Li and his teammates gave an outstanding performance, earning the gold medal at the men's team event. Li also won an individual gold medal in parallel bars. After winning two gold medals for men's team and parallel bars at the Beijing Olympics, he surpassed Li Ning by holding 16 world titles, more than any other gymnasts in China.

Rhythmic Gymnastics

Part One Listening and Speaking

Activity 1

🎧 Listen to the following conversation, and then work in pairs to act it out.

(Lisa and Katie are practicing rhythmic gymnastics together. Lisa can't do her calf raise with the turn perfectly, so she is asking for Katie's suggestions on how to improve it.)

A: How about your calf raise with the turn?

B: It's OK. And you?

A: It seems that I can't do it well.

B: Why?

A: The center of my body weight is always unbalanced, so I fall down. Plus, I can't make a full turn.

B: Well, it sounds like your calf raise isn't sufficient. But don't worry. I made the same mistake when I learned to do it at the very beginning.

A: OK, I'll just keep practicing it then. Would you like to give me some tips?

B: Absolutely!

Words and Expressions

calf /ka:f/ *n.* 小腿肚，腓	plus /plʌs/ *adv.* 此外
calf raise 侧吸腿	tip /tɪp/ *n.* 提示
unbalanced /ˌʌnˈbælənst/ *adj.* 不平衡的	absolutely /ˈæbsəluːtlɪ/ *adv.* 完全地

Activity 2

👥 Work in pairs and make conversations according to the given situations.

Situation 1: A gymnast injured her knee and fell down during the rope exercise. You accompanied her to see the doctor.

Situation 2: A gymnast performed the wrong action on the ball exercise. Point it out and give her some advice.

Part Two Reading

Passage 1

Directions: Read the passage about rhythmic gymnastics and discuss the following questions with your partners.

Rhythmic Gymnastics I

Rhythmic gymnastics is a women-only sport that combines elements of dance, gymnastics, acrobatic routines, and apparatus manipulation. Gymnasts perform to music with bare hands or a light apparatus such as rope, hoop, ball, clubs, and ribbon in their hands. The victor is the participant who earns the most points, determined by a panel of judges, for leaps, balances, pivots, apparatus handling, and execution. The choreography must cover the entire floor. Physical abilities needed by a rhythmic gymnast include strength, flexibility, endurance and hand-eye coordination.

Rhythmic gymnastics evolved from a host of related disciplines. It incorporates elements from classical ballet, as well as the German and Swedish gymnastics. The sport is governed by the International Gymnastics Federation (FIG), which designs the Code of Points and regulates all aspects of international elite competitions.

Words and Expressions

manipulation /məˌnɪpjʊˈleɪʃn/ *n.* 操控，处理

bare /beə(r)/ *adj.* 空的；赤裸的

rope /rəʊp/ *n.* 绳子

hoop /huːp/ *n.* 箍，环，圈

club /klʌb/ *n.* 棍棒

ribbon /ˈrɪbən/ *n.* 绸带，缎带

leap /liːp/ *n.* 跳跃

pivot /ˈpɪvət/ *n.* 旋转运动

execution /ˌeksɪˈkjuːʃn/ *n.* 执行；完成

physical /ˈfɪzɪkl/ *adj.* 身体的；物理的

flexibility /ˌfleksəˈbɪlətɪ/ *n.* 灵活性

coordination /kəʊˌɔːdɪˈneɪʃn/ *n.* 协调

incorporate /ɪnˈkɔːpəreɪt/ *v.* 包含，囊括

regulate /ˈregjuleɪt/ *v.* 控制，管理

elite /eɪˈliːt/ *n.* 精英

Questions:

1. What apparatuses are used in rhythmic gymnastics?

2. How is the rhythmic gymnast's performance judged?

3. What physical abilities are required by the rhythmic gymnasts?

Passage 2

Directions: Read the passage about rhythmic gymnastics and discuss the following questions with your partners.

Rhythmic Gymnastics II

Competitive rhythmic gymnastics began in the 1940s in the Soviet Union. The FIG formally recognized this discipline in 1961, first as modern gymnastics, then as rhythmic sportive gymnastics, and finally as rhythmic gymnastics. The first World Championships for individual rhythmic gymnasts was held in 1963 in Budapest, Hungary. Groups were introduced at the same level in 1967 in Copenhagen, Denmark. The number of athletes grew as interest spread to other parts of the world, and not until 1984 was rhythmic gymnastics added as an Olympic sport in Los Angeles. Competition was held in the individual all-around, and participants are female, who must be at least 16 years old by the end of the Olympic year in order to compete. The group competition was officially listed at the Olympic Games in 1996 in Atlanta, which marked a new stage in its history and promoted further development of rhythmic gymnastics. Besides the Olympic Games and World Championships, other largest events in this sport are European Championships, World Cup and Grand-Prix Series.

Questions:

1. When did rhythmic gymnastics become the Olympic event?

2. Who is your favorite rhythmic gymnast? Introduce her to your classmates.

Part Three Exercises

Directions: Do the following exercises.

1. Give a brief introduction to some of the major international events in rhythmic gymnastics.

2. Watch one of the individual events in rhythmic gymnastics and write a 250-word article about your opinion of that event.

Part Four Rules and Concepts

1. There are two programs of rhythmic gymnastics: individuals and groups. The program for senior and junior individual gymnasts usually consists of four exercises. The length of each exercise is from 1'15" to 1'30". The program for senior groups usually consists of two exercises: one with a single type of apparatus and the other with two types of apparatuses. The length of each exercise is from 2'15" to 2'30".

2. The stopwatch will start as soon as the gymnast or the first gymnast in the group begins to move and will be stopped as soon as the gymnast or the last gymnast in the group is totally motionless. 0.05 point for each additional or missing second will be penalized by the Coordinator Judge.

3. The music can be interpreted by one or several instruments or a musician, including the voice used as an instrument. All instruments are authorized provided that they express music with the characteristics necessary to accompany a rhythmic gymnastics exercise: clear and well-defined in its structure.

4. Each jury (individuals and groups) consists of two groups of judges: Difficulty and Execution. Each group will be assisted by a D1 Coordinator Judge who will apply the penalties indicated in the Annex. The Superior Jury must confirm the penalties

given by the Coordinator Judge.

5. No penalty will be applied if the apparatus passes the boundary of the floor area without touching the ground.

6. The gymnast or the group will not be penalized for the broken apparatus or the apparatus caught in the small beams of the ceiling, but will only be penalized for the consequences of various technical errors.

7. A correct gymnastics leotard must be of a non-transparent material; leotards that have some part in lace have to be lined (from the trunk to the chest).

8. Individual gymnasts and the six gymnasts of the group should be present in the competition area only once they have been called either by microphone or by the Coordinator Judge, or when the green light is showing.

9. During the actual performance of the exercise, the coach of the gymnast or group (or any other member of the delegation) may not communicate with their individual gymnast, group gymnasts, the musician, or the judges in any manner.

10. Any difficulty executed with greater amplitude than required by the definition of the corresponding difficulty will not change its value.

Part Five Further Reading

Deng Senyue

Deng Senyue is a Chinese individual rhythmic gymnast. She is the 2014 Asian Games silver medalist and finished 4th in the all-around at the 2013 World Championships. She is considered as China's most successful rhythmic gymnast.

Deng started rhythmic gymnastics at six years old. In 1999, she went to Beijing to pursue gymnastics and was recruited by the China Rhythmic Gymnastics Team. She made her senior international debut at the 2007 Aeon Cup.

In 2009, Deng won the gold medal at the 11th National Games, raising her national ranking to first. She finished 21st in the all-around final at the 2010 World Championships in Moscow. Deng won a bronze medal in hoop at the 2011 Summer Universiade and won the bronze medal in the all-around at the 2011 Asian Championships. She then represented China at the 2011 World Championships where she finished 13th in the all-around.

Lesson 9

Aerobics

Activity 1

🎧 Listen to the following conversation, and then work in pairs to act it out.

(Jane and Julie are teammates of the aerobics team. At this moment, they are discussing how to perform double pirouette turns better.)

A: How's your double pirouette turn going?

B: Not bad. How about you?

A: Lately I haven't been able to perform it well. I always lose my center of body weight after one and a half turns. I usually can't even execute two turns. Could you give me some advice?

B: OK. Give it another try, and I will try to figure out what's wrong.

A: You see, I have a tendency to wobble and lose focus when doing a turn.

B: I see. I think the main reason is that you don't have enough power in your ankles.

A: What should I do?

B: You can strengthen your legs and ankles by doing calf raises. Focus on controlling your arm swings and shifting your center of body weight.

A: Got it. Thank you for your help!

B: You are welcome.

Words and Expressions

pirouette /ˌpɪruˈet/ *n.* （芭蕾舞）脚尖旋转	**tendency** /ˈtendənsɪ/ *n.* 趋势
execute /ˈeksɪkjuːt/ *v.* 执行；完成	**wobble** /ˈwɒbl/ *v.* （使）摇晃，摇摆
figure out 弄清楚，弄明白	**focus** /ˈfəʊkəs/ *n.* 重心；中心
	ankle /ˈæŋkl/ *n.* 脚踝

Activity 2

👤 Work in pairs and answer the following questions.

> **Question 1:** Can you tell the differences between gymnastics with bare hands and aerobic gymnastics in terms of the rhythm, the direction of movements, the lines and the formation?
>
> **Question 2:** Which event do you prefer to watch, gymnastics or aerobic gymnastics? Why?

Part Two Reading

Passage 1

Directions: Read the passage about aerobics and discuss the following questions with your partners.

Aerobics

Aerobics, originating in 1968, is a popular sport worldwide which typically combines the elements of gymnastics, dance and music with various movement patterns for the practical purpose of keeping fit, shaping one's character and experiencing pleasure according to the choreographic routine.

The first official aerobics competition was held in the U.S. in 1983, and the first Far-East Bodybuilding Competition was held in Japan in 1984, both of which led to aerobics' thriving and prosperity around the world.

In terms of its purpose or its kind, aerobics has gradually evolved into either fitness aerobics or aerobic gymnastics. Fitness aerobics has so many advantages that it has gained great popularity around the world. For example, it is easy and simple to learn without any specified requirements. It is performed at a slightly slow rhythm. Furthermore, its performance time may vary from person to person. On the contrary, gymnasts perform perfect and difficulty-based routines to music in aerobic gymnastics in order to show their talents for constant, complicated and high-intensity performance. It is worth mentioning that the routine must perfectly combine the elements of the music and the performance to display its originality. In addition, some requirements and evaluation criteria must be taken into consideration, such as the permitted time, the competitive area, costume, music, choreographic routine, the high-quality execution of the routine, the number of difficulties, style, and so on.

Words and Expressions

combine /kəm'baɪn/ *v.* （使）结合

pattern /'pætn/ *n.* 模式，方式；范例，典范

shape /ʃeɪp/ *v.* 塑造

choreographic /ˌkɒrɪə'græfɪk/ *adj.* 舞蹈的，编舞的

thrive /'θraɪv/ *v.* 兴盛，兴旺

prosperity /prɒ'sperətɪ/ *n.* 兴旺，繁荣

advantage /əd'vɑːntɪdʒ/ *n.* 优势，优点

popularity /ˌpɒpju'lærətɪ/ *n.* 普及，流行

specified /'spesɪfaɪd/ *adj.* 规定的，详细说明的

rhythm /'rɪðəm/ *n.* 节奏，韵律

on the contrary 相反

constant /'kɒnstənt/ *adj.* 连续发生的，不断的

intensity /ɪn'tensətɪ/ *n.* 强度

display /dɪ'spleɪ/ *v.* 表现，显露；陈列，展示

originality /əˌrɪdʒə'nælətɪ/ *n.* 独创性，创意

criteria /kraɪ'tɪərɪə/ *n.* （单数 criterion）标准，准则；原则

costume /'kɒstjuːm/ *n.* 服饰，着装

Sports Terms

fitness aerobics 健身健美操   **aerobic gymnastics** 竞技健美操

Questions:

1. Can you describe the development of aerobics?

2. How many types can aerobics be divided into? What are they?

Passage 2

Directions: Read the passage about aerobic gymnastics and discuss the following questions with your partners.

Aerobic Gymnastics

Aerobic gymnastics is a competitive sport with complex, high-intensity movement patterns and elements of varying difficulties that is performed to music. It also combines elements of acrobatic gymnastics and rhythmic gymnastics, along with music, dance, etc.

The performances are made up of the following elements: dynamic strength, static strength, jumps and leaps (power), kicks (dynamic strength), balance and flexibility. Additionally, a maximum of ten elements from following families are allowed: push-ups, supports and balances / holds, kicks and splits, jumps and leaps. Performances are scored according to artistic quality, creativity, execution, and difficulty. Artistic quality is the composition of the routine. Creativity is the variety of movements, lifts in pairs, trios and groups. Execution is the perfection of each movement. Difficulty is the number of required gymnastic elements demonstrating strength, flexibility and local muscular endurance.

Words and Expressions

dynamic /daɪˈnæmɪk/ *adj.* 动态的；动感的

static /ˈstætɪk/ *adj.* 静态的

kick /kɪk/ *n. & v.* 踢

push-up /pʊʃ-ʌp/ *n.* 俯卧撑

composition /ˌkɒmpəˈzɪʃn/ *n.* 组成，构成

trio /ˈtriːəʊ/ *n.* 三人小组

muscular /ˈmʌskjələ(r)/ *adj.* 肌肉的

Questions:

1. What elements make up the performances of aerobic gymnastics?

2. How are the performances in aerobic gymnastics scored?

Part Three Exercises

Directions: Do the following exercises.

1. Make a 250-word commentary on the aerobics team for the Art Department of your university.

2. Talk about the development of aerobic gymnastics in China.

Part Four Rules and Concepts

1. The official FIG aerobic gymnastics competition is the Aerobic Gymnastics World Championships, which is held every two years.

2. The Aerobic Gymnastics World Championships comprises the following categories: individual women, individual men, mixed pair, trio, group.

3. For the health and safety of gymnasts, the FIG has accepted that gymnasts competing in multiple finals require 10 minutes to recover before competing again.

4. Should a competitor fail to appear on stage within 20 seconds after being called, a deduction of 0.5 point shall be made by the Chair of Judges Panel. Should a competitor fail to appear on stage within 60 seconds after being called, the start will be deemed as a Walk Over. Upon announcement of such a Walk Over, the competitor loses her right to participate in the category in question.

5. Coaches have to remain in the waiting area while competitors are competing. Coaches, competitors, and all unauthorized persons are restricted from entering the competition area. Disregard of these restrictions may lead to the disqualification of the competitor by the Superior Jury.

6. For each exercise, total scores, penalties, final score and the rank must be displayed to the public. After the qualification round, each participating member federation must receive a complete copy of the results but not the detailed results. At the end of the competition, a complete set of all detailed results must be given to each participating member federation.

7. The routine must show a balance between aerobic movement patterns and difficulty elements. Arm and leg movement patterns must be strong and with a definite

shape. The length of the routine is 1'30" for all categories with a tolerance of plus or minus 5 seconds (beep sound not included).

8. Aerobic movement patterns are combinations of basic aerobic steps together with arm movements; all are performed to music in order to create dynamic, rhythmic and continuous sequences of high and low impact movements. Routines should display a high level of intensity.

9. Difficulty requirements in all categories:

   —A maximum of 10 difficulty elements from different families from the Element Pool including 1 element from each group;

   —A maximum of 5 difficulty elements on the floor;

   —A maximum of 2 difficulty elements from Group C landing in push-up position;

   —A maximum of 2 difficulty elements from Group C landing in split position.

10. The A-score, E-score, and D-score are added together and constitute the total score. The deductions made by the D-Judges, the Line Judges and the Chair of Judges Panel are deducted from the total score to give the final score.

Part Five Further Reading

Huang Jinxuan

Known as China's aerobics queen, Huang Jinxuan is a world-class athlete and world champion. She is the only female athlete in the national aerobics team and the only woman champion in China's aerobics area. In the 26th World University Games, she won four gold medals and finished second in the 9th World Aerobics Championships. After the National University Games in 2012, she finished her master degree and retired. Now, she is a teacher in Civil Aviation University of China.

Born in 1988, Huang Jinxuan started with gymnastics at an early age and then switched to aerobics, which paved the way for her great success in aerobics. She once said: "As a college student, I am supposed to balance study and training. To achieve good training effect, I have to keep practicing a daily routine, while I also need to maintain focused on the study so as to earn credits. It's not easy to handle this."

Acrobatic Gymnastics

Part One Listening and Speaking

Activity 1

🎧 Listen to the following conversation, and then work in pairs to act it out.

(After watching William's acrobatic performance, Joe has become greatly intrigued. He asks William about acrobatics, and considers joining William in learning acrobatics.)

A: Hey, William. Could you tell me about the different routines in acrobatic gymnastics?

B: Sure, Joe. The acrobatic routines are classified as either dynamic or static routines.

A: What do the dynamic routines involve?

B: They typically involve individual rollings, tumblings, kips, handsprings, somersaults and pairs' and groups' throws and catches.

A: And how about the static routines?

B: They typically contain individual handstands, splits, balance, and pairs' and groups' supports, balance, handstands and figure performances.

A: Oh, so many. Are they easy to learn?

B: Not too difficult, in my opinion. But as with anything else, it takes a lot of practice. Let's meet up and practice when you have enough time, OK?

A: OK! Thank you very much.

Words and Expressions

intrigued /ɪnˈtriːgd/ *adj.* 激起兴趣的，引发好奇心的	handspring /ˈhændsprɪŋ/ *n.* 手翻
rolling /ˈrəʊlɪŋ/ *n.* 翻滚	throws and catches 抛接
tumbling /ˈtʌmblɪŋ/ *n.* 滚翻，翻筋斗；翻腾	handstand /ˈhændstænd/ *n.* 倒立（动作）
kip /kɪp/ *n.* 屈伸起	split /splɪt/ *n.* 劈叉
	figure performance 造型

Activity 2

👥 Work in pairs and answer the following questions.

> **Question 1:** What influence does the frequent and systematic practice of acrobatic gymnastics have on one's physical functioning?
>
> **Question 2:** How many optional routines does each gymnast perform in individual events in acrobatic gymnastics? Can you do some of them?

Part Two Reading

Passage 1

Directions: Read the passage about acrobatic gymnastics and discuss the following questions with your partners.

Acrobatic Gymnastics

Acrobatic gymnastics is a competitive gymnastic discipline where gymnasts work together and perform acrobatic moves, dance and tumbling, accompanied by music. There are three types of routines: a "balance" routine where the focus is on strength, poise and flexibility; a "dynamic" routine which includes throws, catches, and somersaults, and (at FIG level 6 and above) a "combined" routine which includes elements from both balance and dynamic.

The sport is governed by the International Federation of Gymnastics (FIG). At international level, there are four FIG categories of the competition defined by age:

11–16, 12–18, 13–19, and 15+ (Senior). Acrobatic gymnasts perform in pairs or groups. In each partnership, the gymnasts' different sizes and abilities will be balanced to complement each other in order to carry out the complex moves. Some will mainly carry out supporting and pitching roles, which are known as "bases". They are then balanced with smaller gymnasts who become the "tops".

Words and Expressions

accompany /əˈkʌmpənɪ/ v. 伴随；陪伴	补充
poise /pɔɪz/ n. 平衡	complex /ˈkɒmpleks/ adj. 复杂的
complement /ˈkɒmplɪment/ v. 补足；	pitch /pɪtʃ/ v. & n. 投掷；投球

Sports Terms

balance routine 静力性动作	**base** /beɪs/ n. 下面的人
dynamic routine 动力性动作	**top** /tɒp/ n. 上面的人
combined routine 综合动作	

Questions:

1. How many types of routines make up the acrobatic gymnastics? What are they?

2. How are the pairs' roles assigned in acrobatic gymnastics?

Passage 2

Directions: Read the passage about the IFSA and discuss the following questions with your partners.

International Federation of Sports Acrobatics

The International Federation of Sports Acrobatics (IFSA) was established in 1973. The current president is Mr. Stoimenov, a Bulgarian. Its official languages are Russian and English. Its top legislature and executive agency is the congress which is held once every four years. Fewer than three representatives from each of its national associations are sent to the congress with the single vote. When the congress is not in session, its executive committee will be in charge of all affairs. The committee consists of the president, the vice-president, the secretary general and the members, all of whom are elected by the congress with a four-year term.

Currently the IFSA organizes the international events—the Acrobatic Gymnastics World Championships which was held for the first time in the Soviet Union in 1974, and takes place every even-numbered year, and the World Cup held once every odd-numbered year.

The Chinese Association of Sports Acrobatics joined the IFSA in December 1979. Several major events have been held successfully in China since then, such as the 5th World Cup, the 2nd World Youth Championships, the 2nd Asian Championships and the 11th Acrobatic Gymnastics World Championships. The flawless performances by Chinese acrobats have become world renowned.

Words and Expressions

legislature /ˈledʒɪsleɪtʃə(r)/ *n.* 立法机关，立法机构

executive /ɪɡˈzekjətɪv/. *adj.* 决策的；经理的；执行的

agency /ˈeɪdʒənsɪ/ *n.* (代理)机构

congress /ˈkɒŋgres/ *n.* 代表大会；国会

representative /ˌreprɪˈzentətɪv/ *n.* 代表

vote /vəʊt/ *n.* 投票

session /ˈseʃn/ *n.* 会议；（法庭）开庭

elect /ɪˈlekt/ *v.* 选举

flawless /ˈflɔːləs/ *adj.* 完美的，无瑕疵的

acrobat /ˈækrəbæt/ *n.* 杂技演员

renowned /rɪˈnaʊnd/ *adj.* 有名的，闻名的

Sports Terms

International Federation of Sports Acrobatics (IFSA) 国际技巧运动联合会

Acrobatic Gymnastics World Championships 世界技巧锦标赛

Chinese Association of Sports Acrobatics 中国技巧协会

Questions:

1. What does the executive committee of the IFSA consist of?

2. What do you know about the main competitive events organized by the IFSA?

3. What acrobatic gymnastics events have been held in China?

Part Three Exercises

Directions: Do the following exercises.

1. Give your opinion on whether acrobatic gymnastics should be added to the physical education programs of elementary and secondary schools.

2. Read, research and write an article in no less than 250 words on the development of acrobatic gymnastics in China.

Part Four Rules and Concepts

1. There are five event categories included in acrobatic gymnastics' competitions: women's pairs, men's pairs, mixed pairs, women's groups, and men's groups.

2. The Superior Jury is composed of the TC President, two Artistry Experts, two Execution Experts and Difficulty Experts.

3. Artistry Judges evaluate the performed exercises for artistic merit in strict accordance with the Code of Points. Exercises are evaluated without discussion with any other person.

4. All exercises have a maximum duration of 2'30". There is no minimum duration.

5. All pair/group static elements must be held for a minimum of 3 seconds each.

6. There must be a minimum of six pair/group elements, three of which must be static holds and three dynamic elements including one catch. Each element must have a minimum difficulty value of one.

7. The final position of each mount must be held for 1 second for the mount to be given a difficulty value.

8. Criteria for evaluation of execution: logic and efficiency of entries to and exits from elements, efficiency of technical execution, correctness of line and shape, amplitude in execution of pair/group and individual elements, full stretch in balance elements and maximum flight of dynamic elements, stability of static elements, confident and effective catching and throwing, and landing control.

9. Balance exercises must demonstrate strength, balance, flexibility and agility.

10. In the dynamic exercises, competitors must demonstrate assisted and individual flight, using a variety of directions, rotations, twists, different body shapes and springs.

Part Five Further Reading

Arthur Davis

Arthur Davis is a retired U.S. acrobatic gymnast who won two world championship titles while competing in a mixed pair with top Shenea Booth (also retired from athletic competition).

Davis and Booth were the first U.S. athletes to win the mixed-pair all-around gold medals at the 2002 Acrobatic Gymnastics World Championships in Riesa, Germany. Also in 2002, the pair placed second all-around at the 2002 Machuga Cup in Krasnodar, Russia.

The pair won the all-around at the U.S. National Sports Acrobatic Championships in 2002, 2003 and 2004. Davis and Booth also won national awards for performance, skill difficulty and choreography.

Lesson 11 Trampolining

Part One Listening and Speaking

Activity 1

🎧 Listen to the following conversation, and then work in pairs to act it out.

(In a school's trampolining class, Edward is consulting the teacher about the components of trampolining routines, the features of this sport and the rules of trampolining competition.)

A: Sir, can you tell me something about the trampolining routine? What is it exactly?

B: OK. It's pretty simple. The whole routine consists of front or back somersaults with or without twists.

A: Oh, sounds simple enough. And what features does it have?

B: It has quite a few, actually. There's the splendid performance of the routine in the air, which is great to watch. And then there's the rhythmical connections and changes of the moves, especially the take-off with feet, backdrop, front drop, and seat drop.

A: Another thing I was wondering is whether a pause in the air is allowed in the match?

B: No, I'm afraid not.

A: Really? Why?

B: According to the rules, pausing in the air is not allowed in the routine of a match. That's it.

A: Oh, I see. Thank you very much.

Words and Expressions

consult /kən'sʌlt/ v. 咨询，请教

trampolining routine 蹦床动作

feature /'fiːtʃə(r)/ n. 特性，特征

twist /twɪst/ n. 弯曲，扭曲；扭转，
转动

splendid /'splendɪd/ adj. 辉煌的，壮
丽的

rhythmical /'rɪðmɪkl/ adj. 有节奏
的，有韵律的

backdrop /'bækdrɒp/ n. 背弹；（舞
台）背景幕

front drop 腹弹

seat drop 坐弹

pause /pɔːz/ n. 暂停，间歇

Activity 2

👥 Work in pairs and answer the following questions.

Question 1: Have you ever played on a trampoline in amusement parks? What moves can you make?

Question 2: What physical qualities do you think are essential for trampolinists?

Part Two Reading

Passage 1

Directions: Read the passage about trampolining and discuss the following questions with your partners.

Trampolining I

Trampolining, part of gymnastics, is a competitive sport in which athletes perform acrobatic skills while bouncing on a trampoline. Thus it is also called a rebounce acrobatic sport. Trampolining is the perfect combination of sport and art, so it is well-known as the "air ballet".

Its acrobatic routine consists of ten basic skills of different somersaults and tumblings. The gymnast should finish all the acrobatics movements, including free bounce, tuck jump, pike jump, front and back somersault or some more complicated combined movements. A routine on the trampoline is characterized by high, continuous rhythmic jumping elements, without hesitation or intermediate straight bounces.

During a routine no element may be repeated, otherwise the difficulty of the repeated element will not be counted.

The first national trampolining exhibition took place in Texas, U.S. in 1947, and trampolining was listed as an official sport in 1948. Soon afterwards it was brought to Europe. The first World Championships was held in Britain in 1964. The sport was first held at the Summer Olympic Games in 2000.

Since trampolining became an Olympic sport, China has made a very successful effort to develop world-class trampolinists. The first major success was in the 2007 Men's World Championships and later in the 2008 Olympic Games with two gold medals in individual men and individual women.

Words and Expressions

bounce /baʊns/ *v.* 弹跳，弹回

trampoline /ˈtræmpəliːn/ *n.* 蹦床

combination /ˌkɒmbɪˈneɪʃn/ *n.* 结合

ballet /ˈbæleɪ/ *n.* 芭蕾

complicated /ˈkɒmplɪkeɪtɪd/ *adj.* 复杂的

characterize /ˈkærəktəraɪz/ *v.* 以……为特征

hesitation /ˌhezɪˈteɪʃn/ *n.* 犹豫

exhibition /ˌeksɪˈbɪʃn/ *n.* 展览

Sports Terms

free bounce 自由弹跳

tuck jump 抱膝跳

pike jump 屈体跳

front somersault 前空翻

back somersault 后空翻

trampolinist /ˈtræmpəliːnɪst/ *n.* 蹦床运动员

Questions:

1. What are the characteristics of trampolining?

2. When was trampolining competed in the Olympic Games?

Passage 2

Directions: Read the passage about trampolining and discuss the following questions with your partners.

Trampolining II

The first modern trampoline was built by George Nissen. In the early 1930s, George Nissen observed trapeze artistes performing tricks when bouncing off the safety net. He made the first modern trampoline in his garage to reproduce this on a smaller scale and used it to help with his diving and tumbling activities. He formed a company to build trampolines for sale and used the trampoline to entertain audiences and also let them participate in his demonstrations as part of his marketing strategy. This was the beginning of the new sport.

In the U.S., trampolining was quickly introduced into school physical education programs and was also used in private entertainment centers. Elsewhere in the world the sport was most strongly adopted in Europe and the Soviet Union. Since trampolining became an Olympic sport in 2000, many more countries have started developing programs.

Words and Expressions

reproduce /ˌriːprə'djuːs/ v. 复制

entertain /ˌentə'teɪn/ v. 娱乐

marketing /'mɑːkɪtɪŋ/ n. 营销

strategy /'strætədʒɪ/ n. 策略

Questions:

1. Who built the first trampoline?

2. How did trampolining come into being?

Part Three Exercises

Directions: Do the following exercises.

1. Write a 250-word news report about the fact that He Wenna and Lu Chunlong won the gold medals respectively in trampolining at the Beijing Olympic Games in 2008.

2. Give a brief description of the kids' playing trampolining in the park in no less than 250 words.

Part Four Rules and Concepts

1. Trampolining competitions are comprised of three routines with ten elements in each routine.

2. The starting order for the final will be in order of merit, the gymnast with the lowest score in the qualifying round going first.

3. The first routine in the qualifying round includes both free elements and special requirements. The order in which the elements are performed is at the discretion of the gymnast.

4. Immediately prior to the qualifying round and the final, each gymnast will be allowed maximally 30 seconds to warm up on the competition apparatus. In the event that a gymnast abuses this time limit, the Chair of Judges Panel may instruct the Chief Recorder to deduct a penalty of 0.3 point from the total score of the following routine.

5. In all positions, the feet and legs should be kept together (except straddle jumps), with the feet and toes pointed.

6. Elements having the same amount of rotation but performed in the tucked, piked and straight positions are considered to be different elements and not repetitions. The tucked and pucked positions are considered to be the same position.

7. The routine must end under control in an upright position, with both feet on the trampoline bed, otherwise there will be a deduction.

8. After the final landing on the bed, the gymnast must stand upright and show stability for approximately 3 seconds, otherwise there will be a deduction for lack of stability.

He Wenna

He Wenna is a female Chinese trampolining gymnast. She competed in the 2008 Beijing Summer Olympics, where she won the gold medal with a score of 37.80. This was the first gold medal for Chinese trampolining team.

She won a gold medal in the team event at the 2007 Trampoline World Championships and 2009 Trampoline World Championships. In 2009, she also won a silver medal in individual. In the 2011 Trampoline World Championships, she won both team and individual gold medals and secured a place for China in the Olympics.

In the 2012 Summer Olympics, she was leading after the preliminary round but fell on her out bounce at the end of her routine and finished in the third place. In the 2016 Rio Olympics, she ranked the fourth place. Soon after that, she announced her retirement.

3
Chapter

Ball Games

Football

Part One Listening and Speaking

Activity 1

Listen to the following conversation, and then work in pairs to act it out.

(In an ongoing football match, a footballer is arguing with the referee over whether or not he deserves the yellow card.)

A: Referee, I'm confused. Why did you show me a yellow card? Did I foul?

B: Yes, I'd already blown my whistle to stop the match, but you kept on playing.

A: How come you blew your whistle?

B: You were offside. The assistant referee raised his flag.

A: The fans were too noisy, and I didn't hear the whistle. Could you cancel the yellow card?

B: Sorry, I can't. I must abide by the rules fairly.

A: OK, no problem.

Words and Expressions

ongoing /'ɒngəʊɪŋ/ *adj.* 持续存在的；仍在进行的，进行中的	whistle /'wɪsl/ *n.* & *v.* 口哨
argue with 与……争论	offside /ˌɒf'saɪd/ *adj.* 越位的
referee /ˌrefə'riː/ *n.* 裁判员	assistant /ə'sɪstənt/ *n.* 助手；助理
deserve /dɪ'zɜːv/ *v.* 值得；应得，应受	raise /reɪz/ *v.* 举起
confused /kən'fjuːzd/ *adj.* 疑惑的，困惑的	cancel /'kænsl/ *v.* 取消
foul /faʊl/ *v.* 犯规	abide (by) /ə'baɪd/ *v.* 遵守，遵循（法律、协议、协定等）

Activity 2

👤 Work in pairs and make conversations according to the given situations.

Situation 1: A football player fell down and got injured in a football match. The referee asked the player: "Can you continue? If not, please send for another player. You can come back after treatment."

Situation 2: The referee blew the whistle to suspend the match, ran to the player who committed the foul and showed him the yellow card.

Part Two Reading

Passage 1

Directions: Read the passage about football and discuss the following questions with your partners.

Football

Football is a kind of ball game in which the ball is controlled mainly by players' feet. Modern football is one of the most popular and influential sports in the world. It is called "the first sport of the world" and "King of Sports".

In 1848, *The Cambridge Rules* was drawn up, bringing out a code of common rules for football. In 1857, the first football club, Sheffield Football Club, was founded in England. On 26 October, 1863, the Football Association (FA)—the first football organization in the world—was formed by 11 English soccer clubs in London to agree on common rules. The date is widely regarded as the birthday of modern football. Later on 8 December, the University of Cambridge revised the world's first written football rules, *The Cambridge Rules*, stipulating that in football matches players can only dribble the ball with their feet, and no hand is allowed to touch the ball. They also named "football" as "association football" while in schools it was called "soccer".

After the establishment of the Football Association, football began to be popular throughout the country and spread to the European continent and the rest of the world via sailors, soldiers, businessmen, engineers and priests. With the establishment of the FIFA in 1904, the World Cup has been held every four years, and the rules of football have been constantly modified and improved. All of these have promoted the innovation of football tactics. In 1974, the Dutch invented the "total football works", bringing the game of football into a "comprehensive" era. Since then, international football has ushered in a brand-new beginning, and the sport has continued growing steadily.

Words and Expressions

influential /ˌɪnfluˈenʃl/ *adj.* 有影响的

draw up 草拟，起草

widely /ˈwaɪdlɪ/ *adv.* 广泛地，普遍地

revise /rɪˈvaɪz/ *v.* 修改，校订

stipulate /ˈstɪpjuleɪt/ *v.* 规定，明确要求

throughout /θruːˈaʊt/ *prep.* 各处，遍及

spread /spred/ *v.* 传播；扩展

constantly /ˈkɒnstəntlɪ/ *adv.* 不断地，持续地

modify /ˈmɒdɪfaɪ/ *v.* 调整；对……稍作修改

innovation /ˌɪnəˈveɪʃn/ *n.* 创新；改革

comprehensive /ˌkɒmprɪˈhensɪv/ *adj.* 综合的，全面的

era /ˈɪərə/ *n.* 时代

usher /ˈʌʃə(r)/ *v.* 引导，引领

brand-new /ˈbrændnjuː/ *adj.* 崭新的

steadily /ˈstedəlɪ/ *adv.* 稳定地，稳步地

Sports Terms

Sheffield Football Club 谢菲尔德足球俱乐部

The Cambridge Rules 《剑桥规则》

Football Association (FA) 英格兰足球协会

FIFA 国际足球联合会（国际足联）

Questions:

    1. What's the most popular sport in the world?

    2. What is *The Cambridge Rules*?

    3. How does the FIFA promote the development of football?

Passage 2

Directions: Read the passage about the FIFA and discuss the following questions with your partners.

International Federation of Football Association

The Fédération Internationale de Football Association (FIFA), which is called International Federation of Football Association in English, is an international sport organization made up of national football associations from all over the world. It is headquartered in Zurich, Switzerland and currently consists of 209 members. The FIFA was founded in Paris in 1904, and its current president is Joseph Blatter (Swiss). It organizes worldwide football matches and is responsible for the rules of player transfer, awards the FIFA Player of the Year and publicizes the world rankings monthly. The laws of the game are made by the IFAB (International Football Association Board).

The main matches organized by the FIFA are: FIFA World Cup (starting in 1930, held once every four years); football events at the Summer Olympics (listed in the Olympics officially in 1912, held once every four years); FIFA U-20 World Cup (Coca-Cola Cup, staging in 1977, held once every two years) ; FIFA U-17 World Cup (starting in 1985, held once every two years); FIFA Futsal World Cup, etc.

The FIFA World Cup is the main marketing tool with massive audience, and gains huge profits by tickets, broadcasting rights, sponsorships and transactions. In addition, part of its funding comes from membership and registration fees.

China joined the FIFA in the 1930s, but the Chinese Football Association announced its withdrawal in 1958. In 1979, the legal seat of the Chinese Football Association was restored.

Words and Expressions

be made up of 由……构成，由……组成

transfer /træns'fɜː(r)/ *n. & v.* 转会（尤指职业足球队）；转移

award /ə'wɔːd/ *v.* 奖励；判给

publicize /'pʌblɪsaɪz/ *v.* 宣传，推广

ranking /'ræŋkɪŋ/ *n.* 等级；排名

massive /'mæsɪv/ *adj.* 巨大的；大量的

audience /'ɔːdɪəns/ *n.* 观众

profit /'prɒfɪt/ *n.* 利益，收益

broadcast /'brɔːdkɑːst/ *v.* 转播

sponsorship /'spɒnsəʃɪp/ *n.* 赞助

transaction /træn'zækʃn/ *n.* 交易；事务

registration /ˌredʒɪ'streɪʃn/ *n.* 登记，注册

withdrawal /wɪð'drɔːəl/ *n.* 撤退，收回

restore /rɪ'stɔː(r)/ *v.* 恢复（某种情况或感受）

Sports Terms

International Federation of Football Association (FIFA) 国际足球联合会（国际足联）

FIFA Player 世界足球先生

International Football Association Board (IFAB) 国际足球联合理事会

FIFA World Cup 世界杯足球赛

FIFA U-20 World Cup 世界青年足球锦标赛

FIFA U-17 World Cup 世界少年足球锦标赛

FIFA Futsal World Cup 五人足球世界杯赛

Chinese Football Association 中国足协

Questions:

1. When and where was the FIFA founded?

2. What are the major responsibilities of the FIFA?

3. Can you list the main competitions organized by the FIFA?

Part Three Exercises

Directions: Do the following exercises.

1. Watch a CSL football match and give your opinion on the present situation of Chinese football.

2. If a substitute uses offensive, insulting or abusive language, or makes obscene gestures, can the referee show him a red card to send him off the pitch?

Part Four Rules and Concepts

1. A football game is played on a rectangular grass or artificial turf field, which is 105 meters long and 70 meters wide. In the international matches, the field can range from 100 meters to 110 meters in length and 64 meters to 75 meters in width.

2. A player must not use equipment or wear anything which is dangerous to himself or another player. The basic compulsory equipment of a player is a jersey or shirt, shorts, stockings, shinguards and footwear.

3. Each match is controlled by a referee who has full authority to enforce the rules of the game in connection with the match. The officials wear uniforms that distinguish them from the players on both teams.

4. The team that wins the coin toss has the right to choose the kickoff or the side. All players of the two teams must stay on their own half of the field before the kickoff takes place.

5. If the ball completely crosses the goal line between the goalposts and under the crossbar, the goal will be awarded.

6. A ball is in play when it is within the boundaries of the field and/or the play has not been stopped by the referee. A ball is out of play when the ball completely crosses the touch line or goal line, or the play has been stopped by the referee.

7. An attacking player is in the offside position when he is closer to the goal line than either the ball or an opposing defender.

8. A penalty kick is awarded if any of the most severe rule violations is committed by the defense inside its own penalty area.

9. Free kicks are awarded for fouls or violations of rules. When a free kick is taken, all players of the offending side must be 10 yards (9 meters) away from the ball. Free kicks may be either direct or indirect.

10. In a direct free kick, the ball may be kicked straight into the net of the offending team to score a goal while in an indirect free kick, a goal can be scored only if the ball subsequently touches another player before it enters the goal.

Part Five Further Reading

Ronaldo

Ronaldo Luís Nazário de Lima, commonly known as Ronaldo, is a retired Brazilian footballer. Popularly dubbed "the phenomenon", he is considered by experts and fans to be one of the greatest football players of all time. A three-time FIFA World Player of the Year and two-time Ballon d'Or recipient, Ronaldo was named in the FIFA 100, a list of the greatest living players compiled in 2004, and was inducted into the Brazilian Football Museum Hall of Fame and the Italian Football Hall of Fame.

Ronaldo played for Brazil in 98 matches, scoring 62 goals, and is the second-highest goal scorer for his national team. Aged 17, he was a member of the Brazilian squad that won the 1994 FIFA World Cup. At the 1998 World Cup, he received the Golden Ball for player of the tournament in helping Brazil reach the final where he suffered a convulsive fit hours before the defeat to France. He won a second World Cup in 2002 where he scored twice in the final, and received the Golden Boot as top goal scorer. During the 2006 FIFA World Cup, Ronaldo scored his 15th World Cup goal, which was a World Cup record at the time.

Basketball

Part One Listening and Speaking

Activity 1

🎧 Listen to the following conversation, and then work in pairs to act it out.

(During a basketball game, the coach substitutes player No. 15 for No. 10. He then tells No. 15 what he should do after he enters the court.)

A: No. 15, get ready to go onto the court and substitute No. 10.

B: OK, coach.

A: When you get out there, tell No. 8 to keep an eye on the other team's right guard.

B: Sure thing.

A: Are you clear about your position on the court?

B: Yes, I'll take the power forward (No. 4) position and help No. 8 do the center-pivot play.

A: Good. Be careful out there on defense, keep moving your feet quickly.

B: Copy that, coach. Can I go out there now?

A: Yeah, get going. Head to the scorer's table.

Words and Expressions

substitute /'sʌbstɪtjuːt/ *v.* 替代，替换；
n. 替代品

court /kɔːt/ *n.* 球场

keep an eye on sb. 盯住某人

guard /gɑːd/ *n.* 防卫，防守

power forward 大前锋

center-pivot /'sentə(r)-'pɪvət/ *n.* 中锋

defense /dɪ'fens/ *n.* 防守，防御

scorer /'skɔːrə(r)/ *n.* 记分员，记录员

Activity 2

👤 Work in pairs and make conversations according to the given situations.

Situation 1: Please organize some pre-game warm-up exercises. The team captain is responsible for the warm-up, including running, drills without arms, shooting and action shot.

Situation 2: It is time for a time-out. The coach and players are discussing changing from a zonal defense to a man-to-man defense, so players will need to keep a close watch on their defensive players and assist each other.

Part Two Reading

Passage 1

Directions: Read the passage about basketball and discuss the following questions with your partner.

Basketball

The game of basketball was invented in 1891 by an American Dr. James Naismith, a physical education professor and instructor at the International Young Men's Christian Association Training School (YMCA) (Springfield College) in Springfield, Massachusetts. Dr. Naismith sought a vigorous indoor game to keep his students occupied and at proper levels of fitness during the long New England winters. After rejecting other ideas as either too rough or poorly suited to gymnasiums, he imitated the actions of peach growers picking the peaches and throwing them into baskets, and nailed a peach basket onto a 3-meter elevated track, in order to let the students throw the ball into the basket. This was the beginning of a new sport.

After experiencing the periods of starting up, trying out, improving, spreading, popularizing, innovating and overall developing, the game has gradually evolved into the modern basketball game. When playing the game, players coordinate, fight, offend, defend and move dynamically. It is a comprehensive, professional and commercial game loved deeply by the masses.

There are many techniques for ball-handling—shooting, passing, dribbling, and rebounding. Basketball teams generally have player positions. The tallest and strongest members of a team are called center forward or power forward, while slightly shorter and more agile players are called small forward, and the shortest players or those who possess the best ball-handling skills are called point guard or shooting guard. The point guard directs the on-court action of the team, implementing the coach's game plan, and managing the execution of offensive and defensive plays (player positioning).

Words and Expressions

seek /siːk/ *v.* 寻求，寻找；探索

vigorous /'vɪgərəs/ *adj.* 有力的；有精力的，充沛的

occupied /'ɒkjupaɪd/ *adj.* 无空闲的；占用的

imitate /'ɪmɪteɪt/ *v.* 模仿，效仿

popularize /'pɒpjələraɪz/ *v.* 使大受欢迎，使流行

innovate /'ɪnəveɪt/ *v.* 革新，创新

coordinate /kəʊ'ɔːdɪneɪt/ *v.* 协调，配合

offend /ə'fend/ *v.* 进攻；攻击

defend /dɪ'fend/ *v.* 防守；防卫

professional /prə'feʃənl/ *adj.* 专业的

commercial /kə'mɜːʃl/ *adj.* 商业的

implement /'ɪmplɪment/ *v.* 履行，执行

Sports Terms

ball-handling /bɔːl-'hændlɪŋ/ *n.* 运球

shooting /'ʃuːtɪŋ/ *n.* 投球

passing /'paːsɪŋ/ *n.* 传球

dribbling /'drɪblɪŋ/ *n.* 控球

rebounding /rɪ'baʊndɪŋ/ *n.* 篮板球

center forward/ power forward 中锋

small forward 小前锋

point guard/ shooting guard 得分后卫

Questions:

1. When and where was basketball first invented?

2. What are the techniques for ball-handling in basketball?

Passage 2

Directions: Read the passage about the FIBA and discuss the following questions with your partner.

International Basketball Federation

The International Basketball Federation (FIBA) is an international organization comprised of many basketball associations in the world, with its headquarters in Geneva, Switzerland. It was founded in 1932, four years before the sport was officially recognized by the IOC. There are currently 215 members, and they are divided into five regional zones or commissions: Africa, Americas, Asia, Europe, and Oceania. Each of them is responsible for the basketball affairs of its own area.

The FIBA is responsible for establishing the international rules of basketball, specifying the equipment and facilities required (e.g. the height of the basketball hoop, the length and width of the basketball court, the size of the penalty area, the distance from the three-point line, etc.), regulating the transfer of players across countries, appointing referees in international basketball competitions, and organizing large-scale games of basketball.

The FIBA Basketball World Cup is a world tournament for men's national teams which is held every four years. Teams compete for the Naismith Trophy. A parallel event for women's teams, the FIBA Women's Basketball World Cup, is also held every four years. It was held in the same year as the men's event but in a different country.

Words and Expressions

regional /'riːdʒənl/ *adj.* 地区性的，区域性的

commission /kəˈmɪʃn/ *n.* 委员会；佣金

affair /əˈfeə(r)/ *n.* 事务

specify /ˈspesɪfaɪ/ *v.* 具体说明，明确规定

facility /fəˈsɪlətɪ/ *n.* 设施；设备

penalty /ˈpenəltɪ/ *n.* 惩罚，处罚

appoint /əˈpɔɪnt/ *v.* 约定；任命，指派

tournament /ˈtʊənəmənt/ *n.* 锦标赛；联赛

International Basketball Federation (FIBA) 国际篮球联合会

basketball hoop 篮球筐

basketball court 篮球场

penalty area 禁区

three-point line 三分线

FIBA Basketball World Cup 国际篮联篮球世界杯

Naismith Trophy 奈史密斯杯

Questions:

1. When was the FIBA founded?

2. Can you describe the main responsibilities of the FIBA?

Part Three Exercises

Directions: Do the following exercises.

1. Prepare some questions for a press conference to interview a coach before the CBA League Finals. You can ask the coach about his ideas of this match, his evaluation of the opponents and his prediction of the result.

2. Write a short article on the basketball team of your university. For instance, describe characteristics of the players and the coach, and give some suggestions for their improvement.

Part Four Rules and Concepts

1. Basketball is played by two teams of five players each. The aim of each team is to score in the opponents' basket and to prevent the other team from scoring. The game is controlled by officials, table officials and a commissioner, if present.

2. The playing court shall have a flat, hard surface free from obstructions with dimensions of 28 meters in length by 15 meters in width measured from the inner edge of the boundary line.

3. The captain is a player designated by his coach to represent his team on the playing court. He may communicate in a courteous manner with the officials during the

game to obtain information; however, this can only happen when the ball becomes dead and the game clock is stopped.

4. The game are played in four quarters of 10 minutes (FIBA) or 12 minutes (NBA).

5. A goal is made when a live ball enters the basket from above and remains within or passes through the basket.

6. A dribble is the movement of a live ball caused by a player in control of that ball who throws, taps, rolls the ball on the floor or deliberately throws it against the backboard.

7. A player shall not remain in the opponents' restricted area for more than three consecutive seconds while his team is in control of a live ball in the frontcourt and the game clock is running.

8. An unsportsmanlike foul is a player contact foul which, in the judgment of an official, is not a legitimate attempt to directly play the ball within the spirit and intent of the rules.

9. Charging is illegal personal contact, with or without the ball, by pushing or moving into an opponent's torso.

10. Blocking is illegal personal contact which impedes the progress of an opponent with or without the ball.

Part Five Further Reading

Kobe Bryant

Kobe Bryant is an American professional basketball player for the Los Angeles Lakers of the National Basketball Association (NBA).

The son of former NBA player Joe Bryant, Kobe Bryant enjoyed a successful high school basketball career at Lower Merion High School in Pennsylvania, where he was recognized as the top high school basketball player in the country. He declared for the NBA draft upon graduation, and was selected with the 13th overall pick in the 1996 NBA draft by the Charlotte Hornets, who traded him to the Los Angeles Lakers. As a rookie, Bryant won the 1997 Slam Dunk Contest, and was named an All-Star by his second season.

He has played for the Lakers his entire career, winning five NBA championships. Bryant is an 18-time All-Star, 15-time member of the All-NBA Team, and 12-time member of the All-Defensive Team. He has led the league in scoring twice, and he ranks third on both the league's all-time regular season scoring and all-time postseason scoring lists. At the 2008 and 2012 Summer Olympics, he won gold medals as a member of the U.S. national team.

After beginning his 20th season with the Lakers in 2015–2016, Bryant announced that he would retire after the season.

Lesson 14 Volleyball

Part One Listening and Speaking

Activity 1

🎧 Listen to the following conversation, and then work in pairs to act it out.

(A volleyball match is about to begin. The referee has whistled and ordered the captains of both sides to join in the coin toss.)

A: Captains, let's toss. The Blue Team is pattern. Do you want to serve or receive?

B: I choose to receive.

A: No. 7's necklace is dangerous, and so is No. 8's ring. They must remove them; otherwise, they are not allowed to play.

B: OK. No. 7 has taken the necklace off. But No. 8's ring is too tight to remove. Don't worry, she has it taped.

(The match is ongoing.)

A: Captain, your libero replacement must be quick. It's not allowed after I have whistled, or I will give you a delay penalty next time.

B: Yes, sir. But they always intentionally prevent us from seeing when they serve.

A: I'll pay attention to that.

B: Excuse me, sir. Why did you rule our ball "four hits"?

A: I've explained. Play or appeal, it's up to you. Otherwise, I will give you a sanction.

B: We choose to appeal, sir.

A: OK, please confirm it after the game. Captain, please inform your teammates not to irritate your opponents.

B: Yes, sir. Thank you!

Words and Expressions

captain /ˈkæptɪn/ *n.* 队长	**prevent** /prɪˈvent/ *v.* 阻止；预防
toss /tɒs/ *n. & v.* 扔，抛，掷	**sanction** /ˈsæŋkʃn/ *n.* 制裁，处罚；许可，批准
serve /sɜːv/ *n. & v.* 发球；服务	
receive /rɪˈsiːv/ *v. & n.* 接球；收到，得到	**confirm** /kənˈfɜːm/ *v.* 确认
replacement /rɪˈpleɪsmənt/ *n.* 更换，置换	**irritate** /ˈɪrɪteɪt/ *v.* 使烦恼（尤指不断重复的事情）；刺激（皮肤或身体部位）
delay /dɪˈleɪ/ *n.* 耽搁，延误	
intentionally /ɪnˈtenʃənəlɪ/ *adv.* 故意地，有意地，存心地	**opponent** /əˈpəʊnənt/ *n.* 对手

Activity 2

👤 Work in pairs and answer the following questions.

Question 1: The libero of the team has just been replaced by a player. After the technical time-out, could he or she return to the court immediately?

Question 2: How does the substitution proceed in a volleyball match?

Part Two Reading

Passage 1

Directions: Read the passage about volleyball and discuss the following questions with your partner.

Volleyball

Volleyball is one of the most successful and popular sports in the world. It is competitive, recreational and explosive. It is a team sport in which two teams of six players are separated by a net. Each team tries to score points by grounding a ball on the other team's court under organized rules. It has been a part of the official program of the Summer Olympic Games since 1964.

Volleyball originated from 1895, in Holyoke, Massachusetts. William G. Morgan, a physical education director, created a new game called "Mintonette". Then an observer, Dr. Alfred Halstead, noticed the volleying nature of the game and renamed it as "volleyball". It was brought to China in 1905.

Generally, there are two forms of volleyball. One is competitive volleyball, such as six-players volleyball and beach volleyball. The other is entertainment volleyball, such as soft volleyball, balloon volleyball, four-players volleyball, nine-players volleyball and volleyball for the disabled. A formal six-players volleyball competition starts with the serving team. The back right player throws the ball into the air and attempts to hit the ball so it passes over the net. The opposing team must use a combination of no more than three contacts with the volleyball to return the ball to the opponent's side of the net. Each team is entitled to a maximum of three hits (except for blocking) and each player may not hit the ball twice consecutively (except for blocking). The competition continues until one of the following situations: (1) the ball successfully grounds on the opponent's court; (2) the ball lands out of the court as it touches the arms or the hands of the opposing team players; (3) a player commits a fault. A team scores a point for every successful hit. The first team to score 25 points by a two-point margin is awarded the set. A match is won by the team that wins three sets, and the fifth set is usually played to 15 points by a two-point margin.

Words and Expressions

recreational /ˌrekrɪˈeɪʃənl/ *adj.* 娱乐的，消遣的

explosive /ɪkˈspləʊsɪv/ *adj.* 突增的，猛增的；爆炸性的

score /skɔ:(r)/ *v.* 得分

volley /ˈvɒlɪ/ *v.* 截击，齐发

entertainment /ˌentəˈteɪnmənt/ *n.* 娱乐活动

entitle /ɪnˈtaɪtl/ *v.* 有……的权利

maximum /ˈmæksɪməm/ *n.* 最大值，最大化

consecutively /kənˈsekjətɪvlɪ/ *adv.* 连续不断地

commit /kəˈmɪt/ *v.* 犯……错

competitive volleyball 竞技排球

six-players volleyball 6 人制排球

beach volleyball 沙滩排球

entertainment volleyball 娱乐排球

soft volleyball 软式排球

balloon volleyball 气排球

four-players volleyball 4 人排球

nine-players volleyball 9 人排球

blocking /ˈblɒkɪŋ/ *n.* 拦网

Questions:

1. Can you describe the origin and development of volleyball?

2. Can you list different forms of volleyball?

3. Do you know the rules of volleyball games?

Passage 2

Directions: Read the passage about the International Volleyball Federation and discuss the following questions with your partner.

International Volleyball Federation

The International Volleyball Federation, commonly known by the acronym FIVB, is the international governing body for the sports of indoor, beach and grass volleyball. Its headquarters are located in Lausanne, Switzerland and its current president is Ary Graça. As of 2010, the FIVB counted 220 affiliated national federations.

The FIVB was founded in Paris, France in 1947, by 14 national federations representing five different continents, under the leadership of Paul Libaud. The first World Championships were organized in 1949 for men and 1952 for women and both have remained the biggest events in volleyball, along with the Olympic Games in 1964. Later in 1969, a new international event, the World Cup was introduced. In 1984, the FIVB moved its headquarters to Lausanne, Switzerland and intensified its policy of promoting volleyball on a worldwide basis. Measures taken include the establishment of competitions for men's and women's volleyball, such as the World League and the Grand Prix, the indication of beach volleyball as an Olympic event and a number of changes in the rules of the game with the purpose of enhancing public visibility.

The FIVB's main responsibility is worldwide planning and organization of volleyball events. This involves defining qualification procedures and competition formulae for tournaments, as well as the FIVB's world rankings.

Words and Expressions

as of 到······时候为止	见度
represent /ˌreprɪ'zent/ *v.* 代表	**formula** /'fɔːmjələ/ *n.* (复数 formulae)
intensify /ɪn'tensɪfaɪ/ *v.* 加强，强化	方案，计划；配方；程式
visibility /ˌvɪzə'bɪləti/ *n.* 显示度，可	

Sports Terms

International Volleyball Federation (FIVB) 国际排球联合会

grass volleyball 草地排球

Questions:

    1. When was the FIVB founded?

    2. Can you retell the history of the FIVB briefly?

    3. What are the main responsibilities of the FIVB?

Part Three Exercises

Directions: Do the following exercises.

1. Write an article about the activity of playing volleyball in no less than 250 words. The article should highlight the process of players' communication, emotion and performance, etc.

2. Watch a volleyball match and give a commentary on the players' attacking tactics.

Part Four Rules and Concepts

1. The referee corps for a volleyball match is composed of the following officials: the first referee, the second referee, the scorer and four (two) line judges.

2. Before the match, the first referee carries out a coin toss to decide upon the first service and the sides of the court in the first set. If a deciding set is to be played, a new toss will be carried out.

3. Prior to the match, the team captain signs the score sheet and represents his team in the toss. When the ball is out of play, only the game captain is authorized to speak to the referees.

4. Regular game interruptions are time-outs and substitutions. Each team is entitled to a maximum of two time-outs and six player substitutions per set.

5. A hit is any contact with the ball by a player in play. The team is entitled to a maximum of three hits (in addition to a block) for returning the ball. If more are used, the team commits the fault of "four hits".

6. The ball may touch any part of the player's body. It can rebound in any direction.

7. It is permitted to penetrate into the opponent's space under the net, provided that it does not interfere with the opponent's play.

8. At the moment of the service hit or take-off for a jump service, the server must not touch the court (the end line included) or the floor outside the service zone.

9. Consecutive (quick and continuous) contacts with the ball may occur by one or more blockers provided that the contacts are made during one action. A block contact is not counted as a team hit. Consequently, after a block contact, a team is entitled to three hits to return the ball.

10. For FIVB world competitions for seniors where a team chooses to have more than twelve players, it is compulsory for the team to designate amongst the list of players two specialized defensive players as "liberos". The libero cannot be either team captain or game captain at the same time as performing the libero function.

Part Five Further Reading

Lang Ping

Lang Ping is a former Chinese volleyball player and the current head coach of Chinese women's national volleyball team.

Owing to her central role in the Chinese women's volleyball team in the 1980s, Lang Ping was seen as a cultural icon and is one of the most respected people in modern Chinese sports history. She and the women's volleyball team won the world championships multiple times, concluding with the 1984 Olympics.

In 1995, Lang Ping became the head coach of the Chinese national team and eventually guided the squad to the silver medal at the 1996 Summer Olympics and second place at the 1998 World Championships. Due to health reasons, she resigned from the national team, and went to Italy, and then the U.S. In 2013, she became the head coach of the Chinese national team again and guided the Chinese squad to the gold medal at 2016 Rio Olympics.

She became the first person to have won gold medals at the Olympics both as a player and as a coach.

Lesson 15

Table Tennis

Part One Listening and Speaking

Activity 1

🎧 Listen to the following conversation, and then work in pairs to act it out.

(Harry is meeting his friend Robert after playing a game of table tennis. Now they are discussing the final result together.)

A: Hello, Harry! You have a ruddy face. Have you just finished playing table tennis?

B: Yeah, I'm exhausted! Very hot and sweaty!

A: How did it go?

B: It was fun, but I lost four games to five.

A: Really? But you're such a good player. How could you lose with your versatile changing spins and tricky placements?

B: John is younger and more energetic. He swings very fast, but that's not the point.

A: But you swing just as fast and hard as people younger than you, right?

B: For me, it's the footwork that matters the most. I cannot move as fast as them.

A: He must have played his best to beat you. He's a talented person.

B: I couldn't agree more. Today I got a good sense of real speed, strength, spin, placement and footwork in playing table tennis. All of them are important.

Words and Expressions

ruddy /'rʌdɪ/ *adj.*（面色）红润健康的

exhausted /ɪg'zɔːstɪd/ *adj.* 筋疲力尽的，疲惫不堪的

sweaty /'swetɪ/ *adj.* 汗流浃背的

versatile /'vɜːsətaɪl/ *adj.* 多才多艺的，有多种技能的

tricky /'trɪkɪ/ *adj.* 机警的

placement /'pleɪsmənt/ *n.* 落点；（对人的）安置，安排

energetic /ˌenə'dʒetɪk/ *adj.* 能量充沛的，精力旺盛的

footwork /'fʊtwɜːk/ *n.*（体育、舞蹈的）步法，脚步动作

talented /'tæləntɪd/ *adj.* 有天赋的

Activity 2

👥 Work in pairs and make conversations according to the given situations.

Situation 1: You will help your friend download a training video with which he can conduct a special practice of footwork when playing table tennis.

Situation 2: You are told that there is a kind of glue in an exclusive shop, and brushing it on sponges can increase the ball's speed. You are considering giving it a try.

Part Two Reading

Passage 1

Directions: Read the passage about table tennis and discuss the following questions.

Table Tennis

Table tennis originated in England during the 19th century, where it was played among the upper-class as an after-dinner game. It has been suggested that the game was developed by British military officers in India in around 1860s or 1870s. Soldiers laid a row of books along the center of the table as a net, using two more books as rackets and continuously hit a golf-ball. In modern times, table tennis is a sport in which two or four players hit a lightweight ball back and forth across a table using a small paddle. The game takes place on a hard table divided by a net.

The paddle can be divided into two categories: the pen-hold grip and handshake grip. The basic skills of table tennis include grip, serve, receive, push, block, attack, chop, and loop drive, etc. Speed, strength, spin and placement are the four main influential factors. Meanwhile the tactics in table tennis consist of the serve, service and reception, push attack, and counterattack during chops. Attack after service is the tactic one uses to take the initiative, and it is the most common weapon used in a pen-hold quick attack. Different types of players use this tactic to take the lead over their opponents, and the effect could be seen with a perfect serve during the first three strokes.

The World Table Tennis Championships, World Cup and the Olympics are the three main sporting events in table tennis. Table tennis has been an Olympic sport since 1988, with several event categories. From 1988 to 2004, these were men's singles, women's singles, men's doubles and women's doubles. Since 2008, a team event has been played instead of the doubles.

Words and Expressions

racket /ˈrækɪt/ *n.* 球拍

lightweight /ˈlaɪtweɪt/ *adj.* 重量轻的

back and forth 反复地，来回地

paddle /ˈpædl/ *n.* （乒乓球）球拍

take the initiative 采取主动

take the lead 占上风；带头，为首

stroke /strəʊk/ *n.* 击球动作

Sports Terms

pen-hold grip 直板

handshake grip 横板

grip /grɪp/ *n.* 握拍

push /pʊʃ/ *n.* 推球

block /blɒk/ *n.* 挡球

attack /əˈtæk/ *n.* 攻球

chop /tʃɒp/ *n.* 削球

loop drive 弧圈球

push attack 搓攻战术

counterattack during chops 削中反攻战术

attack after service 发球抢攻

Questions:

 1. How was table tennis brought out?

 2. Can you list some basic skills in playing table tennis?

 3. Which events have been included in the Olympic table tennis competitions since 2008?

Passage 2

Directions: Read the passage about the International Table Tennis Federation and discuss the following questions.

International Table Tennis Federation

 The International Table Tennis Federation, referred to as ITTF, is the governing body for all international table tennis associations. It was founded in Berlin, Germany in 1926, and headquartered now in Lausanne, Switzerland. The current president since 2014 is Thomas Weikert from Germany. It has 222 existing association members belonging to six continental federations: European Table Tennis Union, Asian Table Tennis Union, African Table Tennis Federation, Latin American Table Tennis Federation, Northern American Table Tennis Union and Oceania Table Tennis Federation. The Chinese Table Tennis Association (CTTA) formally joined the ITTF in 1953.

 One of the ITTF's main tournaments is the World Table Tennis Championships (WTTC). They are regarded as the top-level games held by the ITTF and have a worldwide influence. The World Championships include seven formal events, and every event has its specific cup which was named after the donator's name or country's name.

 China is no doubt the strongest member in the ITTF, having many world famous players and coaches, to name a few: Xu Yinsheng—ITTF honorary president, Cai Zhenhua—CTTA president, Zhang Deying—three-time world champion, Kong Linghui—Olympic & world champion, Ma Lin—Beijing Olympic champion in men's single and his partner Chen Qi—Athens Olympic champion in men's doubles, and Guo Yue and Wang Hao—both world champions.

Words and Expressions

donor /ˈdəʊnə(r)/ *n.* 捐赠者　　　honorary /ˈɒnərərɪ/ *adj.* 名誉的，荣誉的

Sports Terms

International Table Tennis Federation (ITTF) 国际乒乓球联合会

Chinese Table Tennis Association (CTTA) 中国乒乓球协会

World Table Tennis Championships (WTTC) 世界乒乓球锦标赛

Questions:

1. What is the most important tournament governed by the ITTF?

2. Can you introduce some famous Chinese table tennis players to your classmates?

Part Three Exercises

Directions: Do the following exercises.

1. Suppose you are going to interview a very famous table tennis coach. Please draft an outline for the interview.

2. Discuss your point of view on the development of Chinese table tennis.

Part Four Rules and Concepts

1. The playing space of table tennis shall be rectangular and not less than 14 m long, 7 m wide and 5 m high. The light source shall not be less than 5 m above the floor.

2. Service shall start with the ball resting freely on the open palm of the server's stationary free hand.

3. The server shall project the ball nearly vertically upwards, without imparting spin, so that it rises at least 16 cm after leaving the palm of the free hand and then falls without touching anything before being struck.

4. The ball, having been served or returned, shall be struck to touch the opponent's court, either directly or after touching the net assembly.

5. A game shall be won by the player first scoring 11 points unless both players score 10 points, when the game shall be won by the first player subsequently gaining a lead of 2 points.

6. A match is usually two games out of three or three games out of five. The player winning the toss has the choice of service or end of table.

7. Players often towel themselves off, tie their shoes, or in some other way attempting to change the pace of the game.

8. When competing against a top table tennis player, a short and low serve is the safest way to get the ball into play.

9. Backspin is applied by hitting through and under the ball with the lower part of the paddle angled ahead of the upper section. The aim is to make the ball slow down and die (bounce as little as possible) on contact with the table.

10. Forehand smash is one of the most devastating shots in any player's armory, in which the ball is hit at a high speed. As well as adding topspin, the player can conceal in which direction the ball will travel by flicking his wrist to direct the ball across the table.

Part Five Further Reading

Zhang Yining

Zhang Yining is a former Chinese table tennis player. She is considered one of the greatest female table tennis players in the history of the sport.

Zhang Yining almost held the ITTF No. 1 ranking continuously from 2003 to 2009, remaining a dominant figure in women's table tennis, with four Olympic gold medals, ten World Championships, and four World Cup wins.

Zhang is the women's singles and doubles gold medals holder at the 2004 Summer Olympics. She participated in the 2008 Summer Olympics in Beijing, winning the gold medals in both the women's singles and women's team competition. Zhang successfully defended her singles Olympic gold medal, defeating compatriot Wang Nan in the finals 8-11, 13-11, 11-8, 11-8, 11-3. During the 2008 Beijing Olympics, she was often referred to by commentators as "The Yellow Beast", denoting her dominance of the sport.

Zhang was married in October 2009 and has not been present in table tennis tournaments since then. She announced her retirement from international play on March, 2011.

Lesson 16

Tennis

Part One Listening and Speaking

Activity 1

🎧 Listen to the following conversation, and then work in pairs to act it out.

(Magee is a good tennis player, and Allen is a beginner. Allen is consulting Magee about the tennis serve.)

A: Hi, Magee, I've heard that you're a good tennis player. I'm having trouble understanding the serve in tennis. Could you explain it to me?

B: Sure. The server stands behind his own baseline to one side of the center mark, and then hits the ball over the net into whichever service court is diagonally opposite.

A: OK. Then how about that for the first point of the game?

B: For the first point of each game, the player stands right of the center mark to serve. For the second, to the left; for the third, back to the right and so on alternately.

A: When I watch a tennis match on TV, I often hear "let". I was wondering what "let" means.

B: If the service ball touches the net, but still goes into the correct service court, it is called a "let". This means the server can serve again.

A: What if it's a "let" on the first serve?

B: If it happens on the first serve, the server still has two attempts to make a good service.

A: I see. And how does the scoring system work? It's so confusing.

B: It may seem that way at first, but in fact it's quite simple.

A: OK, but I'm not familiar with it.

B: No worries. Let me clarify. In each game, a player begins with no score, which is called "love". The first point he wins in the game gives him a total score of 15. The second brings the total to 30, and the third to 40. After this, the next point wins him the game unless his opponent also reaches 40, in which case, one of them has to get a two-point lead to win.

A: Got it. Thanks for your explanations!

B: You're welcome!

Words and Expressions

baseline /'beɪslaɪn/ n. 端线；底线；基线

service court 发球区

diagonally /daɪ'ægənəlɪ/ adv. 斜着地，呈对角线地

alternately /ɔːl'tɜːnətlɪ/ adv. 交替地，轮流地

let /let/ n.（网球或羽毛球发球时的）触网重发

confusing /kən'fjuːzɪŋ/ adj. 令人疑惑的

Activity 2

Work in pairs and answer the following questions.

Question 1: Is the receiver allowed to stand outside the lines of the court?

Question 2: After the server has hit a first serve, the racket falls out of the server's hand and touches the net before the ball has bounced. Is this a service fault, or does the server lose the point?

Part Two Reading

Passage 1

Directions: Read the passage about tennis and discuss the following questions.

Tennis

Tennis is a sport that can be played individually against a single opponent (singles) or between two teams of two players each (doubles). Each player uses a tennis racket to strike a hollow rubber ball covered with felt over or around a net and into the opponent's court. The object of the game is to play the ball in a way that the opponent is not able to play a valid return. The player who is unable to return the ball will not gain a point, while the opposite player will.

Tennis originated from a French court game. Played in the 12th century, the game initially involved hitting the ball with one's palms, until later when rackets were developed. The sport gained popularity in France and England, where it was played by the aristocrats who in turn appealed to the masses by constructing public playing areas. In 1869, Walter Wingfield, a British army officer, invented the game of "Sphairistike", which was the direct predecessor of the modern game of lawn tennis. By 1873, Wingfield began marketing the game together with the racket and rubber balls to the general public, which quickly caught on to its appeal. Now, it is regarded as the second most popular ball game in the world.

Tournaments are often organized by gender and number of players. Common tournament configurations include men's singles, women's singles and doubles. The four Grand Slam tournaments are considered to be the most prestigious tennis events in the world. They are held annually and comprise, in chronological order, the Australian Open played on hard courts, the French Open played on red clay courts, the Wimbledon Open played on grass courts, and the U.S. Open played also on hard courts.

Words and Expressions

hollow /'hɒləʊ/ *adj.* 空的，中空的

object /'ɒbdʒɪkt/ *n.* 目标；物体

valid /'vælɪd/ *adj.* 有效的，合法的

aristocrat /'ærɪstəkræt/ *n.* 贵族

appeal /ə'piːl/ *v.* 对……有吸引力 *n.* 吸引力，兴趣

mass /mæs/ *n.* 群众

lawn /lɔːn/ *n.* 草地，草坪

configuration /kən,fɪɡə'reɪʃn/ *n.* 配置，结构

prestigious /pre'stɪdʒəs/ *adj.* 有声望的

chronological /,krɒnə'lɒdʒɪkl/ *adj.* 按时间先后的

Sports Terms

tennis racket 网球拍

the four Grand Slam 四大满贯

Australian Open 澳大利亚网球公开赛

French Open 法国网球公开赛

Wimbledon Open 温布尔登网球公开赛

U.S. Open 美国网球公开赛

Questions:

1. Can you describe the origin and development of tennis?

2. How can a player get a point in playing tennis?

3. What are the four Grand Slam tournaments?

Passage 2

Directions: Read the passage about world tennis organizations and discuss the following questions.

World Tennis Organizations

The ITF (International Tennis Federation) was established in 1913 and is the oldest international tennis organization, headquartered in London. Its main responsibilities are: in charge of any affairs about the game of tennis; formulating the rules of tennis; promoting the popularization and development of tennis among the youth; organizing the Davis Cup, Fed Cup and Olympic tennis tournament; directing the four Grand Slam tournaments.

The ATP (Association of Tennis Professionals) was formed in 1972. It is an autonomous international organization of male professional tennis players. Its main task is to coordinate partnerships between professional athletes and events. It is also responsible for organizing and managing professional athletes' points, rankings, and bonus distribution, developing competition rules, and qualifying or disqualifying players. It organizes the ATP World Tour Masters 1000 annually.

The WTA (Women's Tennis Association) was founded in 1973. It is an autonomous organization of female professional tennis players around the world. Its main task is to organize a variety of women's professional tournaments. It is responsible for more than

60 games such as the WTA Tour Finals tournament and four Open events. It primarily represents the interests of female professional players worldwide to ensure that they have the opportunity to participate in competitions, and to promote the development of women's tennis.

Words and Expressions

formulate /'fɔːmjʊleɪt/ v. 制定；规划

direct /də'rekt/ v. 管理，监督

adj. 直接的

autonomous /ɔː'tɒnəməs/ *adj.* 有自治

权的，自治的

bonus /'bəʊnəs/ n. 奖金

distribution /ˌdɪstrɪ'bjuːʃn/ n. 分配

primarily /praɪ'merəlɪ/ adv. 主要地；

根本地

Sports Terms

International Tennis Federation (ITF) 国际网球联合会

Davis Cup 戴维斯杯

Fed Cup 联合会杯

Association of Tennis Professionals (ATP) 世界男子职业网球协会

ATP World Tour Masters 1000 ATP 世界巡回赛 1000 大师赛

Women's Tennis Association (WTA) 国际女子网球协会

Questions:

1. When was the ITF founded?

2. What are the responsibilities of the ATP?

3. What are the responsibilities of the WTA?

Part Three Exercises

Directions: Do the following exercises.

1. Suppose you are a journalist and are asked to write an article about Li Na. Think about what kind of information will be included in your article.

2. Watch a tennis match, and write an essay in no less than 250 words.

Part Four Rules and Concepts

1. A standard game is scored as follows with the server's score being called first: NO point—"Love"; First point—"15"; Second point—"30"; Third point—"40"; Fourth point—"Game".

2. A match can be played to the best of 3 sets (a player/team needs to win 2 sets to win the match) or to the best of 5 sets (a player/team needs to win 3 sets to win the match).

3. The player shall change ends at the end of the first, third and every subsequent odd game of each set. During a tie-break game, the player shall change ends after every six points.

4. The choice of ends and the choice to be server or receiver in the first game shall be decided by a coin toss before the warm-up starts.

5. Immediately before starting the service motion, the server shall stand at rest with both feet behind (i.e. further from the net than) the baseline and within the imaginary extensions of the center mark and the sideline.

6. When serving in a standard game, the server shall stand behind alternate halves of the court, starting from the right half of the court in all games. The service shall pass over the net and hit the service court diagonally opposite, before the receiver returns it.

7. The player/team shall stand on opposite sides of the net. The server puts the ball into play for the first point, and the receiver returns the ball served by the server.

8. If a ball touches a line, it is regarded as touching the court bounded by that line.

9. If a player is hindered in playing by a deliberate act of the opponent, the player shall win the point.

10. Coaching is considered to be communication, advice or instruction of any kind to a player.

Part Five Further Reading

Novak Djokovic

Novak Djokovic is a Serbian professional tennis player who is currently ranked World No. 1 in men's singles tennis by the Association of Tennis Professionals (ATP). He is generally considered one of the greatest tennis players of all time. Djokovic holds the best match winning rate (83%) in Open Era, as of August 2016.

Djokovic has won 12 Grand Slam singles titles, the fourth most in history, and has held the No. 1 spot in the ATP rankings for a total of 214 weeks. In majors, Djokovic has won six Australian Open titles, three Wimbledon titles, two U.S. Open titles and one French Open title. In 2016, he became the eighth player in history to achieve the career Grand Slam by winning the 2016 French Open.

Djokovic is the first Serbian player to be ranked No. 1 by the ATP and the first male player representing Serbia to win a Grand Slam singles title. He has won numerous awards, including the 2012, 2015, and 2016 Laureus World Sports Award for Sportsman of the Year, 2011 BBC Overseas Sports Personality of the Year, five-time ITF World Champion, and four-time ATP Year-end No. 1.

Lesson 17 Badminton

Part One Listening and Speaking

Activity 1

🎧 Listen to the following conversation, and then work in pairs to act it out.

(Duncon is a big fan of badminton. He is talking with his coach Mr. Robert about the changes after the implementation of new rules for badminton tournaments.)

A: Coach! What are the big changes in the new rules for badminton?

B: The biggest change is that the serve ace has been cancelled. The singles match has uniformly ruled the win points of each game as 21 points, and more than 2 points is regarded as the winner according to two out of three sets. Meanwhile one minute's technical suspension is added.

A: How about the doubles?

B: It is the same as singles, but the second service is cancelled.

A: Is this supposed to speed up the game?

B: Yes.

A: Do you think it saves time?

B: Yes, it makes the competition faster in pace.

Words and Expressions

badminton /ˈbædmɪntən/ *n.* 羽毛球

serve ace 发球得分

uniformly /ˈjuːnɪfɔːmlɪ/ *adv.* 一致地，

始终如一地，一贯地

suspension /səˈspenʃn/ *n.* 中止，

暂停

pace /peɪs/ *n.* 节奏，速度

Activity 2

Work in pairs and answer the following questions.

Question 1: In the singles matches of badminton, can the winner of the first set serve first in the next set?

Question 2: In the singles matches of badminton, if both sides reach 20, shall a game be won by the player who scores 21 points first?

Part Two Reading

Passage 1

Directions: Read the passage about badminton and discuss the following questions.

Badminton

Badminton is a sport using rackets to hit a shuttlecock across a net. It is often played as a casual outdoor activity in a yard or on a beach; formal games are played on a rectangular indoor court. Points are scored by striking the shuttlecock with the racket and landing it within the opposing side's half of the court.

Each side may only strike the shuttlecock once before it passes over the net. Play ends once the shuttlecock has struck the floor or if a fault has been called by the umpire, service judge, or (in their absence) the opposing side. The shuttlecock is a feathered or (in informal matches) plastic projectile which flies differently from the balls used in many other sports. In particular, the feathers create much higher drag, causing the shuttlecock to decelerate more rapidly. Shuttlecocks also have a high top speed compared to the balls in other racket sports.

The game developed from the earlier game of battledore and shuttlecock. European play came to be dominated by Denmark but the game has become very popular in Asia, with recent competition dominated by China. Since 1992, badminton has been a Summer Olympic sport with five events: men's singles, women's singles, men's doubles, women's doubles, and mixed doubles. At high levels of play, the sport demands excellent fitness: players require aerobic stamina, agility, strength, speed, and precision. It is also a technical sport, requiring good motor coordination and the development of sophisticated racket movements.

Words and Expressions

casual /ˈkæʒuəl/ *adj.* 非正式的；临时的

yard /jɑːd/ *n.* 院子

beach /biːtʃ/ *n.* 沙滩

rectangular /rekˈtæŋgjələ(r)/ *adj.* 矩形的

umpire /ˈʌmpaɪə(r)/ *n.* 裁判

feathered /ˈfeðəd/ *adj.* 羽毛的

projectile /prəˈdʒektaɪl/ *n.* 抛射体，抛体

drag /dræg/ *n.* 拖尾

decelerate /ˌdiːˈseləreɪt/ *v.* 使减速

stamina /ˈstæmɪnə/ *n.* 毅力，精力

agility /əˈdʒɪləti/ *n.* 敏捷，灵活

precision /prɪˈsɪʒn/ *n.* 准确，精准

motor coordination 运动协调

sophisticated /səˈfɪstɪkeɪtɪd/ *adj.* 复杂的

Sports Terms

shuttlecock /ˈʃʌtlkɒk/ *n.* 羽毛球   **service judge** 发球裁判

Questions:

1. What are the basic rules of playing badminton?

2. What badminton events are included at the Olympic Games?

3. Do you think badminton is popular all over the world? Why?

Passage 2

Directions: Read the passage about the Badminton World Federation and discuss the following questions.

Badminton World Federation

The Badminton World Federation is the international governing body for the sport of badminton. It was founded as the International Badminton Federation (IBF) in 1934. In 2006, at the Extraordinary General Meeting in Madrid, it was decided to adopt the new name Badminton World Federation (BWF). There are five regional federations in the BWF: Badminton Asia Confederation (BAC), Badminton Europe (BE), Badminton Pan Am (BPA), Badminton Confederation of Africa (BCA) and Badminton Oceania (BO). Now it has a membership of 176. The Chinese Badminton Association joined the International Badminton Federation in 1981.

The organization's main task is to popularize and develop the sport of badminton around the world, to strengthen the connection between the national badminton associations, and to hold large international events. The BWF regularly organizes six major international badminton events, namely the Olympic badminton games, the World Men's Team Championships (the Thomas Cup), the World Women's Team Championships (the Uber Cup), the World Championships, the Group World Championships (the Sudirman Cup), and the World Junior Championships.

Sports Terms

Badminton World Federation (BWF) 世界羽毛球联合会

Chinese Badminton Association 中国羽毛球联合会

World Men's Team Championships (the Thomas Cup) 世界男子团体锦标赛（汤姆斯杯）

World Women's Team Championships (the Uber Cup) 世界女子团体锦标赛（尤伯杯赛）

Group World Championships (the Sudirman Cup) 世界团体锦标赛（苏迪曼杯）

World Junior Championships 世界青年锦标赛

Questions:

1. When was the BWF founded?

2. What competitions are hosted by the BWF?

Part Three Exercises

Directions: Do the following questions.

1. Watch an international or domestic badminton competition, and write an essay in no less than 250 words.

2. Watch a badminton doubles match with one of your friends and then make a short conversation about the match.

Part Four Rules and Concepts

1. In badminton games, a player of the serving side shall serve or receive in the right service court when the serving side has not scored or has scored an even number of points in that game. A player of the serving side shall serve or receive in the left service court when he has scored an odd number of points in the game.

2. After the ball is served, the server and receiver alternately hit the ball until the ball is dead or one violates the regulations.

3. The server gets one point when the receiver violates the regulations or the ball is dead for touching the receiver's court. Then the server serves the ball from the other service court.

4. The server loses the right to serve when he or she violates the regulations or the ball is dead for touching his or her own court. Then the receiver becomes the server, and neither party scores.

5. When the game starts, the party that wins the right to serve at a time should serve from the right service court. Only the receiver can receive the ball. If his or her partner hits the ball or is touched by the ball, the server gets one point.

6. After the ball is returned, anyone on the serving team can hit the ball, and then anyone on the receiving team can hit the ball, continuing back and forth until the

ball is dead.

7. After the ball is returned, the players can hit the ball from any position of their side.

8. During a serve, the arm must remain below the shoulder, and both feet must be on the ground throughout the stroke; overarm "tennis-style" serves are illegal, and the racket must remain beneath the server's wrist.

Part Five Further Reading

Li Lingwei

Li Lingwei is a Chinese badminton player of the 1980s who ranks among the greatest badminton players in the history of the women's game.

A brilliant all-around player whose court coverage and net play were particularly impressive, she maintained an overall edge on her teammate, rival, and sometimes doubles partner Han Aiping. They dominated international women's badminton during most of the 1980s, each winning the then biennial IBF World Championships (now known as the BWF World Championships) twice, and winning the IBF World doubles, together, in 1985. They also led Chinese teams won the biennial Uber Cup competitions.

Li Lingwei retired in 1989 and was inducted into the Badminton Hall of Fame in 1998.

Li Lingwei never competed in the Olympics because badminton did not become an Olympic sport until 1992. However, she was chosen as one of the five retired athletes to carry the Olympic flag during the opening ceremony of the 2008 Beijing Olympics. In July 2012, she was elected as a member of the International Olympic Committee. The IOC president Jacques Rogge presented her with an "IOC Gold Medal".

Baseball

Part One Listening and Speaking

Activity 1

🎧 Listen to the following conversation, and then work in pairs to act it out.

(Joe is a baseball fan. Today, he has invited his friend Jack to watch a baseball game. Because it's the first time for Jack to watch baseball, Joe is explaining some questions from Jack about the sport.)

A: How many players does a baseball team usually consist of?

B: Nine players. Actually, a team can have more than twenty players, but only nine are allowed on the field at one time.

A: I see. How many substitutions are allowed?

B: There's no limit to the number of substitutions, but substituted players can't re-enter the game.

A: Each team has a pitcher and a batter, right? Where do they stand on the field?

B: Yeah. The pitcher stands on the pitcher's mound, and the batter stands next to the home base plate.

A: How is a run scored?

B: A run is scored when a player makes his way round all of the bases and back to home base without being tagged or thrown out. And after three outs, the teams trade places.

A: It sounds complicated.

B: It may seem so at first. But once you get to know it, I'm sure you'll find it very interesting.

Words and Expressions

baseball /ˈbeɪsbɔːl/ *n.* 棒球

substitution /ˌsʌbstɪˈtjuːʃn/ *n.* 替补；代替

pitcher /ˈpɪtʃə(r)/ *n.*（棒球运动中的）投手

batter /ˈbætə/ *n.*（棒球运动中的）击球员

mound /maʊnd/ *n.*（内场中央高出地面的）投球区土墩

run /rʌn/ *n.*（棒球或板球比赛中跑动得到的）一分

base /beɪs/ *n.* 垒

trade places 换位置

Activity 2

Work in pairs and answer the following questions.

Question 1:　What are the basic rules of playing baseball?

Question 2:　How many possible ways can a run be scored?

Part Two Reading

Passage 1

Directions: Read the passage about baseball and discuss the following questions.

Baseball

Baseball is played between two teams, each comprising nine players, that take turns playing offense (batting and base running) and defense (pitching and fielding). A pair of turns, one at bat and one in the field, by each team constitutes an inning. A game consists of nine innings. The pitcher of one team throws the ball to a batter from the other team and the batter tries to hit the ball. If he misses, it is called a strike. If a batter gets three strikes, he loses his turn at bat and is called out. The batter is also out if he hits the ball in the air and an opposing player catches it. But if the batter hits the ball and it is not caught, the batter tries to run to one or more of the four bases on the field counter-clockwise. The batter can run to all four bases if he hits the ball over the fence or out of the ballpark. A run is scored when a player makes his way round all of the bases and back to the home plate without being put out.

Baseball evolved from older bat-and-ball games already being played in England by the mid-18th century. This game was brought by immigrants to North America, where the modern version developed. By the late 19th century, baseball was widely recognized as the national sport of the United States. Baseball is now popular in North America and parts of Central and South America, the Caribbean, and East Asia.

Baseball was first admitted to the Olympics at the 1992 Games, and was dropped from the 2012 Summer Olympic Games at the 2005 International Olympic Committee Meeting.

Words and Expressions

constitute /ˈkɒnstɪtjuːt/ v. 组成，构成   immigrant /ˈɪmɪɡrənt/ n. 移民

take turns 轮流，依次

Sports Terms

bat /bæt/ v. & n. 攻击   **strike** /straɪk/ n. 好球

field /ˈfiːld/ v. & n. 守备   **ballpark** /ˈbɔːlpɑːk/ n. 棒球场

inning /ˈɪnɪŋ/ n.（棒球、垒球比赛的）   **home plate** 本垒
一局

Questions:

1. How many players are there in each team in a baseball game?

2. How many innings is a baseball game usually composed of?

3. What is the national sport of America? Why?

Passage 2

Directions: Read the passage about the IBAF and discuss the following questions.

International Baseball Federation

The International Baseball Federation (IBAF), founded in 1938, was the former worldwide governing body recognized by the International Olympic Committee as overseeing, deciding and executing the policy of the sport of baseball.

The IBAF has since become the international baseball "division" of the World Baseball Softball Confederation (WBSC), the officially recognized world governing body for baseball (and softball). One of its principal responsibilities under the WBSC is to organize, standardize and sanction international competitions among baseball's 124 national governing bodies through its various tournaments to determine a world champion and calculate world rankings for both men's and women's baseball. Prior to the establishment of the WBSC in 2013, which has since superseded its authority, the IBAF had been the lone entity that can assign the title of "world champion" to any baseball team delegated to represent a nation. Its offices are housed within the WBSC headquarters in Lausanne, Switzerland. The main events under the jurisdiction of the IBAF are the Olympics baseball games, the World Championships, the World Cup and the World Club Cup.

On 1 April, 2011, the IBAF and the International Softball Federation announced that they were studying how to prepare a joint proposal in order to revive play of both sports at the 2020 Summer Olympics. As part of that proposal, in April 2013, the two organizations began the process of merging into a new combined federation that will govern both sports, the World Baseball Softball Confederation (WBSC).

Words and Expressions

standardize /'stændədaɪz/ *v.* 使规范化

supersede /ˌsuːpə'siːd/ *v.* 代替，取代

entity /'entətɪ/ *n.* 实体

assign /ə'saɪn/ *v.* 指定；分派

delegate /'delɪgeɪt/ *v.* 委派……为代表

jurisdiction /ˌdʒʊərɪs'dɪkʃn/ *n.* 权限，权力

joint /dʒɔɪnt/ *adj.* 联合的；合办的

proposal /prə'pəʊzl/ *n.* 提议，建议

revive /rɪ'vaɪv/ *v.* 使复兴，使苏醒

merge /mɜːdʒ/ *v.* 合并

Sports Terms

International Baseball Federation (IBAF) 国际棒球联合会

World Baseball Softball Confederation (WBSC) 世界棒球垒球联盟

Baseball World Club Cup 棒球世界俱乐部杯赛

Questions:

1. What are the main events hosted by the IBAF?

2. What are the responsibilities of the IBAF?

Part Three Exercises

Directions: Do the following exercises.

1. Briefly state the development of the sport of baseball in China.

2. Watch a baseball game, and write a review on it in about 250 words.

Part Four Rules and Concepts

1. A base-runner is out if any of the following occur: (1) The base runner is forced out before arriving at the next base; (2) The base runner is tagged out while being off the base.

2. A foul ball is one that is hit when it rolls to the outside of the line from home plate to 1st base or outside the line from home plate to 3rd base. A batter never receives a third and final strike for hitting a foul ball.

3. If a foul ball is hit twice, the batter will keep batting. The exception is that if a foul hit ball (or fair ball) is caught before it strikes the ground, the batter will be out.

4. After a fair ball is hit, the batter proceeds to run to 1st base.

5. Any player of the fielding team may tag any runner out by touching the player with the ball in hand or the glove containing the ball provided the runner is off base with exception of the first base over-run.

6. A pop fly ball is a ball hit into the air and caught by a fielder before it hits the ground.

7. Baseball is a contest between the speed of the batter's feet and that of the fielder's throwing arm.

8. Baserunners can be tagged or forced out when they are not touching a base.

Part Five Further Reading

Jackie Robinson

Jack Robinson, nicknamed "Jackie" Robinson, was an American professional baseball player who became the first African American to play in Major League Baseball (MLB) in the modern era.

Robinson had an exceptional baseball career. He was the recipient of the inaugural MLB Rookie of the Year Award in 1947, was an All-Star for six consecutive seasons from 1949 to 1954, and won the National League Most Valuable Player Award in 1949—the first black player so honored. Robinson played in six World Series and contributed to the Dodgers' 1955 World Series Championships. He was inducted into the Baseball Hall of Fame in 1962. In 1997, MLB "universally" retired his uniform number, 42, across all major league teams. They also adopted a new annual tradition, "Jackie Robinson Day", for the first time on 15 April, 2004, on which every player on every team wears No. 42.

Robinson's character and his unquestionable talent challenged the traditional prejudice of racial segregation which then influenced many other aspects of American life. He influenced the culture of and contributed significantly to the Civil Rights Movement. Robinson was also the first black television analyst in MLB. In the 1960s, he helped establish the Freedom National Bank, an African-American-owned financial institution based in Harlem, New York. In recognition of his achievements on and off the field, Robinson was posthumously awarded the Congressional Gold Medal and Presidential Medal of Freedom.

Lesson 19 Softball

Part One Listening and Speaking

Activity 1

🎧 Listen to the following conversation, and then work in pairs to act it out.

(Dan likes playing softball, while Mark is fond of playing baseball. They are discussing differences between softball and baseball.)

A: I know softball is very popular in the United States.

B: Yeah, we've mentioned that before. Do you remember the differences between softball and baseball?

A: Sure. There are three main differences: the field size, equipment and pitch.

B: Good memory!

A: Thank you. But there are some additional explanations.

B: Oh, such as?

A: Softball has three major classifications: fast-pitch, slow-pitch, and modified-pitch.

B: So that's how it's done!

A: Do you play softball?

B: Actually, I play baseball more than softball. It's not bad, you know, it's popular in China.

A: True, but softball is not that popular in China mainly because there's not enough promotion for it.

B: I absolutely agree.

A: Maybe we can try to promote it ourselves.

B: Emm, sounds good, and these kids will definitely like it because it really is so much fun.

Words and Expressions

softball /'sɒftbɔːl/ *n.* 垒球

be fond of 喜欢

mention /'menʃn/ *v.* 提到，提及

field size 场地大小

pitch /pɪtʃ/ *n.* 投球

additional /ə'dɪʃənl/ *adj.* 额外的，附加的

modified /'mɒdɪfaɪd/ *adj.* 修改的，改进的

promotion /prə'məʊʃn/ *n.* 广告宣传；促销；提倡

Activity 2

👤 Work in pairs and answer the following questions.

Question 1: What are the differences between baseball and softball?

Question 2: What equipment do you think should be prepared in playing softball?

Part Two Reading

Passage 1

Directions: Read the passage about softball and discuss the following questions.

Softball

Softball is a variant of baseball played with a larger ball on a smaller field. It was invented in 1887 in Chicago as an indoor game. It was at various times called indoor baseball, mush ball, playground, soft bund ball, kitten ball and ladies' baseball (because it was also played by women). The name "softball" was given to the game in 1926. A tournament held in 1933 at the Chicago World's Fair spurred interest in the game.

There are three types of softball: slow-pitch softball, fast-pitch softball and modified-pitch softball. The ball of slow-pitch softball is larger than the standard 12 inches; there are 10 players in a team; and bunting and stealing are prohibited. In fast-pitch softball, the pitch is fast; there are 9 players on the field at one time, and bunting and stealing are permitted. Softball rules vary somewhat from those of baseball. Two major differences are: (1) the ball must be pitched underhand—from 46 ft (14 m) for men or 43 ft (13.1 m) for women as compared with 60.5 ft (18.4 m) in baseball; (2) there are seven innings instead of nine in softball.

Despite the name, the ball used in softball is not very soft. The infield in softball is smaller than a standard baseball diamond; each base is 60 ft (18 m) from the next, as opposed to baseball's 90 ft (27 m).

Words and Expressions

variant /'veərɪənt/ *n.* 变体

spur /spɜː(r)/ *v.* 刺激，鞭策

bunt /bʌnt/ *v.* 触击

prohibit /prə'hɪbɪt/ *v.*（以法令、规

则等）禁止

underhand /ˌʌndə'hænd/ *adv.* 下手地，

以下手投

infield /'ɪnfiːld/ *n.* 内场

Sports Terms

slow-pitch softball 慢速垒球

fast-pitch softball 快速垒球

modified-pitch softball 变换式垒球

baseball diamond 棒球内场

diamond /'daɪəmənd/ *n.*（棒球）内

野，棒球场

Questions:

1. When and where was softball invented?

2. Do you know the different types of softball?

3. What are the differences in rules between softball and baseball?

Passage 2

Directions: Read the passage about the International Softball Federation and discuss the following questions

International Softball Federation

The International Softball Federation (ISF) is a division of the World Baseball Softball Confederation (WBSC)—the governing body of baseball and softball internationally recognized by the International Olympic Committee (IOC) and Sport

Accord. It was founded in 1952 and headquartered in Florida, the U.S. There are 127 national governing bodies.

The 117th meeting of the International Olympic Committee, held in Singapore in July 2005, voted to drop softball and baseball from the 2012 Summer Olympic Games. As part of a campaign to return softball to the Olympic Games in time for 2020, in April 2013, the ISF began a process of merging with the International Baseball Federation to form a new combined federation for both sports—the World Baseball Softball Confederation (WBSC).

Through the WBSC, the ISF organizes and conducts world championship competitions in women's and men's fast pitch, junior women's and men's fast pitch, women's, men's and coed slow pitch and women's and men's modified pitch. It also sanctions regional championships and provides technical support to Regional (Multi-Sport) Games. The ISF provides the official playing rules for international competitions including but not limited to the Olympic Games, World Championships, regional championships, regional games and other sanctioned competitions.

Words and Expressions

campaign /kæmˈpeɪn/ *n.* 运动；竞选活动

coed /ˈkəʊed/ *adj.* 男女都参加的

Sports Terms

International Softball Federation (ISF) 国际垒球联合会

Questions:

1. When was the ISF founded?

2. What sporting events does the ISF mainly organize?

3. Is softball an Olympic event now?

Part Three Exercises

Directions: Do the following exercises.

1. Write an essay in no less than 250 words about the scene at a softball event.
2. Watch a softball game, and prepare a commentary about players' offensive tactics.

Part Four Rules and Concepts

1. The number of umpires on a given game can range from a minimum of one to a maximum of seven. There is never more than one "plate umpire"; there can be up to three "base umpires", and up to a further three umpires positioned in the outfield.

2. Official umpires are often nicknamed "blue" because of their uniforms. In many jurisdictions, the plate umpire often uses an indicator (sometimes called a clicker or counter) to keep track of the game.

3. Decisions are usually indicated by the use of hand signals and the call. Safe calls are made by stretching hands horizontally with the palm downward and waved up and down, with a verbal call of "Safe". Out calls are made by raising the right hand in a clenched fist, with a verbal call of "Out".

4. Strikes are called by the plate umpire, who uses the same motion as the out call with a verbal call of "Strike". Balls are only called verbally, with no hand gesture. The umpire also has the option of saying nothing on a ball.

5. Foul balls are called by extending both arms up in the air with a verbal call of "Foul ball", while fair balls are indicated only by pointing towards fair territory with no verbal call. Only hand signal but no verbal signal is given for balls that are close to the borderline.

6. All decisions made by the umpires are considered to be final. Protests are never allowed on what are considered "judgment calls"—balls, strikes, and fouls.

7. A softball game can last anywhere from 3 to 9 innings, depending on the league, rules, and types; however, 7 innings is the most common.

8. In each inning, each team bats until three batters have been put out. The teams take turns batting. In the event of a tie, extra innings are usually played until the tie is broken except in certain tournaments and championships.

Part Five Further Reading

Jennie Lynn Finch

Jennie Lynn Finch is an American softball pitcher and first-baseman. She pitched for the Arizona Wildcats, the U.S. national softball team and the Chicago Bandits.

Finch won the 2001 Women's College World Series and helped lead Team USA to the gold medal at the 2004 Summer Olympics and a silver medal at the 2008 Summer Olympics. *Time* magazine described her as the most famous softball player in history. In 2010, Finch retired from softball to focus on her family. She leaves with a spotless personal reputation and the knowledge that she has inspired other girls who play for the love of the game.

Lesson 20 Golf

Part One Listening and Speaking

Activity 1

Listen to the following conversation, and then work in pairs to act it out.

(Patrick invited his friend Xiao Lee to play putt-putt golf. But when Xiao Lee arrived, he felt disappointed because it was not a true golf course. So Patrick started to explain to Xiao Lee about putt-putt golf.)

A: Here we are.

B: Patrick, are you sure this is a golf course?

A: Oh, this isn't an actual golf course. This is putt-putt golf. It's sort of like an amusement park.

B: Putt-putt golf?

A: Putt-putt golf means miniature golf.

B: Oh, mini golf. So it's not a real golf course for matches.

A: If we went to a real golf course, we would be the worst players on the course. Now grab a club, and let's tee off.

B: Tea? But I'm not thirsty.

A: No, you spell this tee T-E-E, it's a small peg that holds the golf ball. Tee off means to start a round of golf. You can also use it in daily life when you start to do something. For example, yesterday our boss teed off the staff meeting with a great speech.

B: OK. Got it. Let's tee off.

Words and Expressions

putt-putt golf 迷你高尔夫

golf course 高尔夫球场

amusement park 游乐园

miniature /'mɪnətʃə(r)/ *n.* 缩图；微型画

grab /græb/ *v.* 抓住，抓起

club /klʌb/ *n.* 杆

tee off 发球，开球

peg /peg/ *n.* 桩

Activity 2

👤 Work in pairs and answer the following questions.

Question 1：What is the meaning of the word "golf"?

Question 2：It is unclear and much debated about the origins of golf. What's your opinion?

Part Two Reading

Passage 1

Directions: Read the passage about golf and discuss the following questions.

Golf

While the modern game of golf originated in 15th-century Scotland, the game's ancient origins are unclear and much debated. The first written record of golf is James II's banning of the game in 1457, as an unwelcome distraction to learning archery. James IV lifted the ban in 1502 when he became a golfer himself. The world's oldest golf tournament in existence, and golf's first major, is The Open Championship, which was first played on 17 October, 1860 at Prestwick Golf Club, in Ayrshire, Scotland, with Scottish golfers winning the earliest majors.

Golf is a club and ball sport in which players use various clubs to hit balls into a series of holes on a course in as few strokes as possible. It is one of the few ball games that do not require a standardized playing area. The game is played on a course with an arranged progression of either 9 or 18 holes. Each hole on the course must contain a tee box and a putting green. Also, each hole is unique in its specific layout and arrangement.

Golf is played for the lowest number of strokes by an individual, known as stroke play, or the lowest score on the most individual holes in a complete round by an individual or team, known as match play. Stroke play is the most commonly seen format at all levels.

For the first time since 1904, golf has been considered an Olympic sport. After a 112-year absence from the Olympic Games, golf makes its comeback at the 2016 Rio Games.

Words and Expressions

ban /bæn/ *v.* 禁止

distraction /dɪ'strækʃn/ *n.* 注意力分散

archery /'ɑːtʃərɪ/ *n.* 箭术

lift /lɪft/ *v.* 解除（法令等）

existence /ɪg'zɪstəns/ *n.* 存在

terrain /tə'reɪn/ *n.* 领域；地形

layout /'leɪaʊt/ *n.* 设计，布局；安排

format /'fɔːmæt/ *n.* 版本；格式

absence /'æbsəns/ *n.* 缺席

Sports Terms

major /'meɪdʒə(r)/ *n.* （高尔夫球或网球中的）大赛；（棒球中的）职业总会；专业

tee box 开球区，发球区

putting green 果岭区

stroke play 比杆赛

match play 比洞赛

Questions:

1. When and where was the first golf tournament held?

2. What are the forms of golf games?

Directions: Read the passage about the golf organizations and discuss the following questions.

Golf Organizations

Golf tournaments, in nature, can be divided into professional games and amateur games. In rank, they can be classified as international games, provincial games and club games. In form, they can be categorized into Open Tournaments, Championship Tournaments, Invitational Tournaments, Golf Tour and Masters Tournament.

As the most popular and influential golf games, they are also called the four Grand Slam events, namely the U.S. Masters, U.S. Open, British Open and the U.S. PGA Championship. Golfers regard victories at all four major golf tournaments as the supreme award.

The R&A was formed in 2004, based in St Andrews. It takes its name from the Royal and Ancient Golf Club of St Andrews. It was responsible for administrating the rules of golf, running The Open Championship and other key events, and developing the game in existing and emerging golfing nations.

The R&A is the governing body of golf worldwide except in the United States and Mexico, where the governing organization is the United States Golf Association. The United States Golf Association (USGA) was formed in 1894. It is headquartered at Golf House in Far Hills, New Jersey, and serves as the governing body of golf for the U.S. and Mexico. It is a non-profit organization managed by and for golfers.

Words and Expressions

provincial /prəˈvɪnʃl/ *adj.* 省的

invitational /ˌɪnvɪˈteɪʃənl/ *adj.* 邀请的

supreme /suːˈpriːm/ *adj.* 至高的，无

上的，最高的

emerging /ɪˈmɜːdʒɪŋ/ *adj.* 新兴的

Sports Terms

Open Tournaments 公开赛

Championship Tournaments 冠军赛

Invitational Tournaments 邀请赛

Golf Tour 高尔夫巡回赛

Masters Tournament 大师赛

U.S. Masters 美国名人赛

U.S. Open 美国公开赛

British Open 英国公开赛

U.S. PGA Championship 美国 PGA 锦标赛（美巡赛）

Royal and Ancient Golf Club of St Andrews (R&A)
圣安德鲁斯皇家古老高尔夫俱乐部

United States Golf Association (USGA) 美国高尔夫球协会

Questions:

1. What are the most influential golf games?

2. Who makes the rules for golf games?

3. What is the governing body of golf for the U.S. and Mexico?

Part Three Exercises

Directions: Do the following exercises.

1. What's your opinion on golf's return to the Olympics in 2016?

2. Search for a piece of the latest news about golf, and discuss your ideas about the future of golf in China.

Part Four Rules and Concepts

1. Golfers are allowed to carry a maximum of 14 clubs in a match. It is illegal to play any practice shots during the play of a hole.

2. If a golfer plays a tee shot from outside the designated area, in match play there is no penalty, but the opponent may require him to replay a stroke immediately; in stroke play, the golfer incurs a two club-stroke penalty and must play a ball from within the correct area.

3. When making a stroke on the putting green, the golfer should ensure that the flagstick is removed or attended by someone. The flagstick may also be removed or attended to when the ball lies off the putting green.

4. If a golfer's ball at rest is moved by someone other than himself, his partner or caddies, the golfer may replace his ball without penalty.

5. If a ball at rest is moved by the wind or moves of its own accord, the player should play it as it lies without penalty.

6. If a ball struck by a golfer is deflected or stopped by himself, his partner, caddies or equipment, the golfer incurs a penalty of one stroke and play the ball as it lies.

7. If a ball struck by a golfer is deflected or stopped by another ball at rest, there is normally no penalty and the ball is played as it lies.

8. Movable obstructions (i.e. artificial movable objects such as rakes, bottles, etc.) located anywhere may be moved by a golfer without penalty. If the ball moves as a result, it must be replaced without penalty.

9. If a ball is lost outside a water hazard or out of bounds, the golfer must play another ball from the spot where the last shot was played, under penalty of another, i.e. stroke distance.

10. A golfer is allowed 5 minutes to search for a ball. If the ball is not found within 5 minutes, it is lost.

Part Five Further Reading

Tiger Woods

Eldrick Tont "Tiger" Woods is an American professional golfer who is among the most successful golfers of all time. He has been one of the highest-paid athletes in the world for several years.

Woods has broken numerous golf records. He has been awarded PGA Player of the Year eleven times, the Byron Nelson Award for lowest adjusted scoring average eight times, and has the record of leading the money list in ten different seasons. He has won 14 professional major golf championships, the second highest of any player (Jack Nicklaus leads with 18), and 79 PGA Tour events, second all time behind Sam Snead, who had 82 wins.

He is the youngest player to achieve the career Grand Slam, and the youngest and fastest to win 50 tournaments on tour. Additionally, Woods is only the second golfer, after Jack Nicklaus, to have achieved a career Grand Slam three times. Woods has won 18 World Golf Championships after they began in 1999.

4
Chapter

Dance

Dancesport

Part One Listening and Speaking

Activity 1

🎧 Listen to the following conversation, and then work in pairs to act it out.

(Lisa is practicing dancesport turns. But she finds she can't turn stably and fast enough. So she is asking for her coach's advice.)

A: Sir, why do I always lose my balance when I try to turn?

B: That is because your body axis is not perpendicular to the floor. You need to keep your back straight.

A: Oh, I see. Then how do I turn faster?

B: Tighten your body while rotating.

A: How about now? Any better this time?

B: Better, but it will be much better if you straighten your pivoting leg.

A: Ah! I see. I feel more stable.

B: Good, now pay more attention to your head. Turn it with clear direction and keep your eyesight focused.

A: Thanks for your help. I will practice harder.

Words and Expressions

stably /'steɪblɪ/ *adv.* 平稳地，稳定地

axis /'æksɪs/ *n.* 轴心

perpendicular /ˌpɜːpən'dɪkjələ(r)/ *adj.*
垂直的，正交的

tighten /'taɪtn/ *v.* 绷紧

rotate /rəʊ'teɪt/ *v.* 旋转

pivot /'pɪvət/ *v.* 在枢轴上转动

stable /'steɪbl/ *adj.* 稳定的，稳固的

Activity 2

👤 Work in pairs and make conversations according to the given situations.

Situation 1: Explain how to keep balance when turning around in circles.

Situation 2: Now that the Latin Dance Final is upcoming, tell the participants to change their costume as soon as possible and get ready for the competition.

Part Two Reading

Passage 1

Directions: Read the passage about dancesport and discuss the following questions with your partner.

Dancesport

Dancesport, also known as the International Standard Dance, originated in London in 1924. It was initiated by the British, while European and American dancers regulated and refined it, based on a wide range of research on traditional court dance, ballroom dance and country dance with various styles of the Latin American countries. In 1925, Standard Dance was formally promulgated, including the Waltz, Tango, Foxtrot, and Quickstep. Some competitions were first held in Western Europe before spreading to other countries, where they quickly became popular and well-loved.

Dancesport is classified into Standard Dance and Latin Dance with ten species, according to their style and technical structure. Standard Dance includes Waltz, Tango, Foxtrot, Quickstep and Vienna Waltz, which originated in Europe (except Tango), and are known for their graceful, subtle, sedate and elegant styles. Latin Dance includes

Samba, Cha Cha, Rumba, Paso Doble and Jive, which were derived from the countries of Latin America (except Paso Doble), and are known for their warm, lively and romantic styles.

According to the competition events, there are Standard Dance, Latin Dance and group dance. Group dance is a mixture of Standard Dance and Latin Dance, and it involves music, posture, queue pattern and players' harmonious cooperation. Each species has its own dance, footwork and style. Different sets are formed according to different music and movement requirements.

Words and Expressions

refine /rɪˈfaɪn/ v. 完善，改进

range /reɪndʒ/ n. 范围

promulgate /ˈprɒmlgeɪt/ v. 公布，发表

graceful /ˈgreɪsfl/ adj. 优雅的，端庄的

subtle /ˈsʌtl/ adj. 含蓄的

sedate /sɪˈdeɪt/ adj. 稳重的，沉着的

elegant /ˈelɪgənt/ adj. 高雅的，典雅的

warm /wɔːm/ adj. 热情的；温暖的

lively /ˈlaɪvlɪ/ adj. 奔放的，活泼的

romantic /rəʊˈmæntɪk/ adj. 浪漫的

posture /ˈpɒstʃə(r)/ n. 姿势，姿态

harmonious /hɑːˈməʊnɪəs/ adj. 和谐的

Sports Terms

dancesport /dɑːnsˈspɔːt/ n. 体育舞蹈

International Standard Dance
国际标准舞

court dance 宫廷舞

ballroom dance 交谊舞，交际舞

country dance 士风舞

Standard Dance 摩登舞

Latin Dance 拉丁舞

Waltz /wɔːls/ n. 华尔兹

Tango /ˈtæŋgəʊ/ n. 探戈

Foxtrot /ˈfɒkstrɒt/ n. 狐步

Quickstep /ˈkwɪkstep/ n. 快步

Vienna Waltz 维也纳华尔兹

Samba /ˈsæmbə/ n. 桑巴舞

Cha Cha /ˈtʃɑː tʃɑː/ n. 恰恰

Rumba /ˈrʌmbə/ n. 伦巴

Paso Doble 斗牛舞

Jive /dʒaɪv/ n. 牛仔舞

group dance 集体舞

1. How did dancesport come into being?

2. What are the different types included in Standard Dance?

3. What are the different types included in Latin Dance?

Passage 2

Directions: Read the passage about the Blackpool Dance Festival and discuss the following questions with your partner.

Blackpool Dance Festival

The Blackpool is called the "City of Entertainment" in Europe and the "Las Vegas" of the United Kingdom. The Blackpool Dance Festival was first held in 1920, and then each year in May in the Empress Ballroom at the Winter Gardens in Blackpool, England. It lasts for more than a week and is the oldest dance festival in British history. Known as "the Olympic Games of the dance", it serves as a sort of palace in contestants' hearts worldwide, and as an important stage to show the development of dances in different countries. It is the world's first and most famous ballroom dance competition of international significance.

The Blackpool Dance Festival covers Ballroom and Latin American dancing, and incorporates the British Open Championships in categories of adult amateur and professional couples and formation teams. In 2005, two new categories were introduced: the British Rising Star Amateur Ballroom and Latin Competitions. Two invitation events, the Professional Team Match and the Exhibition Competition, create much interest. The Junior Dance Festival, Blackpool Sequence Dance Festival which incorporates the British Sequence Championships, and British National Dance Festival are also held annually in Blackpool.

In 2004, Luan Jiang and Zhang Ru of China won first place in the Professional Latin Rising Star Competitions, performing best among the Asian performers who participated at the Blackpool Open Championships.

Sports Terms

Blackpool Dance Festival 黑池舞蹈节

Empress Ballroom 皇后舞厅

British Rising Star Amateur Ballroom and Latin Competitions
英国新星业余交谊舞 / 拉丁舞大赛

Professional Team Match 职业团体赛

Blackpool Sequence Dance Festival 黑池序列舞舞蹈节

British National Dance Festival 英国国家舞蹈节

Questions:

1. When and where is the Blackpool Dance Festival held annually?

2. What's the significance of the Blackpool Dance Festival?

3. What competitions are held in the Blackpool Dance Festival?

Part Three Exercises

Directions: Do the following exercises.

1. What kind of dance style do you like best? Why?

2. What do you think is important to improve dancing skills?

Part Four Rules and Concepts

1. The World Dancesport Championships are held in the Standard Dances (Waltz, Tango, Viennese Waltz, Slow Foxtrot and Quickstep), and the Latin American Dances (Samba, Cha Cha, Rumba, Paso Doble and Jive).

2. A minimum of three out of five competition dances from the selected discipline must be included in any performance and must be danced for 75% of the duration of the performance. Elements of other dances and dance forms may be included up to a maximum of 25% of the duration of the performance.

3. Competitors must provide the organizers with two copies of a compact disc (CD) recording of their selected music, and a full, accurate and latest list of the selected music including title(s), composer(s), arranger(s), publisher(s) and CD or record number(s).

4. A competition may comprise a maximum of a first round and a final. Competitors must perform the same choreography in the same order and with the same musical arrangement in every round.

5. A maximum of three lifts is permitted during each performance. Each lift may not exceed 15 seconds in duration.

6. No props are permitted at any time during the performance.

7. The dress regulations ordered by the World Dancesport Federation apply to all competitions held under its rule. A couple's competition dress may demonstrate or suggest the theme of the choreography or performance but must be in either Latin or Standard style.

8. The order of contestants' performances shall be decided by drawing lots by the Chairman or a person approved by the Chairman, at which all the contestants or their representatives must be present.

Part Five Further Reading

Hanna Karttunen

Hanna Karttunen is a Finnish professional Latin dancer. She also trained in ballet as a child with a love of dance.

Specializing in Latin American and representing England with Paul Killick, she won the titles of United Kingdom Open Champion, International Champion, World Series Champion, World Masters Champion, etc. and also became the British National Champion four times. Together they were also runner-up in every major professional championship, such as the World Championship, European Championship and also the British Open Championship, where in 2002 they came close to taking the title, after being placed first in two out of five dances: Rumba and Paso Doble.

Appreciation of Dancesport

Part One Standard Dance

Waltz: Waltz is characterized by elegance, ornateness and colorfulness. When the male partner dances like a prince, his companion resembles a princess with gentle and generous grace. Its action is smooth, mildly varied, elegant and beautiful, quiet and soft, like water or clouds. Casual and elegant, it mimics successive waves with its dashing rotations. It enjoys a reputation of the "Dancing Queen". Doing round exercises, the body smoothly rotates in small amplitude and elegant and charming fashion. It typically has a 3/4 time signature, so the rhythmic beat of each measure is 1, 2, 3. The first beat is accented. The second and third shots are mute with a rate of 28 to 30 bars per minute.

Tango: Tango dance is unique, as its movement is intertwined and uninhibited, oblique at every step. This is commonly known as the "crab catwalk". Tango's actions are characterized by strength and sharpness, and its speed of movement is extraordinarily changeable, varying from sudden quickness to slowness. Its steadiness is accompanied by boldness while its brilliance co-exists with variety. Its dance involves a 2/4 beat, and 30 to 34 bars per minute. The dance is classified into sub-S (Slow Walk) and Q (Quick Quickstep), which accounts for a beat for S, while Q accounts for half a beat. Tango music is thought of as moderate under a solemn atmosphere, and it stimulates the spirits.

Foxtrot: It is a dance style characterized as soft and changeable. A sudden lifting and lowering of the dance steps occurs frequently in the cohesion of actions. When moving forward, the step is accompanied by gentle friction on the ground, and the heel cannot be towed on the floor forcibly while moving backward. The steps cannot be interrupted and must continue smoothly; furthermore, they are fluid and changeable. In the process of moving forward or backward continuously, the upper body takes the position of the reverse action by a small margin. With the body forward or backward, the guide power is maintained by the upper body conformably. The musical rhythm of Foxtrot is a 4/4 beat, about 30 bars per minute, and its rhythm is classified into quickness for 1 beat, and slowness for 2 beats.

Quickstep: Quickstep style is characterized by lightness and liveliness, and is full of passion. Dancers move freely and invoke a sense of power and expressiveness. Regarding music, its rhythm is a 4/4 beat with 50 to 52 bars per minute. The music is quite cheerful and has a strong sense of rhythm. The basic rhythm is slowness, quickness, quickness and slowness, or slowness, slowness, quickness and quickness. Its rhythmic form goes usually as follows: at the end of the first step, it starts to rise; for the second and third steps, it continues to rise; and for the fourth step it keeps rising; in the end it falls. Different dance movements have different ways of rising and falling, but the movements mostly follow the form of Foxtrot, and some dance steps are in accordance with the rising and falling of Waltz, so it is necessary to master the use of rising, falling and other various dance skills.

Vienna Waltz: This style is decent, melodic, graceful, fluid and rotational. Its basic action involves rotating towards the left or right quickly, completing the skills of reversal, tilt, swing, rising and falling. The dance step is smooth, rotational and enthusiastic. Vienna Waltz is elegant and solemn. Its music is breezy, and has a 3/4 beat with 56 to 60 sections per minute. Each section is made up of three bars. The first bar is accented, and the fourth bar is secondarily accented. The basic footwork is six steps for six beats, two sections forming a cycle, and the first section is a fluctuation.

Part Two Latin Dance

Samba: Its action is rough and full of fierce ups and downs, and its dance step is bold, swift and infectious. Its musical rhythm is a 2/4 beat with 48 to 56 bars per minute.

Cha Cha: Its music is interesting and its action is characterized by the style of humor and fancy. The arrangement of Cha Cha does not require consistent performances of the male and female dancers. In most cases, the female dancer is followed by the male dancer and their steps are very cohesive. Its dance steps originated from jazz, which has a strong vitality, explosive force and infection. The musical rhythm is a 4/4 beat with a speed of 29 to 32 bars per minute, and the rhythm is "1, 2, 3, 4 &1". The first step is for "1, 2, 3" of the beat, and the fourth beat is two steps. Therefore, each section of Cha Cha consists of five steps.

Rumba: Its romantic music is accompanied by graceful movements. The Cubans are accustomed to walking with items on top of their heads, with hips twisting toward both sides to adjust paces and keep their bodies in balance. Rumba adheres to this characteristics. The original style has been melted into the modern elements. Its action is characterized by the charming twists of the hip and free stretch of the upper body, which can fully display the beauty of women. Moreover, the theme of love is expressed through pretty charm and a romantic atmosphere. With mild love music, the dance is full of romantic sentiment. Its musical rhythm is a 4/4 beat, and the rate is about 27 bars per minute. The first beat is accented. Its basic step is three steps for 4 beats.

Paso Double: The dance posture is straight with no hip actions or excessive flexions and extensions of the knees. The ankle and foot are flat on the ground to complete the steps. It has vivid movements, a strong sense of strength, quick forces and agile steps. With mighty and majestic music, it is full of masculine flavor. The magnificent melody is accompanied by the vigorous Spanish march. Its musical rhythm is a 2/4 beat, 60 to 62 bars per minute. The basic step is one step for one beat and eight beats for a cycle.

Jive: Its style is characterized by lively music and an uninhibited state. The dance steps are agile, relaxed and cheerful. The basic dance steps are composed of treading, merging steps, jumps and spins. The bottoms of the feet are required to tread upon the ground, while the waist and hip swing like a pendulum. It resembles the energetic, romantic, and forthright style of the American cowboys. It has cheerful melodies and strong jumps, with the rhythm of a 4/4 beat, and the second beat is a big beat. There are 42 to 44 bars per minute with eight steps for six beats.

Folk Dance

Part One Listening and Speaking

Activity 1

Listen to the following conversation, and then work in pairs to act it out.

(Peter is having a dance lesson. There are some dancing terms he doesn't know. Now he is referring to his teacher about them.)

A: Sir, I don't know the meaning of the stage directions. Would you please explain?

B: OK. It refers to eight directions on the stage, positions 1 to 8. These are professional terms to regulate the dancers' body positions and step directions.

A: Oh, so what are positions 1–8?

B: Facing the LOD is "position 1"; the right forward, right side, and right back are "positions 2, 3, and 4"; facing away from the LOD is "position 5"; and the left back, left side, and left forward are the "positions 6, 7, and 8".

A: Got it. But there is another problem. How do I distinguish between the "facing" and "visual"?

B: Facing refers to the direction of the front of your body, and visual means the line of sight. For example, "look at 8" means both the face and eyes are in position 8.

A: Thank you, sir. I just have one more question. How can I understand the difference between "keep head" and "shake head"?

B: "Keep head" means the body begins to turn, while the head stays in its original position; "shake head" means the head turns to another direction quickly, which is used in the appearance.

A: I see, thank you sir.

Words and Expressions

stage direction 舞台方位

distinguish /dɪˈstɪŋɡwɪʃ/ v. 区分

line of sight 视线

keep head 留头

shake head 甩头

Activity 2

Work in pairs and answer the following questions.

Question 1: One of the prominent features of Chinese folk dance is the close integration of dancing and singing. What is your opinion?

Question 2: How many types does classic dance include?

Part Two Reading

Passage 1

Directions: Read the passage about folk dance and discuss the following questions with your partners.

Folk Dance

Folk dance originated from and was passed down through the folk peoples of various countries. It is restricted by each individual culture with its impromptu performances but stable style for self-entertainment. Due to the living environment, customs, habits, life styles, national character, cultural traditions, religious beliefs, and other physiological factors such as the performer's age and gender, folk dance in different areas and countries has significant differences in performance skills and styles. With its chastity, various forms, rich content, and vivid images, folk dance is the indispensable source for classic dance, court dance and professional dance.

With a vast territory, a large population, a long history and rich cultural heritage, China is unique in humanity, landscapes, languages, customs, cultures, and religious beliefs. Owing to the different ethnic groups with their own ways of production and religious cultures, Chinese folk dance is brilliant in its content, form, rhythm and style, and it is generally classified into ritual (religious) dance, entertainment dance, ceremonial dance and history (labor) dance, all of which play an important role in promoting the development of Chinese dance.

Words and Expressions

pass down 流传，传承

restrict /rɪˈstrɪkt/ *v.* 限制

impromptu /ɪmˈprɒmptjuː/ *adj.* 即兴的

national character 国民性格

physiological /ˌfɪzɪəˈlɒdʒɪkl/ *adj.* 生理的

gender /ˈdʒendə(r)/ *n.* 性别

vivid /ˈvɪvɪd/ *adj.* 生动的，形象的

indispensable /ˌɪndɪˈspensəbl/ *adj.* 不可缺少的，必不可少的

territory /ˈterətrɪ/ *n.* 领土

heritage /ˈherɪtɪdʒ/ *n.* 遗产

humanity /hjuːˈmænətɪ/ *n.* 人文

landscape /ˈlændskeɪp/ *n.* 风景，景色

brilliant /ˈbrɪlɪənt/ *adj.* 灿烂的，闪耀的

ritual /ˈrɪtʃuəl/ *adj.* 仪式的

ceremonial /ˌserɪˈməʊnɪəl/ *adj.* 仪式的；礼仪的

Sports Terms

folk dance 民间舞

classic dance 古典舞

ritual (religious) dance 祭祀（宗教）性舞蹈

entertainment dance 娱乐性舞蹈

ceremonial dance 礼仪舞蹈

history (labor) dance 历史（劳动）舞蹈

Questions:

1. What is folk dance?

2. What are the characteristics of folk dance?

3. What are the different types of Chinese folk dance?

Passage 2

Directions: Read the passage about the Peach and Plum Cup, Lotus Award and CCTV National Dance Competition and discuss the following questions with your partners.

Peach and Plum Cup, Lotus Award and CCTV National Dance Competition

The "Peach and Plum Cup Dance Competition" is the highest-level youth dance competition in China, and is one of the most important awards of the Chinese government award for culture and art (Splendor Award, for professional theatrical artworks) in the sub-category for cultural and artistic colleges and universities. In 1985, Beijing Dance Academy initiated this competition, and it is held every three years. It enjoys a fine reputation as China's "Dance Oscars".

The "Lotus Award Dance Competition" was approved in 1996 as the national professional dance award. In principle it is held every two years, and the ballet competition is held every three years.

The "CCTV National Dance Competition" is a dance contest for national professional organizations and many dance lovers. Sponsored by the CCTV, it follows the principles of "fairness, justice and openness" and the principle of fully encouraging mass participation. It is held every two years. As the only national television dance competition, it is famous for its authority and richness. By virtue of its advantages as a television show, it gained the favors of many dancers and choreographers, and has become highly acclaimed among dance circles and the audience.

Words and Expressions

splendor /'splendə(r)/ *n.* 光辉，壮丽

theatrical /θɪˈætrɪkl/ *adj.* 戏剧的

artwork /'ɑːtwɜːk/ *n.* 艺术作品

sub-category /sʌb-ˈkætəgərɪ/ *n.* 子范畴

initiate /ɪˈnɪʃɪeɪt/ *v.* 发起；启动

reputation /ˌrepjuˈteɪʃn/ *n.* 名誉，声望

sponsor /'spɒnsə(r)/ *v.* 赞助，资助

by virtue of 由于，凭借

choreographer /ˌkɒrɪˈɒɡrəfə(r)/ *n.* 编舞者，编导

acclaim /əˈkleɪm/ *v.* 称赞，喝彩

Peach and Plum Cup Dance Competition "桃李杯" 舞蹈比赛

Lotus Award Dance Competition "荷花奖" 舞蹈大赛

CCTV Dance Competition CCTV 电视舞蹈大赛

Splendor Award 文华奖

Questions:

1. What's the "Peach and Plum Cup Dance Competition"?

2. What's the "Lotus Award Dance Competition"?

3. What's the "CCTV Dance Competition"?

Part Three Exercises

Directions: Do the following exercises.

1. Watch a folk dance performance and try to learn some dancing movements.

2. Pole dancing is a kind of dance that uses a vertical pipe as a prop for climbing, revolving and standing upside down, and is one of the world's top ten folk dances. Please discuss the value of pole dancing for fitness and entertainment.

Part Four Rules and Concepts

1. Judging criteria of a dance competition is mainly in choreography, uniformity, execution, dress collocation, and musicality.

2. Scoring rules generally consist of six elements.

3. The choreography should be reasonable, consistent, complete, and creative.

4. Performers must have an accurate understanding of the music, and their actions must match up with the rhythm. Movement should appear to be smooth, effortless, rhythmic, expressive and technical.

5. The performance should have a sense of the times and be healthy and elegant.

6. Costumes must reflect the dance style as designated.

7. Performers should be full of spirit, decorous and artistic.

8. Performers should mobilize the atmosphere by interacting with the audience, and properly cope with emergency.

9. The maximum score is 10 points. The final score will be rounded to two decimal places, minus the highest and lowest points to produce an average score.

10. The term "folk dance" is reserved for dances which are to a significant degree bound by tradition and which originate in the times when the distinction existed between the dances of "common folk" and the "high society".

Part Five Further Reading

Yang Liping

Yang Liping is the director, choreographer and star of a performance art show called *Dynamic Yunnan* that has drawn sellout crowds all over China. Between 2004 and 2008, Yang Liping directed and choreographed a trilogy—*Dynamic Yunnan*, *Echoes of Shangri-la* and *Tibetan Myth*. In 2004, *Dynamic Yunnan* won five major awards at the National Lotus Awards, including Gold Award for Dance Spectacular, Best Choreography and Best Female Performer. To create the exotic song and spectacular dance, Yang spent years travelling to remote villages of the 26 ethnic minority tribes in Yunnan and selected over 60 peasants who had the natural gift of song and dance, from whom she built an archive recreating this rich feast of sight and sound.

Appreciation of Ethnic and Folk Dance

Part One Tibetan Dance

Tibetans live mainly in Tibet, as well as Qinghai, Gansu, Sichuan, and Yunnan. The Tibetan folk dance is a combination of farming and religious culture. With great variety, it is classified into self-entertainment dance and religious dance, both of which have richly cultural connotations, beautiful and natural fluttering, and unique dance styles and forms.

Form: Self-entertainment dance is classified into two categories: *Xie* and *Zhuo*, and the main performance forms include Reba, Tap dance, *Lexie*, *Duixie*, *Guoxie*, *Xuanzi*, *Guozhuang*, etc.

Characteristics: At the knees there are continuous, small and quick elastic vibrations, or continuous and flexible flexions, showing the differences in speed, strength and scope. The movement of gravity formed by the step leads to the movement of the relaxed upper limbs. Rhythm varies from slow to quick, from small to large, and from light to heavy.

Representative works: The most representative work is *Guozhuang*, in which men and women dancers stand separately, hand in hand or shoulder to shoulder, and take turns to sing and dance, usually accompanied by the call sign. *Guozhuang* is an amusement dance of the ancient people in the shape of a circle around the bonfire or pots. It includes the *Nishou* and other words to show love. *Qiangmu*, commonly known as *Tiaoshen*, is the most important sacrificial dance in the temple among the religious dances.

Part Two Mongolian Dance

The Mongolian nationality mainly lives in the north of China. The residents took up nomadic and hunting activities, which created the brilliant grassland culture. Mongolian folk dance is a unique, beautiful flower in the grassland culture.

Form: The vibration of the shoulders and the turn of the wrists are used to express the cheerful and enthusiastic personalities of the Mongolian girls. The men's dance posture is upright and heroic, and their paces are swift and carefree, showing the boldness and power of Mongolian men.

Characteristics: Mongolian dance is characterized by a lively rhythm, enthusiastic music, novel lyrics and unique style.

Representative works: These include the chopsticks dance, sabre dance, horse dance, bowl dance, milk dance, eagle dance, etc. The chopsticks dance is very amusing as it evolved from sitting during performance, to crouching, standing, then walking while beating freely against the bodies, and its visual forms are changeable, which vividly expresses the herdsmen's love of life, optimistic and cheerful personalities and emotions.

Part Three Dance of the Uygur Nationality

Xinjiang Uygur region is known as "the town of song and dance". Historically, "the Silk Road" brought the prosperity of commerce and agriculture, which helped to shape the unique tradition and style of Xinjiang folk dance.

Form: The main forms of folk dances popular in Xinjiang include *Sainaimu*, multi-Lang Dance, Samar dance, *Xiadiyana*, Nazirkom, plate dance, hand-drum dance, and other dances for performances.

Characteristics: All parts of the body coordinate with the eyes' movements. The head, shoulder, waist, and arms to the toes are all in action. Holding the head, chest, and waist straight is the basic feature of the body. By combining the dynamic and static movements, comparing big and small movements, and adding the neck shift and turning over of the wrists, Xinjiang folk dance is characterized by enthusiasm, boldness, prudence and softness.

Representative works: These include the hand-drum dance *Picking Grapes*, song and dance *Kashi Sainaim* and large-sized dances *Duolangmaixilaifu*, *Lark* and *Drum Dance*, *Women Labors of Tianshan* and so on.

Lesson 25

Modern Dance

Part One Listening and Speaking

Activity 1

Listen to the following conversation, and then work in pairs to act it out.

(Jim is a beginner of modern dance and is not very clear about the classification of it. Now he is consulting his dancing teacher.)

A: Sir, I was wondering: what are the different types of modern dance?

B: There are various modern dances. If we base it on dance features, there are three types: professional dance, international standard ballroom dancing, and fashion dance.

A: Oh. So what is professional dance?

B: Professional dance includes classic dance, ethnic dance, folk dance, modern dance, tap dance and jazz.

A: I see. And what is the international standard ballroom dancing?

B: We can also call it the international standard dance. It includes Latin Dance (Rumba, Samba, Cha Cha, Paso Doble and Jive) and Standard Dance (Waltz, Vienna Waltz, Tango, Quickstep and Foxtrot).

A: What does the fashion dance refer to?

B: Fashion dance usually refers to disco, rave, street dance, Bala Bala, cheerleading and hot dance.

A: Wow! I didn't realize there's so much! I see. Thank you.

B: Sure!

Words and Expressions

professional dance 专业舞蹈	jazz /dʒæz/ n. 爵士
international standard ballroom dancing	disco /ˈdɪskəʊ/ n. 迪斯科
国际标准交谊舞	rave /reɪv/ n. 锐舞
fashion dance 时尚舞蹈	street dance 街舞
ethnic dance 民族舞	Bala Bala 芭啦芭啦
tap dance 踢踏舞	hot dance 热舞

Activity 2

Work in pairs and answer the following questions.

Question 1: Modern dance is unique because "there is no rule, every artist is creating his own codes." Discuss your view on this statement.

Question 2: As the first person to popularize Chinese modern dance, Jin Xing is an outstanding modern dancer with numerous honors. Do you know her famous works?

Part Two Reading

Passage 1

Directions: Read the passage about modern dance and discuss the following questions with your partners.

Modern Dance

Modern dance, which primarily arouse out of Germany and the United States in the late 19th and early 20th centuries, is also called "contemporary dance", "new dance", and "modern trends dance". Modern dance, as a direct rebellion against classical ballet, refused the formula and constraint of classical ballet and broke away from codified movements and balletic narrative structures. It instead revealed the freedom of emotions and living attitude while reflecting social contradictions and westerners' psychological characteristics.

In the past hundred years, along with the exploration of Duncan, Laban, Denis,

Shawn, Han Fuli, Graham, Cunningham, etc., modern dances have spread across the globe as an art form of the world.

Chinese modern dance, based on a broad cultural background, was created with Chinese characteristics to show a New-Era outlook, time consciousness and the thoughts and feelings of the masses.

Words and Expressions

arise /əˈraɪz/ v. 兴起，崛起

rebellion /rɪˈbeljən/ n. 反抗；叛乱；不服从

refuse /rɪˈfjuːz/ v. 抵制，拒绝

constraint /kənˈstreɪnt/ n. 束缚，约束

codify /ˈkəʊdɪfaɪ/ v. 编成法典

balletic /bəˈletɪk/ adj. 芭蕾的

narrative /ˈnærətɪv/ adj. 叙事的

freedom /ˈfriːdəm/ n. 自由

attitude /ˈætɪtjuːd/ n. 态度

contradiction /ˌkɒntrəˈdɪkʃn/ n. 矛盾

psychological /ˌsaɪkəˈlɒdʒɪklɪ/ adj. 心理的

exploration /ˌekspləˈreɪʃn/ n. 探索

outlook /ˈaʊtlʊk/ n. 风貌

time consciousness 时代意识

Sports Terms

modern dance 现代舞

classical ballet 古典芭蕾

Questions:

   1. When and where did modern dance arise?

   2. What is the difference between modern dance and classical ballet?

   3. What are the characteristics of modern dance?

Passage 2

Directions: Read the passage about the the pioneer of the American modern dance and discuss the following questions with your partners.

The Pioneer of the American Modern Dance

Ted Shawn is one of the first notable male pioneers of American modern dance.

Along with creating Denishawn School with his ex-wife Ruth St. Denis, he is also responsible for the creation of the well known all-male company Ted Shawn and His Men Dancers. With his innovative ideas of masculine movement, he is one of the most influential choreographers and dancers of his day. He is also the founder and creator of Jacob's Pillow Dance Festival in Massachusetts.

The Denishawn School of Dancing and Related Arts, founded in 1915 by Ruth St. Denis and Ted Shawn in Los Angeles, California, helped many dancers perfect their dancing talent. Some of the school's more notable pupils include Martha Graham, Doris Humphrey, Lillian Powell, Charles Weidman, Jack Cole, and silent film star Louise Brooks. The school was especially renowned for its influence on ballet and modern dance.

Due to marital problems of Ruth St. Denis and Ted Shawn and financial difficulties, Denishawn concluded in 1929. Consequently, Shawn went on to form an all-male dance company, made up of athletes he taught at Springfield College in Massachusetts. Shawn's mission in creating this company was to fight for acceptance of the American male dancer and to bring awareness of the art form from a male perspective.

Words and Expressions

notable /'nəʊtəbl/ *adj.* 著名的；显著的

pioneer /ˌpaɪə'nɪə(r)/ *n.* 先驱

innovative /'ɪnəveɪtɪv/ *adj.* 创新的，有创造力的

masculine /'mæskjəlɪn/ *adj.* 男性的，阳性的

marital /'mærɪtl/ *adj.* 婚姻的

financial /faɪ'nænʃl/ *adj.* 财政的

conclude /kən'kluːd/ *v.* 结束，终止

mission /'mɪʃn/ *n.* 任务；使命

acceptance /ək'septəns/ *n.* 接受

Questions:

1. Who is the pioneer of the American modern dance?

2. Do you know any famous pupils of the Denishawn School?

3. What's the purpose of Shawn's creating of the all-male dance company?

Part Three Exercises

Directions: Do the following exercises.

1. Write an essay in about 250 words about college students doing modern dance.
2. Talk about the development of modern dance in China.

Part Four Rules and Concepts

1. Modern dance includes black dance, Korean dance, Disco and so on.
2. According to the performance forms, there are break dance, mechanical dance, lock and jazz.
3. Break dance (Breaking): It is performed with both hands and feet on the floor, depending on B-boys' power, and is character-driven. It is considered the first hip-hop dance style.
4. Mechanical dance: Imitating the robot motion and shape, this style is based on the technique of quickly contracting and relaxing muscles to cause a jerk in a dancer's body and a hit of the joint.
5. Locking: Originally called Campbellocking, it includes distinct street dance style. The body makes quick movements of the hands and feet, along with the more relaxed buttocks and legs, and there is smiling and hands clapping (giving a high five) to mobilize the atmosphere by interacting with the audience.
6. Jazz: Originating from European classical ballet, jazz is classified into three types: Street Jazz, Modern Jazz and Pop Jazz.
7. Street Jazz, mixed with hip-hop elements, is widely used in pop music. Modern Jazz, a blend of ballet and modern dance, is artistic and very skillful. The dancers mainly stretch the body with soft music. Pop Jazz, a kind of pop music, is changeable and emphasizes the combination of strength and shape. Commercially, the main objective is for stage performances.
8. House: Originating in 1880s, it is a blend of African aboriginal dance, Latin dance, and European tap dance. The characteristics embodied are the quick foot and smooth kick, and the rhythm of the body.

Part Five Further Reading

Jin Xing

Jin Xing is a Chinese ballerina, modern dancer, choreographer, actress, and owner of the contemporary dance company "Shanghai Jin Xing Dance Theatre". Jin Xing is the first woman in China to get the government's approval to undergo a sex change, and she is also one of the first few trans women to be officially recognized as a woman by the Chinese government.

Jin expressed high enthusiasm in dance performance. At the age of 9, she joined the People's Liberation Army to receive dance and military training. In 1987, she went to New York to study modern dance for four years, and then traveled and performed in Europe, and taught dance in Rome from 1991 to 1993, followed by a world tour, and returned to China at the age of 26. She underwent sex reassignment surgery in 1996. Her left leg was paralyzed for a while after the surgery. After the recovery, she went to Shanghai to choreograph and train students.

5
Chapter

Wushu and Other Traditional Sports

Lesson 26 Chinese Martial Arts

Activity 1

🎧 Listen to the following conversation, and then work in pairs to act it out.

(John is a Wushu fan. He is turning to a coach for information about the martial arts.)

A: Excuse me, sir. May I ask you a question?

B: Sure, go ahead.

A: I was wondering, what are the main events in martial arts competitions?

B: The main events include sabreplay, spearplay, swordplay, cudgelplay, unarmed combat, armed combat and team events, etc.

A: Hmm. So, which events are considered unarmed combat?

B: The unarmed combat includes long boxing, southern-style boxing, shadowboxing and so on.

A: Oh, I see. Shadowboxing sounds interesting. Could you teach it to me?

B: Of course.

A: Thank you very much!

Words and Expressions

martial arts 武术

sabreplay /ˈseɪbəpleɪ/ *n.* 刀术

spearplay /ˈspɪəpleɪ/ *n.* 枪术

swordplay /ˈsɔːdpleɪ/ *n.* 剑术；击剑

cudgel /ˈkʌdʒəl/ *n.* 棍棒

unarmed /ˌʌnˈɑːmd/ *adj.* 没有武装
的；徒手的

combat /ˈkɒmbæt/ *n.* 战斗

armed /ɑːmd/ *adj.* 武装的

long boxing 长拳

southern-style boxing 南拳

shadowboxing /ˈʃædəʊˈbɒksɪŋ/ *n.* 太
极拳

Activity 2

👤 Work in pairs and answer the following questions.

Question 1: Have you learned shadowboxing? What do you think of the combat and morals involved in martial arts?

Question 2: A player injured his left leg during martial arts training and fell to the ground. Now he can't move. How should we deal with it?

Part Two Reading

Passage 1

Directions: Read the passage about Chinese martial arts and discuss the following questions with your partner.

Chinese Martial Arts

Chinese martial arts, popularly referred to as Chinese Wushu or Kung Fu, are the several hundreds of fighting styles that have developed over a long historical period in China. These fighting styles are often classified according to common traits, identified as "families", "sects" or "schools" of martial arts. Its main content is attacking skills, and it takes routines and combat as sports forms. It is a Chinese traditional sporting event which pays equal attention to inner and outer practice.

Chinese martial arts is rich in content with different classifications. Traditionally, it is divided into internal and external schools according to its main purpose of fighting with or without an opponent; and it is divided into Shaolin, Wudang, and Emei schools according to different mountains and regions. Besides, it is summed up as "Southern fists and Northern kicks". Nowadays it is classified as competitive martial arts, school martial arts, traditional martial arts and military martial arts according to different fields.

The most obvious characteristics of Chinese martial arts is that there are both combat and routine forms of Wushu for practice. Wushu movements involve offensive and defensive skills, such as kicking, punching, throwing, catching, chopping, stabbing, all of which have respective traits and attacking skills.

"We should carry out training in the coldest and the hottest days of the year." Wushu is not only able to develop one's bravery and fortitude, but is also a good way to promote self-cultivation. "Never learn skills before learning courtesy; never learn martial arts before learning its morals." By learning martial arts and its morals, the youth will respect teachers and confirm with social norms, and they will grow into reasonable, trustworthy, righteous and courageous men that will never bully others.

Words and Expressions

trait /treɪt/ *n.* 品质

military /ˈmɪlətrɪ/ *adj.* 军事的

punch /pʌntʃ/ *v.* 打

chop /tʃɒp/ *v.* 劈

stab /stæb/ *v.* 刺

respective /rɪˈspektɪv/ *adj.* 各自的

bravery /ˈbreɪvərɪ/ *n.* 勇敢，勇气

fortitude /ˈfɔːtɪtjuːd/ *n.* 刚毅，不屈不挠

self-cultivation /selfˌkʌltɪˈveɪʃn/ *n.* 自我修养

moral /ˈmɒrəl/ *n.* 道德

reasonable /ˈriːznəbl/ *adj.* 理性的，通情达理的

trustworthy /ˈtrʌstwɜːðɪ/ *adj.* 可靠的，可信赖的

righteous /ˈraɪtʃəs/ *adj.* 正直的；正义的

courageous /kəˈreɪdʒəs/ *adj.* 有胆量的，有勇气的

bully /ˈbʊlɪ/ *v.* 欺凌，欺压

inner and outer practice 内外兼修

internal school 内家

external school 外家

Southern fists and Northern kicks 南拳北腿

offensive and defensive skills 攻防技巧

We should carry out training in the coldest and the hottest days of the year.
冬练三九，夏练三伏

Never learn skills before learning courtesy; never learn martial arts before learning its morals. 未曾学艺先学礼，未曾习武先习德

Questions:

1. What are the main content and sports forms of Chinese martial arts?

2. How is Chinese martial arts classified?

3. What are the most obvious characteristics of Chinese martial arts?

Passage 2

Directions: Read the passage about the International Wushu Federation and discuss the following questions with your partner.

International Wushu Federation

The International Wushu Federation (IWUF) was established on 3 October, 1990, and is based in Beijing, China. Its official working languages are Chinese and English. Currently, the IWUF has 146 members, across five continental federations worldwide. Under the IWUF, there are the executive committee, technical committee, traditional Wushu committee, medical committee and marketing and development committee. The successive presidents of the IWUF are Li Menghua, Wu Shaozu, Li Zhijian and Yu Zaiqing (present).

In August 1985, the Chinese Wushu Association hosted the first session of the International Wushu Invitational Tournament in Xi'an and founded the preparatory committee of the International Wushu Federation. At the 28th congress of the General Association of International Sports Federations, which was held in Monaco on 22

October, 1994, the IWUF was accepted as an official member. The resolution to admit the IWUF was adopted at the 109th session of the IOC held on 20 June, 1999, in Seoul, South Korea. On 10 December, 2001, the International Wushu Federation signed an agreement with the World Anti-Doping Agency.

The IWUF is in charge of events such as the World Wushu Championships (every two years), World Junior Wushu Championships (every two years), World Traditional Wushu Championships and World Traditional Wushu Festival (every two years), Wushu Sanshou World Cup (every two years), World Shadowboxing Health Conference (every two years) and so on.

Words and Expressions

committee /kə'mɪtɪ/ *n.* 委员会

preparatory /prɪ'pærətrɪ/ *adj.* 预备的

resolution /ˌrezə'luːʃn/ *n.* 决议

agreement /ə'griːmənt/ *n.* 协议

Sports Terms

International Wushu Federation (IWUF) 国际武术联合会

International Wushu Invitational Tournament 国际武术邀请赛

General Association of International Sports Federations 国际单项体育联合会总会

World Anti-Doping Agency 世界反兴奋剂机构

Wushu Sanshou World Cup 世界杯武术散打比赛

Questions:

1. When and where was the IWUF founded?

2. What competitions are held by the IWUF?

Part Three Exercises

Directions: Do the following exercises.

1. Translate the following martial arts terms: hand forms, namely, palm, fist, and hook; fist techniques: punching fist, sweeping side punch, uppercut fist; leg techniques, namely, snap kick, sideward sole kick and back sweep; and stances,

stepping methods, balance, jump and tumbles.

2. What's your opinion about the following sayings? "Heart in the paper, moral in Wushu"; "The master initiates the apprentices, but their skill depends on their own efforts"; "We should carry out training in the coldest and the hottest days of the year"; "External exercise is aimed at strengthening the muscles, bones and skin, and internal exercise at *Qi*"; "Sitting like a bell, standing like a pine, walking like the wind, and lying like a bow".

Part Four Rules and Concepts

1. Wushu competition events include long boxing, southern-style boxing, shadowboxing, swordplay, sabreplay, spearplay, cudgelplay, Taiji swordplay, southern-style sabreplay, southern-style cudgelplay, etc.

2. *Duilian* (dual event) is subdivided into *Duilian* without weapons; *Duilian* with weapons; and *Duilian* with bare hands against weapons, and group events.

3. Each competitor shall choose the degree of difficulty and compulsory movements according to the competition rules and regulations.

4. The competition is classified into individual, team, and individual/team events.

5. The duration of routines lasts for no less than 1 minute and 20 seconds for the seniors, and for no less than 1 minute and 10 seconds for the juniors and children.

6. The individual event is conducted on a 14 m × 8 m court, surrounded by a 2 m-wide safety area.

7. Contest judges consist of one chief referee and one or two assistant chief referees.

8. The head judge shall subtract his deduction from a competitor's actual score, and add the bonus points, if any, for the innovative movements, and the sum will be the competitor's final score.

Part Five Further Reading

Bruce Lee

Bruce Lee was a Chinese-American martial artist, action film actor, martial arts instructor, philosopher, filmmaker, and the founder of Jeet Kune Do. Lee is widely considered by commentators, critics and media as one of the most influential martial artists of all time, and a pop culture icon of the 20th century. He is often credited with helping to change the way Asians were presented in American films.

Lee was born in Chinatown, San Francisco on 27 November, 1940 and was raised in Kowloon, Hong Kong with his family until his late teens. He was introduced to the film industry by his father, a Cantonese opera star, and appeared in several films as a child actor. Lee moved to the United States at the age of 18 to receive his higher education, and it was during this time that he began teaching martial arts. He was trained in the art of Wing Chun and later combined his other influences from various sources, in the spirit of his personal martial arts philosophy, which he dubbed Jeet Kune Do (The Way of the Intercepting Fist).

His Hong Kong and Hollywood-produced films elevated the traditional Hong Kong martial arts film to a new level of popularity and acclaim, sparking a surge of interest in Chinese martial arts in the West in the 1970s. The direction of his films changed and influenced martial arts and martial arts films in the U.S., and the rest of the world. He is noted for his roles in five feature-length films: Lo Wei's *The Big Boss* (1971) and *Fist of Fury* (1972); *Way of the Dragon* (1972), directed and written by Lee; *Enter the Dragon* (1973) and *The Game of Death* (1978), both directed by Robert Clouse.

Lesson 27

Wushu Sanshou

Part One Listening and Speaking

Activity 1

Listen to the following conversation, and then work in pairs to act it out.

(John suffered a muscle strain during his Sanshou lesson. Now he is with the doctor and discussing his injury.)

A: Hello, doctor!

B: Hello, what can I do for you?

A: My inner thigh has been hurting these days. I think I might have injured it.

B: OK. Have a seat and don't move. How do you think it got injured?

A: I think it happened while I was doing vertical splits at my Sanshou lesson.

B: I will take a CT check of your bones first.

(After taking a CT)

B: There is nothing wrong with your bones. The problem appears to be your muscle. I think your excessive vertical splits led to a muscle strain.

A: Oh, I see.

B: Put some mercurochrome on your thigh. And for the next few days you need to do less physical exercise.

A: OK. Thank you, doctor!

Words and Expressions

muscle strain 肌肉拉伤

Sanshou 散打

thigh /θaɪ/ *n.* 大腿

vertical split 竖叉

excessive /ɪk'sesɪv/ *n.* 过度的；过多的，大量的

Activity 2

👤 Work in pairs and make conversations according to the given situation.

Situation 1: When doing Sanshou training, one student suffers a leg strain, and now he cannot do any excessive exercise.

Situation 2: You have had a fever and felt dizzy these days. You decided to see a doctor.

Part Two Reading

Passage 1

Directions: Read the passage about Wushu Sanshou and discuss the following questions with your partner.

Sanshou

Sanshou, Chinese boxing, or Chinese kickboxing is a Chinese self-defense system and combat sport. Sanshou was originally developed by the Chinese military based upon the study and practices of traditional Kung Fu and modern combat fighting techniques. It combines full-contact kickboxing, which includes close-range and rapid successive punches and kicks, with wrestling, takedowns, throws, sweeps, kick catches, and in some competitions, even elbow and knee strikes.

Sanshou is the essence of Chinese martial arts and a sporting event with unique national styles. It has evolved as a treasure of the splendid cultural heritage of the Chinese nation. According to historical records, Chinese unarmed combat spread to Japan as early as one thousand years ago. At that time, it was called "Tang Shou", and was changed to "Kong Shou" later. Now, Sanshou is a Chinese Wushu combat event, in which two fighters use martial arts techniques such as kick, strike, throw and defense to compete under restrictions and regulations.

In 1979, Sanshou became an official competitive event in China. In 2000, the first China Wushu Sanshou Championships was held in Changsha, Hunan. This championship was a milestone in the history of Sanshou development, and Chinese Wushu Sanshou had thus entered the era of professional competition system. Now there are lots of martial arts enthusiasts from different countries who love not only Chinese Wushu routine techniques, but also Sanshou. Through international martial arts exchanges, Chinese Sanshou has continued to spread throughout the world.

Words and Expressions

self-defense /ˌself dɪ'fens/ *n.* 防御，自卫

full-contact /fʊl 'kɒntækt/ *adj.* 全接触的

close-range /ˌkləʊs 'reɪndʒ/ *adj.* 近距离的

punch /pʌntʃ/ *n.* 出拳

takedown /'teɪkdaʊn/ *n.* 摔倒

sweep /swiːp/ *n.* 扫腿；扫

elbow /'elbəʊ/ *n.* 手肘

strike /straɪk/ *n.* 击打

essence /'esns/ *n.* 精华

treasure /'treʒə(r)/ *n.* 宝藏

milestone /'maɪlstəʊn/ *n.* 里程碑

enthusiast /ɪn'θjuːzɪæst/ *n.* 爱好者

Sports Terms

boxing /'bɒksɪŋ/ *n.* 拳击

kickboxing /kɪk'bɒksɪŋ/ *n.* 散打，跆拳道

Tang Shou 唐手

Kong Shou 空手

China Wushu Sanshou Championships 中国武术散打王争霸赛

professional competition system 专业赛制

Questions:

1. What's Sanshou?

2. What are the techniques used in Sanshou competitions?

Passage 2

Directions: Read the passage about the WKA and discuss the following questions with your partner.

World Kickboxing and Karate Association

The World Kickboxing Association (WKA) is one of the oldest and the largest amateur and professional kickboxing organizations in the world. Its official name is "World Kickboxing and Karate Association".

The WKA was created in the United States as the World Karate Association in 1976 by Howard Hanson, a Karate black belt holder. It was based in Massa Carrara, Italy. Howard Hanson later sold the WKA to Dale Floyd in 1991. In 1994, Paul Inghram took over the organization. From 29 September, 2012, WKA has a new management, with Michele Panfietti as president.

The organization was the first non-profit governing body to use an independently controlled rating list, the first to establish a world championship division for women and the first to include countries from Asia. The organization eventually became one of the major sanctioning bodies for professional karate. Early stars of the WKA included "The Jet" Benny Urquidez, "The Dragon" Don Wilson, Kevin Rosier and Graciela Casillas.

The WKA is popular throughout Europe, Asia, Oceania, Africa, and North America.

Words and Expressions

take over 接手，接管

independently /ˌɪndɪ'pendəntlɪ/ *adv.* 独立地，自立地

rating list 评级表

division /dɪ'vɪʒn/ *n.* 分支机构，分部

Sports Terms

World Kickboxing Association (WKA) 世界自由搏击协会

karate /kə'rɑːtɪ/ *n.* 空手道

black belt 黑带

Questions:

1. When was the WKA founded?

2. Can you list some stars of the WKA?

Part Three Exercises

Directions: Do the following exercises.

1. Write a piece of news release to describe the current development of Chinese Sanda in no less than 250 words.

2. What do you think of the popularity of kickboxing learning among children nowadays?

Part Four Rules and Concepts

1. Offensive and defensive techniques of various Wushu schools, such as kick, strike and throw, can be used in Sanshou competitions.

2. Qinna (catch and tumble), attacking the vitals of the head, neck, or the groin are prohibited in Sanshou.

3. The effective scoring areas include the head, the trunk and the thighs in Sanshou competitions.

4. Personal fouls include attacking the opponent before the call of "Start" or after the call of "Stop", hitting the opponent on prohibited areas, or hitting the opponent with any prohibited method.

5. Technical fouls include holding the opponent passively or running away from the opponent, raising the hand to request a timeout when at a disadvantage, delaying the fight intentionally, wearing no gum shield or spitting out the gum shield, or loosening the protective gear intentionally, and acting impolitely towards the judges or disobeying their decisions.

6. A competitor who hurts the opponent intentionally will be disqualified from the whole competition, with all his results annulled.

7. A competitor who uses prohibited drugs or inhales oxygen during the break will be

disqualified from the whole competition, with all his results annulled.

8. The competitor whose opponent is knocked down and fails to get to his feet within ten seconds after receiving the heavy blows (except for personal fouls), or who manages to get to his feet but remains in an abnormal state of consciousness, will be declared the winner of the bout.

Part Five Further Reading

Liu Hailong

Liu Hailong is a Chinese Sanshou kickboxer. Liu's rise to fame came in 2000 at the inaugural King of Sanda Tournament when he won the gold medal of 75 kg division. Liu not only won his weight class, but went on to win a grueling one-night open weight round-robin tournament against much stronger fighters as well. He was credited with the title Sanda "King of Kings". Exciting and charismatic, Liu is almost certainly China's most recognized combat athlete.

In 2003, Liu faced a fellow King of Sanda Yuan Yubao in the promotion's first "Superfight", defeating him to earn the title of "Super King of Sanda". At the 2003 Sanshou World Championships in Macau, Liu defeated Salihov in amateur rules competition and won the 80 kg division gold medal. After an injury in 2005, Liu retired from the sport. In 2009, he made a comeback facing and defeated Japanese fighter Iga Koji.

Lesson 28 Folk Wushu

Part One Listening and Speaking

Activity 1

🎧 Listen to the following conversation, and then work in pairs to act it out.

(John is talking about shadowboxing with Peter.)

A: Have you learned martial arts before?

B: Not really. A friend once taught me a little shadowboxing.

A: Really? Would you mind showing me? Maybe I can give you some tips.

B: OK, but can you explain the essentials to me again?

A: Of course. You have to raise your head and keep your shoulders upright and hips withdrawn, and land on your heels first when moving.

B: It seems that you are good at shadowboxing. Will you please teach me if you're ever available?

A: Sure, next time I can introduce my teacher to you. Then we can learn from each other, and make progress together.

B: That's great, thank you very much.

A: You're welcome.

Words and Expressions

essential /ɪ'senʃl/ *n.* 基础，基本要素

raise head 抬头

upright /'ʌpraɪt/ *adj.* 直立的；垂直的

hip /hɪp/ *n.* 臀部

withdraw /wɪð'drɔː/ *v.* 收回；撤退；离开

available /ə'veɪləbl/ *adj.* 有空的；可获得的

Activity 2

👤 Work in pairs and answer the following questions.

Question 1: What preparations should be made before practicing shadowboxing, and what is the purpose?

Question 2: When practicing shadowboxing, why do you need to raise your head with your shoulders upright?

Part Two Reading

Passage 1

Directions: Read the passage about shadowboxing and discuss the following questions with your partner.

Shadowboxing

Shadowboxing is a major division of Chinese martial arts, whose literal meaning is "supreme ultimate fist".

There have been different claims about the origin of shadowboxing. The traditional legend goes that the wise man Zhang Sanfeng of the Song Dynasty created shadowboxing after he had witnessed a fight between a sparrow and a snake; meanwhile, most people have agreed that the modern shadowboxing originated from Chen style shadowboxing, which first appeared during the 19th century in the Daoguang Reign of the Qing Dynasty.

Shadowboxing has its philosophical roots in Taoism and is considered an internal martial art, utilizing the internal energy, or *Qi*, and following the simple principle of "subduing the vigorous by the soft". Taoism is the oldest philosophy of China and is represented by the famous symbol of the *Yin* and *Yang*. This expresses the continuous flow of *Qi* in a circular motion that generates two opposite forces, plus and minus, which interact and balance with each other to bring existence to the physical world.

The most famous forms of shadowboxing practiced today are the Chen, Yang, Woo, Sun and Wu styles. All these five styles can be traced back to the Chen style shadowboxing. According to historical records, shadowboxing was founded by Chen Wangting, who lived in Chenjiagou Village, in today's Henan province in China. Based on Chen style and created by Yang Luchan, a Hebei native of the Qing Dynasty, Yang style is now the most popular style worldwide. Woo style is based on Chen and Yang styles and was created by Woo Yuxiang. Sun style is derived from Chen and Woo styles and was created by Sun Lutang. It is a combination of the more famous internal Chinese martial art forms of *Bagua*, *Xingyi* and shadowboxing. Wu style is based on Chen and Yang styles and was created by Wu Jianquan.

Nowadays, when most people talk about shadowboxing, they are usually referring to Yang style, which has already spread throughout the world and is practiced by millions of people.

Words and Expressions

ultimate /'ʌltɪmət/ *adj.* 最终的；极限的

claim /kleɪm/ *n.* 陈述，声称；要求

legend /'ledʒənd/ *n.* 传说

witness /'wɪtnəs/ *v.* 目睹；证明

sparrow /'spærəʊ/ *n.* 麻雀

snake /sneɪk/ *n.* 蛇

reign /reɪn/ *n.* 统治时期

philosophical /ˌfɪlə'sɒfɪkl/ *adj.* 哲学的

Taoism /'daʊɪzəm/ *n.* 道家

utilize /'juːtəlaɪz/ *v.* 使用，利用

subdue /səb'djuː/ *v.* 征服，抑制

flow /fləʊ/ *n.* 流动；潮流

generate /'dʒenəreɪt/ *v.* 产生；诞生

derive /dɪ'raɪv/ *v.* 源自，发源；获取

Sports Terms

Chen style shadowboxing 陈氏太极拳

subdue the vigorous by the soft 以柔克刚

Questions:

    1. Do you know the legend of the origin of shadowboxing?

    2. What are the philosophical ideas in shadowboxing?

    3. What are the schools of modern shadowboxing?

Passage 2

Directions: Read the passage about the HBWA and discuss the following questions with your partner.

Hebei Wushu Association

The Hebei Wushu Association (HBWA) is a mass organization for Hebei martial arts under the leadership of the Hebei Sports Bureau, which is independently incorporated. The highest authority of the HBWA is the representative assembly held every five years. Its divisions include executive committee, secretariat, technical committee, coach committee, referee committee, publicity committee, and marketing committee. Every city and district has its subdivisions.

The main tasks of the HBWA are to actively promote and carry out Wushu activities, to accelerate vigorously the implementation of "The National Fitness Program", and to give impetus to the development of Wushu in Hebei province. And according to the regulations of the General Administration of Sport of China and Hebei provincial sports administrative departments, the HBWA is responsible for coordinating and organizing provincial, national and international Wushu competitions, laying out competition institutions, preparing competition plans and programs, and so on.

Words and Expressions

leadership /ˈliːdəʃɪp/ *n.* 领导

bureau /ˈbjʊərəʊ/ *n.* 局，部

assembly /əˈsemblɪ/ *n.* 集会；大会；议会

promote /prəˈməʊt/ *v.* 促进；提升

accelerate /əkˈseləreɪt/ *v.* 加速，促进

implementation /ˌɪmplɪmenˈteɪʃn/ *n.* 实施；履行

administrative /ədˈmɪnɪstrətɪv/ *adj.* 行政的；管理的

Sports Terms

"National Fitness Program"《全民健身计划纲要》

General Administration of Sport of China 国家体育总局

Questions:

1. What's the highest authority of the HBWA?

2. What are the divisions of the HBWA?

3. What are the responsibilities of the HBWA?

Part Three Exercises

Directions: Do the following exercises.

1. Offer your advice on how to promote folk Wushu.

2. Do you think it's a good idea for college students to learn shadowboxing?

Part Four Rules and Concepts

1. The Open Palm and Fist Salute is widely recognized in Chinese martial arts, and it is the required salute for Wushu competitions.

2. The salute with the cudgel and the spear requires the competitor to hold the weapon with the right fist covered by the left palm.

3. All competitors are required to adhere to the rules and regulations of the competition and demonstrate sportsmanship towards fellow competitors and respect for judges and other tournament officials.

4. An audible warning will be given 30 seconds prior to the time limit in shadowboxing competitions.

5. The score for a shadowboxing performance is classified into three grades, nine levels. Scores between 8.50 and 10.00 are "excellent", scores between 7.00 and 8.49 are "good", and scores between 5.00 and 6.99 are "acceptable".

6. Re-performing a shadowboxing routine due to forgetfulness will result in a 0.5 point deduction from the final score.

7. If there is any interruption caused by uncontrollable circumstances, such as lighting or computer scoring disorder, the competitor will not be penalized.

8. The judge group does timekeeping with two stopwatches. When the performer violates the time regulation, and the two watches are different in timekeeping, the performer's time is set according to the watch which is closer to the specified time.

9. The preferable costume for traditional Chinese martial arts is either a cotton or silk Chinese-style uniform with frog buttons.

10. Wing Chun competitors must demonstrate good stamina and endurance throughout the demonstration of their form. Any indication that they are tired or exhausted will result in a point deduction.

Part Five Further Reading

Sun Lutang

Sun Lutang was a renowned master of Chinese internal martial arts and was the progenitor of Sun-style shadowboxing. He was also considered an accomplished Neo-Confucian and Taoist scholar, and was a distinguished contributor to the theory of internal martial arts through his many published works.

Sun was well-versed in two other internal martial arts: *Xingyi Quan* and *Bagua Zhang* in his early years. His expertise in these two martial arts is so high that many regarded him as without equal. He learned Wu (Hao)-style shadowboxing from Hao Weizhen. Sun started studying with Hao relatively late in his life, but his accomplishments in the other two internal arts led him to develop his shadowboxing abilities to a high standard more quickly than is usual.

He subsequently was invited by Yang Zhaoxiong and Yang Chengfu to join them on the faculty of the Beijing Physical Education Research Institute where they taught shadowboxing to the public after 1914. Sun taught there until 1928, a seminal period in the development of modern Yang, Wu and Sun-style shadowboxing.

Lesson 29

Dragon-lion Dance

Activity 1

🎧 Listen to the following conversation, and then work in pairs to act it out.

(John wants to learn the dragon-lion dance, but he finds it too difficult. He is considering giving it up. But his teacher Mr. Zhang is encouraging him.)

A: Excuse me, sir. May I have a moment of your time?

B: Yes, please go ahead!

A: I'm really interested in the dragon-lion dance, but it is so difficult!

B: Take it easy! The dragon-lion dance is a part of Chinese traditional culture. It is not something that can be perfected in one or two days.

A: Oh, I see. But I can't help myself. I'm so eager to master it.

B: Well, be patient and don't worry. Also, don't forget the importance of the physical training involved in learning the dance.

A: I see, thank you!

B: My pleasure! I'm confident that someday you'll master the skills, and I hope you'll join the school team soon.

Words and Expressions

dragon-lion dance 舞龙舞狮

give up 放弃

eager /ˈiːgə(r)/ *adj.* 渴望的

master /ˈmɑːstə/ *v.* 掌握

confident /ˈkɒnfɪdənt/ *adj.* 自信的

179

Activity 2

👥 Work in pairs and answer the following questions.

> **Question 1:** What is your impression about the image of the "dragon" and "lion" in the dragon-lion dance?
>
> **Question 2:** Can you describe the skills and basic training methods of the dragon-lion dance?

Part Two Reading

Passage 1

Directions: Read the passage about dragon dance and lion dance and discuss the following questions with your partner.

Dragon Dance and Lion Dance

China is home to the dragon-lion dance. The activity has been welcomed by people from various ethnic groups for generations. Having thrived for thousands of years, it has become an extremely precious cultural heritage. The dragon-lion dance is usually performed during Spring Festival, fairs, carnivals and celebrations.

The "dragon" used in dragon dance is made of straw, bamboo and cloth. Each dragon is different in size, with odd numbers of sections being considered lucky. There are 9-, 11-, 13- and even 29-section dragons. Dragons longer than 15 sections are heavy and difficult to dance with, and are more for decoration than performance. The fire dragon with candles or lamps inside provides viewers and passersby with a spectacular display at night. The movements in the dragon dance vary greatly. Skills are very important for a dancing dragon with nine sections or less. The following movements are very common: a dragon roaming, a dragon moving through arches, the simultaneous movement of the head and tail, a dragon wagging its tail, and a snake sloughing its skin. Performances are stressed for dragons of 11 and 13 sections. For instance, for the movements of "golden dragon chasing treasure pearl", the dragon flies and jumps into the air and then dives into the sea. With the dragon pearls and drum tempos, the dragon dance is an artistic form combining martial arts, drum music, traditional Chinese opera and dragon arts.

The origin of lion dance can be traced back to the Three Kingdoms period, and it became popular in the Southern and Northern Dynasties. It has a history of more than 1,000 years. The dancing lion, with a mighty appearance, features rigid movement and various expressions. There are many different legends of the lion dance. Some are of fables and some are related to history, adding a mysterious element to the dance. People believe that lions are auspicious animals and the lion dance can bring good luck. Nowadays, there are northern and southern schools of lion dancing. The northern school is popular in the north of the Yangtze River while the southern school in the south of the river. They are quite different in styles such as appearances, steps, movements and rhythm of gongs, drums, and cymbals.

Words and Expressions

thrive /θraɪv/ v. 繁荣，兴旺

fair /feə(r)/ n. 集会

carnival /ˈkɑːnɪvl/ n. 联欢；狂欢节

celebration /ˌselɪˈbreɪʃn/ n. 庆典；庆祝

straw /strɔː/ n. 稻草

section /ˈsekʃn/ n. 节，段

decoration /ˌdekəˈreɪʃn/ n. 装饰

passerby /ˌpɑːsəˈbaɪ/ n. 行人，路人

spectacular /spekˈtækjələ(r)/ adj. 壮观的

roam /rəʊm/ v. 漫游，漫步

arch /ɑːtʃ/ n. 弓形

simultaneous /ˌsɪmlˈteɪnɪəs/ adj. 同步

的，同时的

wag /wæg/ v. 摇摆

stress /stres/ v. 侧重；强调

pearl /pɜːl/ n. 珍珠

dive /daɪv/ v. 潜水

drum /drʌm/ n. 鼓

fable /feɪbl/ n. 神话，预言

auspicious /ɔːˈspɪʃəs/ adj. 吉兆的，吉利的

gong /ɡɒŋ/ n. 锣

cymbal /ˈsɪmbl/ n. 钹

Questions:

1. What is made of the "dragon" for the dragon dance?

2. What are the movements in the dragon dance?

3. What's the moral of the lion dance?

Passage 2

Directions: Read the passage about the International Dragon and Lion Dance Federation and discuss the following questions with your partner.

International Dragon and Lion Dance Federation

The International Dragon and Lion Dance Federation (IDLDF) was formally incorporated in Hong Kong on 23 January, 1995. Its predecessor is the International Dragon and Lion Dance Association. In July 1997, the secretariat of the IDLDF executive committee moved to Beijing. The IDLDF is entitled to various rights including the management of dragon-lion dance competitions, the training of referees and coaches, and the promotion of dance skills.

The Chinese Dragon and Lion Dance Sports Association, founded in 1995, consists of various dragon-lion dance associations from provinces, autonomous regions, municipalities and industries. It is a nationwide mass sports society and a voluntary, non-profit organization with independent corporate qualification, and is also a group member of the All-China Sports Federation. The association is the only legitimate organization that represents China to join the IDLDF and participate in international activities of dragon-lion dance.

Words and Expressions

formally /ˈfɔːməlɪ/ *adv.* 正式地 | legitimate /lɪˈdʒɪtɪmət/ *adj.* 法定的；合法的

Sports Terms

International Dragon and Lion Dance Federation (IDLDF) 国际龙狮运动联合会

All-China Sports Federation 全国体育总会

Questions:

1. When was the IDLDF founded?

2. What do you know about the Chinese Dragon and Lion Dance Sports Association?

Part Three Exercises

Directions: Do the following exercises.

1. Watch a dragon-lion dance competition, and compose a commentary of the performance in no less than 250 words.

2. From your perspective, what is the biggest difference between the southern school and northern school of lion dance?

Part Four Rules and Concepts

1. The dragon dance event is divided into four categories including compulsory, optional, traditional and technical routines.

2. Movement difficulty is classified as Level A, B and C. Difficulties of different levels correspond with different scores respectively.

3. The dragon dance is conducted in a 20 m×20 m square venue (under special circumstances, the minimum side length of the square shall not be less than 18 m). The width of the sideline is 0.05 m, inside which is the venue. At least 1 meter outside the sideline is set as a barrier-free zone.

4. Under the supervision of the competition committee, prior to the competition, the representatives sent by every team attend the drawing-lots ceremony for the competition order. The working staff of the organizing committee takes the drawing for the team which does not send any representative to the drawing-lots ceremony.

5. In the competition, athletes shall wear performance costume with special characteristics. They shall wear clean and tidy attire. The style and color of the attire shall be harmonized with the equipment in dragon-lion dances.

6. The music accompaniment is an integral part of the dragon-lion dances in regards to setting an atmosphere, changing rhythm and inspiring spirit. The music rhythm, tempo and transfer shall correspond with the movements.

7. The chief judge has the right to call the judges to consult or display the basic score to adjust when an obviously unfair case or non-allowance difference between the

valid scores occurs.

8. There shall be no change of substitute during the process of the competition. Any offender of this regulation shall be disqualified from the competition.

9. No participants shall impose any influence or disturbance upon the judging staff during the ongoing competition.

10. Dragon-lion dances adhere to the principles of anti-doping. Doping is strictly prohibited in the competition.

Part Five Further Reading

World Dragon and Lion Dance Championships

The World Dragon and Lion Dance Championships is held every two years. Members (friends) of the International Dragon and Lion Dance Federation send teams to participate, and when necessary, non-members (friends) are also invited to play. This sporting event includes dragon dance and lion dance.

Bid for the World Dragon and Lion Dance Championships: the payment of $1,000 for the bid; free accommodations and transportation for prescribed members from all teams for a prescribed period; free accommodations, transportation and game preparation for the officials from the executive committee and representative assembly; responsible for reporting and broadcasting the events and related meetings via government (regional) news media; after payment, the bid winner is entitled to the advertising rights (including television) of the competition and the rights of logo product development of the International Dragon and Lion Dance Federation.

Bid time: The bid for the World Dragon and Lion Dance Championships must be proposed one year before the next executive committee is held. The host of the World Dragon and Lion Dance Championships must submit summary and related materials about the organization and promotion of the competition to the International Dragon and Lion Dance Federation for records within three months after the game.

附录 参考译文

第一章 田径运动

第 1 课 田径运动

听和说

活动 1

🎧 听下面的对话，然后两人一组将其表演出来。

（今天体育理论课的主题是田径运动。张老师解释了为什么田径运动是其他运动的基础后，回答了约翰提出的一些问题。）

A: 为什么说田径运动是体育运动之母呢?

B: 因为从训练方法上来说，它是其他运动的基础。这些方法能够提高人的身体素质。田径运动还能够提高训练水平。

A: 那田径运动是如何分类的呢?

B: 想你也知道，田径运动一般分为田赛、径赛和全能运动三类。

A: 了解了。我对田径运动的历史也很感兴趣。您能告诉我最早的田径比赛是什么吗?

B: 当然啦，是直道短跑，公元前 776 年在希腊奥林匹克村的第一届古代奥运会上举行。

A: 我知道了。

活动 2

👥 两人一组，回答下列问题。

> 问题 1：为什么田径运动是国家运动水平的一项重要指标？
>
> 问题 2：田径运动有哪些突出特点？

第二部分 阅读

文章 1

阅读下面这篇关于世界田径赛事的文章，讨论文后的思考题。

世界田径赛事

奥运会田径赛是世界上最早的田径比赛。1896 年首届奥运会将男子项目列入比赛，1928 年第九届奥运会增设了女子田径项目。田径是奥运会的基石，最能体现"更快、更高、更强"的奥林匹克精神。每四年一届的奥运会促使田径运动成绩不断提高，涌现出许多优秀的田径运动员。

世界田径锦标赛于 1983 年在芬兰赫尔辛基首次举办，之后每四年举办一次，且均在奥运会前一年，1991 年第三届田径锦标赛后改为每两年一届。田径锦标赛项目包括径赛、田赛项目以及马拉松和竞走比赛。事实上，世界田径锦标赛是奥运会前各国田径选手水平的大检阅。世界室内田径锦标赛从 1985 年开始举办，每两年一次，这是唯一一个只进行田径比赛的世界性赛事。

马拉松赛是一项长跑比赛，全长 42.195 公里。该项目得到顾拜旦的大力支持，1896 年第一届奥运会时便被列为比赛项目。女子马拉松比赛直到 1984 年洛杉矶奥运会才被列为正式比赛项目。马拉松赛多为公路赛，采用起、终点在同一地点的往返路线或起、终点不在同一地点的单程路线。马拉松不设世界纪录，只公布世界最好成绩。如今，每年有 500 多场马拉松比赛在世界各地举办，多数参赛者为业余运动员。大型马拉松比赛参赛人数可达万人以上。

思考题:

    1. 田径比赛何时被列为奥运会比赛项目?

    2. 举办世界田径锦标赛的目的是什么?

    3. 马拉松比赛全程有多长?

文章 2

阅读下面这篇关于国际田径联合会的文章,讨论文后的思考题。

国际田径联合会

    国际田径联合会,简称国际田联,是管理田径赛事的国际组织,1912 年 7 月 17 日在瑞典斯德哥尔摩成立,1993 年 10 月起将总部设在摩纳哥。现任主席是英国人塞巴斯蒂安·科。现有会员 215 个,分属欧、亚、非、中北美、南美和大洋洲六个地区联合会。工作用语为英、法、俄、德、西班牙语。国际田联下设五个专业委员会,包括技术委员会、妇女委员会、竞走委员会、越野跑委员会和医务委员会。中国田径协会于 1978 年加入国际田联。

    国际田联负责组织主要的国际性田径比赛。田径比赛是奥运会的主要比赛项目,四年一届。其他主要的国际田径比赛有:世界田径锦标赛、世界杯田径赛、世界青年田径锦标赛、世界少年田径锦标赛、世界室内田径锦标赛、国际田联黄金联赛、国际田径协会决赛、国际田联超级大奖赛、大奖赛和大奖赛总决赛。

思考题:

    1. 国际田联总部设在哪里?现任主席是谁?

    2. 国际田联的工作用语是什么?

    3. 国际田联负责的主要赛事有哪些?

第三部分 练习

请完成以下练习。

1. 请从全运会的视角简述我国田径运动的发展概况。

2. 谈谈你最喜爱的田径项目,并说明理由。

第四部分 规则与概念

1. 田径运动包括：短距离跑、中距离跑和长距离跑、跨栏跑、接力跑、障碍跑、马拉松、跳高、撑竿跳、跳远、三级跳、铅球、铁饼、链球、标枪、竞走、全能等项目。

2. 田径运动的比赛项目包括：

   男子

   - 跑：

     100 米、200 米、400 米、800 米、1500 米、5000 米、10 000 米

     3000 米障碍跑

     马拉松

     4×100 米接力、4×400 米接力

     110 米栏、400 米栏

     20 公里竞走、50 公里竞走

   - 跳：

     跳高

     跳远

     撑竿跳高

     三级跳

   - 投：

     标枪

     铅球

     链球

     铁饼

   - 十项全能

   女子

   - 跑：

     100 米、200 米、400 米、800 米、1500 米、3000 米

     马拉松

     4×100 米接力、4×400 米接力

     100 米栏、400 米栏

- 跳：

  跳高

  跳远

- 投：

  标枪

  铅球

  铁饼

- 七项全能

3. 应给每位运动员分发两块号码布，比赛时分别佩戴在胸前和后背的明显位置，但在跳高和撑竿跳高比赛中，运动员只需在胸前或后背佩戴一块号码布即可。号码必须与秩序册上或规定的号码一致。

4. 如果运动员在比赛中因违反规则而被取消比赛资格，应在官方结果中注明他所违反的那项规则。但这一犯规行为不应影响该运动员参加后续项目的比赛。

5. 如果运动员有违反体育道德或不正当的行为，裁判员将取消其参加其他所有项目比赛的资格。

6. 在以得分决定胜负的比赛中，该计分方法应在比赛前得到所有参赛国家的同意。

7. 所有竞赛项目比赛时，发令员应在确认运动员状态稳定、起跑姿势正确后，使用发令枪朝天鸣放起跑。

8. 在接力比赛中，运动员必须手持接力棒跑完全程。运动员不允许戴手套或在手上放置任何可以助其更好地抓握接力棒的物体。

9. 在所有接力赛跑中，运动员必须在接力区内传递接力棒。在接力区外传接力棒将被取消比赛资格。

10. 比赛开始前，运动员均可在比赛区域练习。投掷练习应在裁判员的监督下按抽签排定的顺序进行。

第五部分 拓展阅读

尤塞恩·博尔特

尤塞恩·博尔特，牙买加短跑运动员，奥运冠军。全自动计时应用以来首位同时保持 100 米和 200 米两项世界纪录的运动员，还是 4×100 米接力世界纪录的保持者，被誉为有史以来最成功的短跑运动员。

2004 年，博尔特参加了在百慕大举行的加勒比共同体运动会，正式成为职业运动员，并在 200 米比赛中跑出了 19 秒 93 的成绩，成为有史以来第一个 200 米跑入 20 秒的青年运动员。2008 年 5 月 31 日，博尔特在纽约锐步田径大奖赛上以 9 秒 72 的成绩打破 100 米世界纪录，创造了属于他的第一个世界纪录。

2008 年北京奥运会上，博尔特获得两项短跑冠军，赢得世界瞩目。在 100 米决赛中，他以 9 秒 69 的成绩打破了自己保持的世界纪录。在随后的 200 米决赛中，他以 19 秒 30 的成绩打破了世界纪录和奥运会纪录。之后，他又与队友合作，以 37 秒 10 的成绩赢得 4×100 米接力金牌并打破世界纪录。博尔特成为第一个在同一届奥运会上包揽 100 米、200 米和 4×100 米接力三项金牌，并同时打破世界纪录的短跑运动员。2012 年伦敦奥运会上，博尔特成功卫冕奥运会男子 100 米、200 米、4×100 米接力冠军。2016 年里约奥运会上，博尔特再次获得男子 100 米、200 米、4×100 米接力冠军，实现奥运三连冠。

9 块奥运金牌、11 块世锦赛金牌，博尔特以其在短跑项目上的巨大成就被誉为"闪电博尔特"。他曾获得"国际田联年度最佳运动员"、"田径年度最佳运动员"称号，三次获得"劳伦斯世界体育奖最佳运动员"荣誉。博尔特已宣布将在 2017 年世锦赛后退役。

第 **2** 课 跑

第一部分 听和说

活动 1

🎧 听下面的对话，然后两人一组将其表演出来。

（在体育课上，张老师正在回答约翰关于跑的问题。）

A: 张老师，什么是径赛？

B: 径赛是以时间计算成绩的跑步运动。

A: 径赛包括哪些项目呢？

B: 很多啊，包括短跑、中长跑、障碍跑、跨栏跑、接力跑和马拉松等。

A: 短距离跑指的是哪些项目呢？

B: 一般包括 50 米、100 米、200 米、400 米、4×100 米和 4×400 米接力跑。

A: 我知道了。那慢跑呢？它算是有氧运动吗？

B: 当然是啊！经常慢跑能够有效地调节人体的机能状态，增强耐力。

A: 真的吗？太棒了！我喜欢慢跑，明天早上我要早点起来慢跑。

B: 非常棒！

活动 2

👤 两人一组，回答下列问题。

> 问题 1: 运动员在短跑训练时右脚受伤，摔倒在地，该如何处理伤痛？
>
> 问题 2: 你知道男子、女子 100 米世界纪录成绩各是多少吗？

第二部分 阅读

文章 1

阅读下面这篇关于跑的文章，讨论文后的思考题。

跑

远在上古时代，人们为了生存，在和大自然及野兽斗争时要经常穿越沼泽平原、跨溪流、越障碍，逐步形成了跑、跳等各种生存技能。随着人类的发展和社会的进步，早期田径运动逐步形成。跑步比赛一直伴随着人类历史的发展，是古代奥运会和现代奥运会的重要组成部分。如今，竞技跑步比赛成为田径运动的核心项目。

跑步时，单腿支撑与腾空相交替，两腿不断重复剪角动作。跑步比赛，或称径赛，是运动员以跑步方式完成规定距离所用时间的长短而分胜负的比赛。比赛主要根据距离，或是设置障碍进行，如障碍跑和跨栏跑中的障碍物。跑步比赛分为不同级别，不同级别要求不同的体格优势，同时也需要不同的运动技巧、训练方法和运动员类型。

短距离跑技术包括起跑、加速跑、稳速跑和冲刺四个部分。成绩的好坏取决于起跑的反应速度、起跑后的加速能力、保持最高跑速的距离以及各部分技术完成的质量。中距离跑、长跑及马拉松跑以培养人的耐力为目的。跑步时，由于氧气的供应不能满足肌肉活动的需要，跑到一定程度就会感到胸闷、呼吸困难，这种现象称为"极点"。因此，练习中长跑时要注意循序渐进。

思考题：

1. 跑步运动如何产生的？
2. 跑步比赛如何分类？
3. 中长跑中的"极点"现象是指什么？

文章 2

阅读下面这篇关于跨栏跑的文章，讨论文后的思考题。

跨栏跑

跨栏起源于英国，由牧羊人跨越羊圈栅栏的游戏演变而来。跨栏指以一定速度奔跑并越过障碍的运动。在田径运动中，跨栏跑是其他高度专业化的障碍赛的基础。跨栏比赛以栏为障碍，按规定高度和距离设置栏杆，运动员跨越各栏完成比赛。

最著名的跨栏比赛项目包括男子 110 米栏、女子 100 米栏和 400 米栏（男女均有），这三种项目都是夏季奥运会和世界田径锦标赛的比赛项目。110 米栏和 100 米栏在直线跑道上进行，400 米栏要绕标准椭圆跑道一周。此外，跨栏比赛也是十项全能和七项全能的比赛项目之一。

在场地赛中，栏高通常在 68 厘米至 107 厘米，按年龄和性别规定。在国际比赛中，男子 110 米栏为高栏，栏高 106.7 厘米；女子 100 米栏为低栏，栏高 83.8 厘米。男女比赛栏数均为 10 个。

思考题：

1. 你知道跨栏跑的起源吗？
2. 最著名的跨栏比赛项目有哪些？
3. 男子和女子跨栏比赛的区别是什么？

第三部分 练习

请完成以下练习。

1. 为一名中学生制定一个晨跑的训练计划。
2. 参加或观看一场马拉松比赛，撰写一篇不少于 250 字的赛后感或观后感。

第四部分 规则与概念

1. 根据径赛规定，比赛在 400 米标准田径场上进行。
2. 短跑口令为"各就各位""预备""鸣枪"，而中长跑口令为"各就各位""鸣枪"。
3. "各就各位"的口令要拉长一些；"预备"口令要平稳短促。
4. 鸣枪后发现运动员犯规，立即鸣枪召回。
5. 短跑比赛中，运动员的名次由终点裁判判定，终点裁判负责在终点记录各道运动员的成绩顺序。中长跑项目裁判一般采取人盯人的计圈以判定运动员到达终点的名次。

6. 检查裁判员的任务是赛前检查径赛场地和设备，比赛中检查运动员是否犯规。例如：短距离跑是否串道，中长距离跑是否发生推撞，跨栏跑是否手推或者脚踢过栏。

7. 运动员以挤撞或阻挡方式妨碍其他运动员走或跑时，应取消其该项目的比赛资格。

8. 运动员自愿离开跑道后将不得继续参加该项目的比赛。

9. 在规定时间的计程比赛中，发令员必须在比赛结束前 1 分钟鸣枪，以警示运动员和裁判员比赛即将结束。

10. 运动员未能跨越每一个栏架，或在过栏瞬间其脚或腿低于栏顶水平面，或者裁判长认为运动员有意撞倒栏架，将被取消比赛资格。

第五部分 拓展阅读

刘翔

刘翔，中国前 110 米栏运动员，奥运金牌获得者，世界冠军。2004 年雅典奥运会上，他为中国男子田径项目赢得了第一块奥运金牌。

刘翔是中国最成功的运动员之一，也是一位文化偶像。他是世界 110 米栏历史上第一位获得"三重冠"的男子运动员：世界纪录保持者、世界冠军、奥运冠军。

2004 年雅典奥运会上，刘翔以 12 秒 91 的成绩追平了由英国选手科林·杰克逊创造的世界纪录，夺得冠军。2006 年，在瑞士洛桑田径超级大奖赛中，他以 12 秒 88 的成绩打破了世界纪录，成功夺冠。北京奥运会上，刘翔被寄予夺金厚望，然而却因最后时刻有人抢跑，使得已发力的他脚伤进一步恶化，最终不得不选择退出比赛。伦敦奥运会上，刘翔再次以夺冠热门身份亮相，却在预赛中攻第一个栏时拉伤跟腱，结束了伦敦奥运会的征程，空手而归。

2015 年 4 月 7 日，刘翔在新浪微博上发表退役通告，正式结束运动生涯。

第 ③ 课 跳跃

第一部分 听和说

活动 1

🎧 听下面的对话，然后两人一组将其表演出来。

（在体育理论课上，张老师正回答学生提出的关于跳跃比赛的问题。）

A: 张老师，什么是田赛？

B: 田赛就是在田径场上举行的比赛。以高度和远度计算成绩，一般包括跳跃和投掷类项目。

A: 跳跃项目有哪些？

B: 跳远和跳高，具体来说，有跳远、三级跳远、跳高和撑竿跳高。

A: 跳高运动员最常用的技术是什么呢？

B: 最常用的是背越式，也称福斯贝利式。

A: 您知道中国有哪些著名跳高运动员吗？

B: 我最先想到的就是朱建华，他曾是世界纪录保持者。

A: 真的吗？他个人最好成绩是多少？

B: 2.39 米。

A: 哇，跳得真高啊！

活动 2

👥 两人一组，回答下列问题。

> 问题 1: 你喜欢跳跃比赛吗？你最喜欢的跳跃比赛项目是什么？
>
> 问题 2: 你要参加学校运动会的跳远或跳高比赛吗？为什么？

第二部分 阅读

文章 1

阅读下面这篇关于跳跃的文章，讨论文后的思考题。

跳跃

跳跃项目包括克服垂直障碍的高度项目和克服水平障碍的远度项目。奥运会的跳跃比赛项目包括跳远、三级跳远、跳高和撑竿跳高。

跳高和跳远既有共同的运动规律，又有各自的运动学和动力学特征。跳远技术包括助跑、起跳、腾空和落地四部分。空中姿势有蹲踞式、挺身式和走步式三种姿势。三级跳远是由助跑开始，沿直线连续进行三次水平跳跃的田赛项目；第一跳为单足跳，第二跳为跨步跳，第三跳为跳跃。运动员必须具备良好的身体素质和较高的技术水平，才能保证取得优异成绩。

跳高的过杆技术有剪式、滚式、俯卧式和背越式，其中背越式跳高最具有代表性，完整技术由助跑、起跳、过杆和落地四部分组成。相比以上三种跳跃项目而言，撑竿跳高在运动结构和技术方面都具有一定的独特性。撑竿跳高分为持竿助跑阶段、插竿准备与插竿、上摆、拉引、转体、蹬伸及过杆等阶段。

思考题：

1. 跳远技术分为哪四步？
2. 什么是三级跳？
3. 跳高的过杆技术有哪些？

文章 2

阅读下面这篇关于撑竿跳高的文章，讨论文后的思考题。

撑竿跳高

撑竿跳高是一项男女均可参加的径赛项目。撑竿跳跃最早是为了跨越沟渠、沼泽等自然障碍而产生的。男子撑竿跳高自第一届现代奥运会起便是正式比赛项目，女子比赛在 2000 年悉尼奥运会上才被列为正式比赛项目。

在撑竿跳比赛中，运动员先要携带一根长而灵便的撑竿进行 40 米至 50 米的冲刺跑，后将撑竿插进插斗内起跳，越过悬于两根跳高架之上的横杆。每轮比赛过后会将横杆高度提高，如果运动员连续三次试跳失败，将被取消比赛资格。裁判在场监督比赛进行，并调整横杆高度。

　　横杆的起始高度和后续增加的高度由裁判决定，运动员可自行选择参加某一高度的比赛。运动员依次进行比赛。如果两名或两名以上运动员过杆成功，裁判将会按规定调整高度，一般一次抬高 5 厘米或 15 厘米。运动员可拒绝参加某一高度的比赛，等待尝试更高的高度。如果比赛出现平局，则将运动员的失败次数计入成绩。如果两名或两名以上的运动员失败次数相同，则进行加时赛，一跳定胜负。

思考题：

　　1. 撑竿跳高何时被列为奥运会的比赛项目？

　　2. 撑竿跳高比赛中两人或两人以上过杆成功后，横杆会被抬高多少？

　　3. 撑竿跳高比赛中出现平局了怎么办？

第三部分　练习

请完成以下练习。

1. 有一场 20 名运动员参加的三级跳比赛，编写一段运动员与裁判员的对话。
2. 你想要参加哪种跳跃运动项目？谈谈你的理由。

第四部分　规则与概念

1. 运动员在规定的场地进行比赛，并按照显示牌上的号码进行试跳。试跳成功举白旗，失败则举红旗。
2. 跳高和撑竿跳高的运动员完成某一高度的比赛后，被淘汰的运动员由裁判员带领退出场地。
3. 跳远和三级跳远运动员每人有 3 次试跳机会，前 8 名运动员可按成绩由低到高的顺序再试跳 3 次。如不足 8 名运动员时，每人试跳 6 次。
4. 在田赛项目中，如果参赛运动员人数较多而无法顺利进行决赛时，应举行预赛。

5. 举行预赛时，所有运动员必须参加，通过预赛获得决赛资格。预赛成绩不计
   入决赛成绩。

6. 在试跳中，如有任何原因使运动员动作受阻，裁判长有权予以补试机会。

7. 每个运动员取其所有试跳中最优成绩。

8. 比赛开始前，主裁判应向运动员宣布起跳高度和每轮结束后横杆的提升
   高度。

9. 所有高度项目的测量均应以厘米为单位，从地面垂直量至横杆上沿最低点。

10. 相关运动员必须试跳所有高度，直至决出名次，或者所有运动员决定不再进
    行试跳为止。

第五部分 拓展阅读

哈维尔·索托马约尔

哈维尔·索托马约尔，古巴田径运动员，职业跳高运动员，也是目前跳高
世界纪录的保持者。1992 年奥运会冠军，20 世纪 90 年代的跳高之王；他以 2.45
米（8.04 英尺）的个人最好成绩成为有史以来唯一一个突破 8 英尺的运动员。

索托马约尔是世界田径锦标赛的两届金牌得主，并在比赛中获得过两枚银
牌。1989—1999 年的世界室内田径锦标赛中，他共获得了四枚金牌；1987—
1995 年的泛美运动会上，他赢得三连冠。他被认为是有史以来最伟大的跳高运
动员。

1984—1988 年，古巴抵制奥运会，1996 年他由于伤病没能再次角逐奥运金
牌，但是在 2000 年悉尼奥运会上，他重回赛场并赢得了一枚银牌。索托马约尔
于 2001 年退役。

第 4 课 投掷

第一部分 听和说

活动 1

🎧 听下面的对话，然后两人一组将其表演出来。

（在投掷课上，张老师正回答约翰关于投掷运动的分类和投铅球的技巧等问题。）

A: 张老师，您能具体给我讲讲投掷比赛吗？比如说都包括哪些项目？

B: 当然了，约翰。投掷比赛有铅球、铁饼、标枪、链球四个项目。

A: 那铅球呢？正式比赛中运动员会采用哪些投掷技术呢？

B: 目前，多数采用背向滑步和旋转式两种。

A: 噢。比赛时铅球投掷圈有多大？

B: 运动员会在直径 2.135 米的圆圈内进行投掷。

A: 您知道比赛器械重量是多少吗？

B: 男子铅球重量为 7.26 公斤，女子铅球重量为 4 公斤。

A: 我知道了，非常谢谢您！

B: 应该的。

活动 2

👥 两人一组，回答下列问题。

> 问题 1: 为什么女子铅球运动员更喜欢采用背向滑步式投掷，而非旋转式投掷技术呢？
>
> 问题 2: 你觉得掷铁饼和掷链球运动危险吗？为什么？

第二部分 阅读

文章 1

阅读下面这篇关于链球运动的文章，讨论文后的思考题。

链球运动

链球是常规田径比赛中投掷比赛的四个项目之一，其他三种是铁饼、铅球和标枪。链球运动起源于苏格兰，当时使用的器械是木柄的铁球，后为便于投掷，将木柄改为钢链。链球比赛是历史最悠久的奥林匹克比赛项目之一，1900 年在法国巴黎的现代奥运会上，链球便成为正式比赛项目。20 世纪 60 年代，由于历史原因，奥运会的优先参赛权由欧洲和东欧国家控制，影响了世界其他地区对链球比赛的关注。

尽管奥运会男子链球比赛从 1900 年开始，但直到 1995 年，国际田联才批准女子参加该项比赛。1999 年首次举办世界锦标赛女子链球比赛；2000 年澳大利亚悉尼奥运会，女子链球第一次出现在奥运赛场上。男子链球的世界纪录保持者是塞迪赫，他在 1986 年斯图加特欧洲田径锦标赛上扔出了 86.74 米的成绩。女子链球的世界纪录保持者是沃达尔奇克，扔出最远距离达 82.98 米。

虽然一般认为链球是一项力量型比赛，但是随着近三十年技术的进步，链球比赛更加重视速度的提升，以扔出最远距离。链球投掷动作包括两圈的原地摆臂，之后以复杂的跟趾运动进行三圈、四圈甚至是五圈的全身旋转。球按圆形路径运动，球体速度随身体的旋转不断提高，球在高速点朝向目标区域，在低速点背对投掷圈，运动员在正对投掷圈时将球扔出。

思考题：

1. 链球何时成为奥运会比赛项目？
2. 男女链球比赛的世界纪录保持者分别是谁？
3. 你能简述一下链球的投掷动作吗？

文章 2

阅读下面这篇关于掷铁饼的文章，讨论文后的思考题。

掷铁饼

掷铁饼是一项田径比赛项目。比赛时，运动员将圆盘，即铁饼，掷出尽可能远的距离。公元前 5 世纪，米隆的雕塑作品《掷铁饼者》证明了这一运动的悠久历史。掷铁饼曾是古代奥运会五项全能的比赛项目，如今已成为一项独立比赛项目。男子比赛自 1896 年第一届夏季奥运会起便是正式比赛项目，女子比赛直至 1928 年才被正式列入奥运会比赛。

掷铁饼的比赛规则与铅球基本一致，只是铁饼比赛的投掷圈稍大一些，没有抵趾板，对于铁饼投掷的方式并没有正式规定。技术环节包括推法、预备姿势、预摆旋转，最后用力和铁饼掷出后的身体平衡四种。掷铁饼的技术很难掌握，需要许多经验累积，因此顶尖铁饼运动员年龄大都在 30 岁以上。

比赛时，运动员站在直径 2.5 米的混凝土板投掷圈内，投掷圈低于圈沿 20 毫米。一般投手在开始时会背对投掷方向，在圈内逆时针旋转一圈半进行预摆发力，最后将铁饼掷出。铁饼要落在 34.92 度的扇形落地区内。测量成绩时从铁圈内沿量至铁饼落地痕迹的最近点，单位精确到厘米。应记录选手试投的最好成绩（通常在 3—6 投中产生）作为其最后成绩。有效投掷距离最远的选手获胜。如果出现平局，则以第二远的成绩决定胜负。

思考题：

1. 掷铁饼运动最早可以追溯到什么时候？
2. 掷铁饼运动何时被列为奥运会比赛项目？
3. 掷铁饼比赛如何计算投掷距离？

第三部分 课后练习

请完成以下练习。

1. 以"滑翔标枪"为题目撰写一篇不少于 250 字的赛事新闻稿。
2. 撰写一篇你喜欢的铅球运动员的励志故事。

第四部分 规则与概念

1. 奥运会投掷项目由六轮组成。标枪是唯一允许助跑的。

2. 每一个比赛项目都只记录运动员在比赛中的最好成绩。三轮过后，每个项目的前 8 名进入决赛，再进行三轮比赛，比赛顺序由前三轮的比赛名次反序排列而成。如果出现平局，则比较运动员第二好的成绩；如果依然出现平局，则比较第三好的成绩，依此类推。

3. 运动员在一分钟内完成投掷。

4. 参赛者可以在动作中途放弃并重新开始，前提是运动员没有将投掷物投出或把脚踏出投掷圈、助跑道以外。

5. 铅球和链球的投掷圈直径为 2.135 米，铁饼的投掷圈直径为 2.5 米。标枪的投掷区是一个有两条边界线的助跑道，边界线的顶端是金属或木质的弧形线，投掷者必须在弧形线后将枪投出。

6. 四种投掷比赛都有一个着陆区，是由煤渣或草坪铺成的平坦区域。

7. 铅球以铁或黄铜制成，是一个表面光滑的金属球。男子比赛中，铅球直径必须在 110 毫米至 130 毫米，女子铅球则在 95 毫米至 110 毫米。

8. 铁饼为圆盘形，中间厚，四周薄，多以金属和木料制成。男子铁饼重约 2 公斤，直径 219 毫米；女子铁饼重约 1 公斤，直径 180 毫米。

9. 国际比赛中，男子标枪长 2.6 米至 2.7 米，重 800 克；女子标枪长 2.2 米至 2.3 米，重 600 克。

10. 链球由球体、金属链和三角形把手构成。男子链球整体重约 7.26 千克，长约 121.3 厘米；女子链球重约 4 千克，长约 119.4 厘米。

第五部分 拓展阅读

李梅素

李梅素，中国著名女子铅球运动员，亚运会冠军，亚洲锦标赛冠军。

李梅素 1976 年进入了河北省田径队。经过严格系统的训练，她的铅球成绩逐年提高。1982 年获第九届亚运会女子铅球冠军，并打破亚运会纪录。她六次刷新女子铅球亚洲纪录。在 1984 年洛杉矶奥运会上以 17.96 米的成绩获得第 5 名；1985 年获亚洲田径锦标赛第 2 名。1987 年在第六届全国运动会上，她两破亚洲纪录并获金牌，世界排名第 7。1988 年，她以 21.76 米的优异成绩又一次刷新了由她保持的亚洲纪录。在第二十四届奥运会上，她以 21.06 米的成绩摘得女子铅球铜牌，实现了中国投掷项目奥运奖牌"零的突破"，这也是亚洲各参赛国在该届奥运会田径比赛中获得的唯一一枚奖牌。

第 5 课 全能运动

第一部分 听和说

活动 1

🎧 听下面的对话，然后两人一组将其表演出来。

（体育理论课上，张老师讲解了全能运动的知识，并回答了约翰提出的问题。）

A: 张老师，什么是全能运动？

B: 全能运动指多种田径运动的组合。如你所想，是由跑、跳、投掷项目组成的，用评分计算成绩的运动项目。

A: 奥运会有哪些全能项目呢？

B: 有男子十项全能和女子七项全能两个大项。

A: 男子十项全能包括哪些单项？

B: Deca 的意思是"十"，因此它包括十项不同的田径比赛：100 米、400 米、1500 米、110 米栏、标枪、铁饼、铅球、撑竿跳高、跳高和跳远。

A: 女子七项全能呢？

B: Hepta- 的意思是"七"，因此包括七个项目，有跳远、跳高、200 米、800 米、100 米栏、铅球和标枪。

A: 我知道了。谢谢您！

活动 2

👥 两人一组，回答下列问题。

> 问题 1： 训练后的拉伸练习能起到消除乳酸堆积、缓解疲劳的作用吗？
>
> 问题 2： 第五届现代奥运会上曾设置过五项全能项目，但后来被取消了。你知道这五项田径项目是什么吗？

第二部分 阅读

文章 1

阅读下面这篇关于男子十项全能的文章，讨论文后的思考题。

男子十项全能

十项全能是一个综合性项目，包括十项田径项目，主要为男子比赛，女子比赛为七项全能。

十项全能起源于古代五项全能。五项全能是古希腊奥运会的比赛项目，包括跳远、铁饼、标枪、短跑和摔跤五个项目。五项全能开始于公元前 708 年，流行数世纪之久。到公元前 6 世纪，这一项目成为宗教比赛的一部分。1884 年，全美业余锦标赛首次举行全能比赛（或称全能锦标赛），包含十个项目，与现代十项全能类似。这一比赛形式延续至 1890 年。1904 年，全能比赛出现在夏季奥运会赛场上，但这是否是奥运会的正式比赛项目尚有争论。1912 年在瑞典斯德哥尔摩举办的第五届奥运会上首次进行了现代十项全能的比赛。

传统上，"全世界最伟大的田径运动员"这一称号是授予奥运会十项全能冠军的。这一传统始于 1912 年斯德哥尔摩奥运会，当时吉姆·索普赢得十项全能冠军，瑞典国王古斯塔夫五世称赞他说："先生，您是全世界最伟大的田径运动员。"

十项全能比赛在两天内完成，以所有项目得分总和计分，分高者获胜。比赛包括四项径赛项目、三项跳跃项目和四项投掷项目，比赛顺序如下：

第一天	第二天
100 米	110 米栏
跳远	铁饼
铅球	撑竿跳高
跳高	标枪
400 米	1500 米

思考题:

　　1. 现代十项全能是何时出现在奥运赛场上的?

　　2. 十项全能运动员需要具备哪些身体素质?

　　3. 十项全能比赛包括哪些项目? 你能按顺序列举出来吗?

文章 2

阅读下面这篇关于女子七项全能的文章,讨论文后的思考题。

女子七项全能

　　七项全能是一项综合性田径赛事,包括七个项目的比赛;分为男子七项全能和女子七项全能,两者比赛项目不同。男子比赛历史更悠久,为室内赛;女子比赛始于 20 世纪 80 年代,为室外赛。

　　女子全能运动 1923 年始于苏联,1948 年得到国际田联的认可,1964 年奥运会将五项全能列为比赛项目,1984 年奥运会改为七项全能,按如下顺序在两天内完成比赛:

第一天	第二天
100 米栏	跳远
跳高	标枪
铅球	800 米
200 米	

　　女子七项全能是一项高难度项目,选手只有经过多年全面系统的训练,在所有项目全面提高的基础上,突出自身强项才能取得优异的成绩。

　　近年来还举行了一些女子十项全能比赛,与男子十项全能比赛项目相同,只是顺序有所不同。国际田联也开始记录这些比赛,但是七项全能依然是世锦赛级别的女子全能项目。

思考题：

    1. 女子七项全能于何时首次出现在奥运赛场上？

    2. 女子五项全能何时被国际田联认可？

    3. 七项全能包括哪些项目？你能按顺序列举出来吗？

第三部分 练习

请完成以下练习。

1. 你最喜欢全能运动中的哪些比赛项目？谈谈你的看法。

2. 你知道为什么人们高度评价全能运动的优胜者吗？

第四部分 规则与概念

1. 十项全能选手和七项全能选手的得分基于他们在每一项比赛中的表现，最后总成绩最高的人获胜。

2. 人们设计了复杂的计分系统以保证只有在每项比赛中都有上佳表现的运动员才能取得最高分。每一项比赛都按奥运会制定的标准来评分。根据世界纪录制定出一个得分对应表格，各项成绩相加得出总分。

3. 全能比赛时，既要采用各有关单项规则，还有一些特殊规定。

4. 径赛项目中，运动员抢跑三次则取消其该单项比赛资格，但仍可参加其余项目比赛。

5. 比赛中途，如运动员的任何一个单项弃权，则其总分和名次不得被计入。

6. 凡需计风速的单项成绩，平均风速在每秒 4 米以下者，其纪录可予以承认。如风速超过每秒 4 米，则不能作为正式全能纪录。

7. 全能运动中的径赛项目采用电子计时或人工计时均可，但不得混合使用。

8. 全能比赛分组时，每组应有 4 名或 4 名以上参赛者，不得少于 3 名。

9. 全能比赛每一项目结束后，由裁判员带领运动员去指定的休息室休息。

10. 现代五项全能的赛事顺序依次为：击剑、游泳、射击、越野跑和马术。

第五部分 拓展阅读

阿什顿·伊顿

阿什顿·伊顿，美国男子十项全能运动员，两届奥运会冠军，十项全能和室内七项全能世界纪录保持者，以9039分的成绩成为继罗曼·谢布尔勒后第二位突破9000分大关的运动员。2015年8月29日，他以9045分的总成绩打破了自己保持的世界纪录。

2011年世锦赛上，伊顿获得男子十项全能银牌，这是他职业生涯中的第一块世界奖牌。2012年，在土耳其室内田径世锦赛上，伊顿以总分6645的成绩打破室内七项全能世界纪录，后在奥运会田径选拔赛上，以9039分的总成绩打破十项全能世界纪录。伦敦奥运会上，伊顿以绝对优势夺得冠军，并打破世界纪录。2016年里约奥运会上，伊顿以追平奥运会纪录的成绩，成功卫冕了男子十项全能冠军。

第 **6** 课 **竞走运动**

第一部分 听和说

活动 1

🎧 听下面的对话，然后两人一组将其表演出来。

（约翰正在操场上锻炼，身边经过一群人在练习竞走技巧。出于好奇，他去找了张老师，询问关于竞走运动的一些问题。）

A: 张老师，您能给我讲讲竞走运动吗？

B: 竞走是一种单脚或双脚落地的步行前进运动。

A: 我之前看过竞走比赛，看上去和跑很像。竞走与跑的区别主要体现在哪里呢？

B: 竞走时，必须始终保持有一只脚落在地面上，双脚不能同时"腾空"，而跑可以。

A: 竞走比赛有不同类型吗？

B: 主要是比赛场地不同，分场地竞走和公路竞走两类。

A: 竞走比赛在距离上是如何划分的呢？

B: 主要分为男子 20 公里、50 公里公路竞走，女子 20 公里公路竞走和 5000 米、10000 米场地竞走。

A: 我明白了，谢谢您！

B: 不客气。如果你想练习竞走的话，直接来找我，我可以给你更深入地讲解。

活动 2

👥 两人一组，回答下列问题。

> 问题 1： 在了解竞走运动规律的基础上，与同伴谈谈竞走与普通走步的区别。
>
> 问题 2： 在竞走训练中，采取哪些方法可以加强髋关节的灵活性？

第二部分 阅读

文章 1

阅读下面这篇关于竞走比赛的文章，讨论文后的思考题。

竞走比赛

竞走是一项长距离田径比赛项目，分为场地赛和公路赛两种。

夏季奥运会的竞走比赛包括男女 20 公里公路赛和男子 50 公里公路赛。两年一次的国际田联世界田径锦标赛的竞走项目也以这三项比赛为主。国际田联竞走世界杯是竞走项目的独立国际赛事，于 1961 年首次举办；除了三项奥运会常规项目外，还增设了青年 10 公里竞走。国际田联世界室内锦标赛还曾设置 5000 米和 3000 米两个竞走小项，但这两项比赛于 1993 年终止。顶级田径锦标赛和其他比赛以 20 公里竞走为主。

在竞走比赛中，运动员必须遵守两项规则。第一，运动员的后脚脚尖在前脚跟离地前不能离地，违反者会被判为"离地"。第二，前腿从着地的一瞬间起必须伸直直到身体越过。是否犯规由裁判亲自做出，不借助任何辅助工具。运动员跨步时可能会出现几毫秒的双脚腾空，这种情况将被电子录像记录下来，但据说人眼是捕捉不到的。

思考题：

1. 竞走项目有哪些国际比赛？
2. 奥林匹克标准的竞走项目有哪些？
3. 竞走比赛的两项基本规则是什么？

文章 2

阅读下面这篇关于竞走运动起源的文章，讨论文后的思考题。

竞走运动的起源

竞走运动起源于英国，是在旅行走路的基础上发展起来的田径运动项目。

这一运动从 19 世纪英国流行的长途竞技走路比赛——"徒步"发展而来。1866 年，英国举行了第一届业余竞走锦标赛，全长 7 英里（约 11.26 公里），约翰·钱伯斯获得冠军。1880 年，英国业余田径协会举办了首次冠军赛，此次比赛也标志着现代田径比赛的开端。

19 世纪末叶，欧洲盛行城市间竞走活动，后传到北美洲、大洋洲国家及其他地区。早期的竞走比赛采取普通走步或任意走的形式，没有严格的技术规则要求。1906 年，在希腊举行的届间奥运会上，竞走被列为比赛项目。

竞走与普通走步不同，其特点是：步频快、步幅大、摆臂有力、节奏感强、脚跟先着地。先进的竞走技术应尽量减少单腿或双腿支撑的时间，在不影响步长的情况下，加快两腿剪角动作，以提高竞走成绩。

思考题：

1. 竞走运动起源于哪里？
2. 最早的竞走赛事是什么？在何时何地举办？
3. 竞走有哪些特点？

第三部分 练习

请完成以下练习。

1. 观看一场电视上的竞走比赛，并与同学进行讨论。
2. 为自己制定一个走步晨练的计划，并提出具体要求。

第四部分 规则与概念

1. 根据竞赛规定，比赛可以在 400 米的田径场或公路上进行。
2. 举行 20 公里以上竞走比赛时，每隔 5 公里设一饮料供给站。饮料有橘汁和加糖、葡萄糖及少量食盐的浓茶等。
3. 在竞走比赛中，运动员必须始终保持至少有一只脚与地面接触。前腿从着地的一瞬间起直到垂直位置必须始终伸直，膝关节不能弯曲。
4. 比赛中有 6—9 名裁判员。按规则规定，他们不能借助任何设备帮助判断，只能依靠自己的眼睛来判断运动员是否犯规。
5. 当竞走裁判员看到竞走运动员的动作有违反竞走技术的迹象时，应予以黄牌警告，并在赛后报告给主裁判。

6. 当竞走裁判员认为某运动员动作不符合规则要求，应靠近该运动员，出示白牌给予警告，并记录下来。

7. 如发现该运动员再次犯规，可出示红牌，并将违规行为记录在该卡上。当裁判收集到某一运动员三张红牌时，将取消其比赛资格。

8. 运动员在出发、互相超越和最后冲刺时易犯规，裁判员应该特别注意。

第五部分 拓展阅读

王镇

王镇，中国田径运动员，主攻 10 公里和 20 公里竞走。他是男子 20 公里竞走亚洲纪录保持者，同时也是男子 10 公里竞走青年赛中国和亚洲纪录保持者。

2010 年，王镇首次入选国家男子竞走队。2012 年 4 月，王镇在奥运选拔赛上打破亚洲纪录，获得第一。同年 5 月，又获得个人首个世界大赛冠军——国际竞走世界杯男子 20 公里比赛冠军。伦敦奥运会上，王镇代表中国队出战，获得男子 20 公里竞走铜牌，与队友陈定（该项目冠军）分享了为中国队收获该项目首枚奥运奖牌的喜悦。2013 年，王镇获得第十二届全国运动会男子 20 公里竞走比赛冠军。2014 年，他获得了仁川亚运会男子 20 公里竞走比赛金牌，并且打破了该项目的亚运会纪录。2016 年 7 月 18 日，王镇随中国体育代表团出征里约奥运会。8 月 13 日，他获得田径男子 20 公里竞走项目冠军，成为继刘翔和陈定之后第三位夺得奥运会田径项目金牌的中国男子运动员。

体操

第 7 课 体操

第一部分 听和说

活动 1

🎧 听下面的对话，然后两人一组将其表演出来。

（艾瑞克是一名年轻的体操运动员。当他在做前空翻时，落地总是不平稳，这令他十分担忧。现在，教练正在给他做一些技术指导。）

A: 老师，有个问题一直困扰着我，能向您请教一下吗？

B: 当然可以，说吧！

A: 我在做前空翻时，落地总是不平稳。

B: 这可能和你的技巧有关。在空翻时，双腿有没有完全蜷曲起来并贴近胸部呢？

A: 我觉得是的呀。

B: 那起跳高度呢？是不是不够高？

A: 这个我不确定，您现在能检查一下我的动作吗？

B: 好的。

（一分钟以后……）

B: 问题就出在起跳高度。空翻技术完成得不错，但起跳高度确实不到位。

A: 我明白了，谢谢您！

活动 2

👤 *两人一组，根据以下所给情景设计对话。*

> ○
> ○ 情景 1： 自由体操训练时，一名体操运动员因重心不稳摔倒，导致右脚
> ○ 踝受伤。
> ○ 情景 2： 你这几天很疲惫，想向教练请假。
> ○

第二部分 阅读

文章 1

阅读下面这篇关于现代体操的文章，讨论文后的思考题。

现代体操

体操是一种徒手或借助器械进行各种身体操练的体育项目。现代体操起源于 18、19 世纪。当时在德国、瑞典、丹麦等国出现了主要的体操流派，不仅推动了体操运动的进一步发展，也为现代体操的形成奠定了基础。

依据目的和任务，现代体操可分为基本体操和竞技性体操两种类型。基本体操是指动作和技术都比较简单的一类体操，其目的是强身健体，培养良好的身体姿态，常见的有广播体操和一些健身体操。竞技性体操是指在赛场上以获得优异成绩、争夺奖牌为主要目的的一类体操，包括竞技体操、艺术体操、健美操、技巧运动和蹦床。值得一提的是，男子和女子竞技体操项目大有不同。男子项目有自由体操、鞍马、吊环、跳马、双杠、单杠；女子项目有跳马、高低杠、平衡木、自由体操，其中女子自由体操需在音乐的伴奏下完成。

现代体操项目在 1840 年以后传入我国，当时体操运动十分落后，没有大规模的群众性体操活动。然而，在 1949 年之后，我国体操运动突飞猛进，目前已成为夺金的主要项目之一。例如，2008 年北京奥运会上，我国体操健儿获得了金牌 9 枚，银牌和铜牌共 14 枚；2012 年伦敦奥运会上，我国获得了 4 枚金牌，3 枚银牌。值得一提的是，中国女子体操队在 2008 年北京奥运会上首次获得女子体操团体金牌。

思考题:

    1. 基本体操和竞技性体操有什么不同?

    2. 你知道男子体操和女子体操竞技项目都包括哪些吗?

    3. 北京奥运会上中国体操运动员共获得多少枚奖牌?

文章 2

阅读下面这篇关于国际体操联合会的文章,讨论文后的思考题。

国际体操联合会

    国际体操联合会,简称国际体联,成立于 1881 年。总部设在瑞士的洛桑,现有会员 142 个。现任主席是意大利人格兰迪。官方用语为法语、英语、德语、俄语和西班牙语。

    国际体操联合会的职责包括:呼吁大众参加各种体操运动;研究体操理论与实践;颁布文件,确定比赛动作和规程;给协会会员以技术援助;举办国际比赛,加强各国运动员之间的友好交往。

    国际体操联合会现管辖五种体操大项,包括:竞技体操、竞技健美操、技巧运动、蹦床和艺术体操。主要国际赛事有:四年一次的奥运会体操比赛;两年一次(单数年)的世界锦标赛;一年一次的世界杯赛;一年一次的世界艺术体操锦标赛;各大洲的锦标赛、体操节(各年龄组运动员的示范表演)等。

    中国体操协会于 1954 年成立,总部位于首都北京,于 1978 年 10 月加入国际体联。

思考题:

    1. 国际体操联合会管辖的体操项目有哪些?

    2. 国际体操联合会主要组织哪些体育赛事?

    3. 国际体操联合会的主要职责是什么?

第三部分 练习

请完成以下练习。

1. 简述国际体操联合会设有哪些专门委员会。

2. 以"快乐的体操课"为题，撰写一篇不少于 250 字的记叙文。

第四部分 规则与概念

1. 依据国际体操联合会《体操技术规程》的规定，竞技体操的比赛共分为四种：团体和个人预赛、个人全能决赛、单项决赛和团体决赛。

2. 在比赛时，各体操项目进行次序如下：男子：自由体操、鞍马、吊环、跳马、双杠、单杠；女子：跳马、高低杠、平衡木、自由体操。

3. 在所有国际体联的正式比赛（世界锦标赛、奥运会、世界杯总决赛）中，单项裁判组由 D 裁判组、E 裁判组、辅助裁判组和助手组构成。

4. 单项项目的成套动作分成两个单独的分数 D 分和 E 分来计算。D 裁判组确定 D 分，即成套动作的内容；E 裁判组确定 E 分，即成套动作的完成情况，涉及编排要求、技术和身体姿势。

5. D 分包括：难度分、连接加分和动作组别分。

6. E 分从 10 分开始，根据成套动作的形式、艺术性、完成情况、技术和编排等方面的失误来扣分。

7. 将 D 分和最后的 E 分相加，即为一套动作的最后分数。

8. 一套自由体操动作主要由技巧动作连接其他体操动作来完成，如力量和平衡、柔韧动作、倒立及舞蹈等，以构成一套韵律和谐、节奏协调的动作组合。一套动作应充分利用整个场地。

9. 现代鞍马项目一套动作的特征，是在鞍马上用不同的支撑姿势完成不同的全旋、单腿摆动和（或）交叉。允许有经手倒立加转体或不转体的动作。所有动作必须通过摆动完成，不能有丝毫的停顿。不允许有力量动作或静止动作。

10. 一套吊环动作由比例大致相等的摆动、力量和静止部分组成。这些动作和连接是通过悬垂、经过或成支撑、经过或成手倒立来完成的，以直臂完成动作为主。

第五部分 拓展阅读

李小鹏

李小鹏，中国体操运动员，特长项目为双杠和跳马。他目前共获得 16 个世界冠军，超过中国其他所有体操运动员。2009 年 8 月 29 日，他担任了香港东亚运动会火炬手。

李小鹏 6 岁开始在湖南省长沙市体校练习体操，12 岁加入湖南省体操队。勤奋和娴熟的技能使他很快在同辈人中脱颖而出，获得了多个省级冠军。15 岁时，他入选国家队。1997 年洛桑世锦赛上，16 岁的李小鹏与队友一起获得了男子团体冠军，成为中国最年轻的世界（团体）体操冠军。同时，他还获得了双杠的银牌（仅次于他的队友张京京），以及自由体操的铜牌。2000 年悉尼奥运会上，李小鹏和队友表现出色，获得男子团体冠军。此外，他还获得了男子双杠冠军。2008 年北京奥运会上，李小鹏获得男子团体和双杠两枚金牌，所获金牌总数达16 枚，超过前辈李宁，成为获得金牌最多的体操运动员。

第 8 课 艺术体操

第一部分 听和说

活动 1

🎧 听下面的对话，然后两人一组将其表演出来。

（丽莎和凯蒂正在一起练习艺术体操。丽莎侧吸腿转体练得不好，因此，她向凯蒂询问提高这一技巧的方法。）

A: 你的侧吸腿转体练得怎么样了？

B: 还可以。你呢？

A: 我练得不太好。

B: 为什么？

A: 我总是重心不稳，容易摔倒，而且还总是转不到位。

B: 我想你可能是提踵没有做充分吧。别担心，刚开始我也是这样。

A: 哦！我想再练习一下，你能帮我指导一下吗？

B: 当然可以！

活动 2

👤 两人一组，根据以下所给情景设计对话。

> **情景 1：** 一名运动员在绳操训练过程中膝盖受伤摔倒在地。你搀扶她找医生检查。
>
> **情景 2：** 一名运动员在球操训练过程中动作出现错误。请你指出其错误动作，并给出建议。

第二部分 阅读

文章 1

阅读下面这篇关于艺术体操的文章，讨论文后的思考题。

艺术体操（一）

艺术体操是一个女子项目，由舞蹈、体操、技巧动作、器械控制等要素组成。运动员徒手或手持轻器械（如绳、圈、球、棒、带等），在音乐伴奏下进行表演。比赛中裁判组根据选手的跳跃、平衡、旋转、器械的使用及整体完成情况进行打分，最终分数最高的选手赢得比赛胜利。舞蹈编排必须贯穿于整个比赛。艺术体操运动员所需的身体素质包括力量、灵巧性、耐力及手眼配合等。

艺术体操从大量相关项目中汲取经验，融合了古典芭蕾、德国式体操和瑞典式体操等运动的元素。艺术体操项目由国际体操联合会管理，包括评分标准的制定和各项国际顶级赛事的管理。

思考题：

1. 艺术体操主要用到哪些器械？
2. 艺术体操运动员的表现是如何评分的？
3. 艺术体操运动员所需的身体素质有哪些？

文章 2

阅读下面这篇关于艺术体操的文章，讨论文后的思考题。

艺术体操（二）

竞技性艺术体操开始于 20 世纪 40 年代的苏联。1961 年，国际体操联合会正式将艺术体操纳入官方比赛项目，最初命名为"现代体操"，后改为"艺术运动体操"，最后改称"艺术体操"。第一届艺术体操世界锦标赛个人项目比赛于 1963 年在匈牙利布达佩斯举行。1967 年在丹麦哥本哈根举行的艺术体操世界锦标赛上新增了团体比赛项目。此后，这项运动开始传播到世界其他地区，运动员数量也大大增加。1984 年，艺术体操终于在洛杉矶奥运会上成为正式比赛项目。不过，当时的艺术体操还只有个人项目，且仅限于奥运会当年年满 16 岁及以上的女性参加。1996 年的亚特兰大奥运会上增加了艺术体操团体项目，这标志着竞技性艺术体操进入了新的发展阶段，也标志着艺术体操运动水平的提高。除了奥运会和世界锦标赛外，艺术体操的国际性比赛还包括欧洲锦标赛、世界杯、大奖赛系列赛等。

思考题:

1. 艺术体操何时成为奥运会的比赛项目？
2. 向同学介绍你最喜欢的艺术体操运动员。

第三部分 练习

请完成以下练习。

1. 简要介绍一下艺术体操的主要国际赛事。
2. 观看一场艺术体操单人项目的比赛，撰写一篇 250 字的观后感。

第四部分 规则与概念

1. 艺术体操比赛项目包括个人项目和集体项目两类。成年和少年个人项目通常包括四套动作，每套动作时间为 1 分 15 秒至 1 分 30 秒。成年集体项目包括两套动作，一套用一种器械，另一套用两种器械，每套动作时长在 2 分 15 秒至 2 分 30 秒。

2. 计时表从运动员或团队第一名运动员开始做动作时开始计时，当运动员或团队的最后一名运动员完全静止时停止。超过或少于规定的时间，每秒扣 0.05 分，由助理裁判员执行。

3. 比赛时，允许播放单一乐器或多种乐器或含有人声吟唱的音乐。音乐所表现出的特质必须结合艺术体操的特性，清楚地诠释出整套动作的内容。

4. 每个裁判组（个人项目和团队项目）由两组裁判组成：难度组和完成组。每个裁判组由一名 D1 协调裁判协助工作。D1 协调裁判按附录标准执行扣分。最高裁判组必须确认协调裁判的扣分。

5. 器械在空中出界但没触地，不扣分。

6. 运动员或团队将不会因器械破裂或挂在悬梁上扣分，裁判仅会对其后造成的技术失误扣分。

7. 体操服不可使用透明材质，有缕纱部位必须衬里布（胸部与躯干）。

8. 个人或团队中的六名选手仅在扩音机宣布或协调裁判示意或绿灯亮起时，才被准许进入比赛场地。

9. 选手上场比赛时，教练（或队职员）不得与选手、乐师、裁判交谈或联系。

10. 如果动作完成难度值大于所申报的难度值，其难度值不变。

第五部分 拓展阅读

邓森悦

邓森悦，中国个人艺术体操运动员，2014 年亚运会艺术体操项目银牌得主；在 2013 年世锦赛上获得个人全能第四名。她被认为是中国最成功的艺术体操运动员。

邓森悦 6 岁开始艺术体操训练。1999 年，她到北京学习体操，并加入了中国艺术体操队。2007 年永旺世界杯是她在艺术体操成年组比赛上的国际首秀。

2009 年第十一届全运会上，邓森悦赢得了金牌，在国内艺术体操的排名升至首位。在 2010 年莫斯科世锦赛上，她荣获了个人全能第 21 名。在 2011 年世界大学生夏季运动会圈操比赛中，她获得了一枚铜牌，同年获得了亚锦赛全能铜牌。随后，她代表中国参加了 2011 年世锦赛，在全能比赛中排名第 13。

第 9 课 健美操

第一部分 听和说

活动 1

🎧 听下面的对话，然后两人一组将其表演出来。

（简和朱蒂是健美操队的队友。此时，她们正在讨论如何把单足立转 720° 做得更好。）

A: 你的单足立转 720° 练得怎么样？

B: 还可以。你呢？

A: 我最近做得不太好，转到 540° 时总是重心不稳，所以转不到 720° 。你有什么建议吗？

B: 好的，你再做一次，我帮你看看问题出在哪儿。

A: 你看，我在转体时总是出现晃动，找不到重心。

B: 我看到了，主要是你的踝关节力量不足。

A: 我该怎么做呢？

B: 你可以加强提踵练习，不断提高腿和踝关节力量。转体时控制好手臂摆动幅度和身体重心。

A: 我知道了，非常感谢。

B: 不客气。

活动 2

👥 两人一组，回答下列问题。

> 问题 1： 你能从动作节奏、运动方向、路线以及造型等方面区分徒手体操与竞技健美操的不同吗？
>
> 问题 2： 你更喜欢看哪个项目，体操还是竞技健美操？为什么？

第二部分 阅读

文章 1

阅读下面这篇关于健美操的文章，讨论文后的思考题。

健美操

健美操，起源于 1968 年，是一项将体操、舞蹈、音乐等元素与各种不同动作类型相结合的运动，以健身美体、陶冶情操、休闲娱乐为实际目的，受到大众广泛欢迎。

1983 年，美国举办了首届健美操比赛；1984 年，日本了举行了首届远东区健美操大赛。这两次比赛促使健美操运动在世界各地全面兴起。

依据锻炼目的或形式的不同，健美操主要分为健身健美操和竞技健美操两类。健身健美操益处多多，在世界范围内得到广泛普及。例如，它没有统一要求，动作简单易学，节奏稍慢，而且时间长短因人而异。相反，竞技健美操是在音乐伴奏下，通过难度动作的完美完成，展示运动员连续表演复杂和高强度动作的能力。值得一提的是，成套动作必须将音乐与动作完美融合以体现创造性。此外，比赛时间、比赛场地、服饰、音乐、舞蹈动作编排、动作完成质量、难度数量以及风格等细节都有相关要求和评价标准。

思考题：

1. 你能概括一下健美操的发展历程吗？
2. 健美操可以分为哪几类？

文章 2

阅读下面这篇关于竞技健美操的文章，讨论文后的思考题。

竞技健美操

竞技健美操是一项需要运动员配合音乐完成具有不同难度的、复杂度的、高强度动作的竞技运动项目。此外，它还综合了技巧运动和艺术体操的元素，结合音乐、舞蹈等发展而成。

竞技健美操动作的完成主要有以下几个指标：动力强度、静力强度、跳跃（力量）、踢蹬（动力强度）、平衡性和灵活性。另外，竞技健美操还从俯卧撑、支撑和平衡、踢蹬和劈叉以及跳跃等运动中借鉴了多达十种动作要素。根据运动员所完成动作的艺术质量、创造性、完成情况和难度进行评分。艺术质量即整套动作的组成编排。创造性指动作种类的多样性，以及双人、三人和多人项目中的托举动作。完成情况指每个动作完成的质量。难度指能展现力量、灵活性和局部肌肉耐力所需的体操动作的数量。

思考题：

1. 竞技健美操动作的完成有哪些指标？
2. 竞技健美操运动员的表现如何评分？

第三部分 练习

请完成以下练习。

1. 为你校艺术系健美操队编写一篇 250 字左右的解说词。
2. 谈谈中国竞技健美操运动的发展。

第四部分 规则与概念

1. 国际体联举办的官方健美操比赛是世界健美操锦标赛，每两年举办一次。
2. 世界健美操锦标赛比赛项目有女子单人操、男子单人操、混合双人操、三人操和集体操。
3. 为了保障运动员的健康和安全，国际体联规定运动员参加多个项目决赛时，两项比赛间需有十分钟的恢复时间。
4. 运动员在开赛叫到后 20 秒不出场，将由裁判长扣除 0.5 分。60 秒后不出场视为弃权，宣布弃权后运动员将失去参加本项比赛的资格。
5. 在运动员比赛时，教练员必须留在等候场地。教练员、运动员等所有未经许可的人员禁止进入比赛场地。违反规定者将由裁判长取消比赛资格。
6. 每场比赛的总分、裁判长扣分、最后得分以及排名都必须公之于众。预赛结束后，各参赛国将得到完整的成绩复印件，但不包括具体评分。在全部比赛结束后，各参赛国将得到一份完整的、包括具体评分的成绩册。
7. 成套动作必须表现出健美操操化动作和难度动作的均衡性。手臂和腿部动作要求有力、定位清晰。所有成套动作的完成时间都为 1 分 30 秒，允许有上下 5 秒浮动（提示声不包括在内）。

8. 操化动作将基本健美操步伐与手臂动作相结合，伴随音乐，创造出动感的、有节奏的、不间断的、包含高低不同运动强度的一串动作。成套动作应达到高运动强度的水平。

9. 难度要求：裁判要求在所有项目中，成套动作最多允许做 10 个难度动作，必须完成每个难度组别中的至少一个难度，所有难度必须来自不同根命组；地面难度最多不超过 5 个；C 组落地成俯撑的难度最多不超过 2 个；C 组落地成劈腿的难度最多不超过 2 个。

10. 艺术分、完成分与难度分相加为总分。从总分中减去难度裁判、视线裁判与裁判长减分为最后得分。

第五部分 拓展阅读

黄晋萱

黄晋萱，被誉为"中国健美操女王"，国际级运动健将，健美操世界冠军。她是国家健美操队唯一的女队员，也是国内健美操界唯一的女冠军。在第二十六届世界大学生运动会上获得四项冠军；第九届世界健美操锦标赛获得第二名。2012 年全国大学生运动会后，她完成硕士学位并宣布退役。现执教于中国民航大学。

黄晋萱生于 1988 年。她很早便开始练习体操，后主攻健美操，这为她之后在健美操上的巨大成就打下了基础。她曾说："作为一名大学生，我要平衡学习和训练的关系。为了达到更好的训练效果，我需要每天坚持制定训练计划，但同时也要努力学习，修满学分。想要两者兼得并不容易。"

第 ⑩ 课 技巧运动

第一部分 听和说

活动 1

🎧 听下面的对话，然后两人一组将其表演出来。

（乔伊看了威廉姆的技巧运动表演后，被深深吸引了。他向威廉姆询问有关技巧运动的问题，还考虑加入其中，和他一起学习。）

A: 你好，威廉姆。你能跟我说说技巧运动成套动作的分类吗？

B: 可以啊，乔伊。技巧运动一般分为动力性动作和静力性动作两大类。

A: 动力性动作具体包含哪些？

B: 通常包括个人项目的翻滚、翻腾、屈伸起、手翻、空翻和双人与集体项目的抛接等动作。

A: 静力性动作又是指哪些动作呢？

B: 主要包括个人项目的倒立、劈腿、平衡以及双人与集体项目的支持、平衡、倒立和造型等。

A: 这么多动作呀，好学吗？

B: 我觉得不是很难。但是同其他事情一样，也需要勤加练习。你有空的时候我们一起练习吧！

A: 好的！非常感谢。

活动 2

👤 两人一组，回答下列问题。

> 问题 1： 频繁系统地练习技巧运动对身体机能状态会产生哪些影响？
>
> 问题 2： 技巧运动个人项目比赛时，每个运动员需要做几套自选动作？你能做吗？

第二部分 阅读

文章 1

阅读下面这篇关于技巧运动的文章，讨论文后的思考题。

技巧运动

　　技巧运动是一项竞技体操项目，运动员伴随音乐相互配合，完成技巧动作、舞蹈和翻腾。技巧运动的动作组合共有三种类型：一是静力性动作，主要考验力量、平衡和灵活性；二是动力性动作，包括抛接和空翻；三是综合动作（国际体联六级及以上难度），综合了静力性和动力性两种类型的动作。

　　技巧运动由国际体联管理，其国际赛事按运动员年龄可分为四种：11—16岁、12—18岁、13—19岁和15岁以上（成人）。技巧运动由双人或多人完成。搭档之间不同的身体条件和能力会得到最好的平衡，以相互补充，完成复杂的动作。有的运动员会主要负责支撑和投掷，称为"下面人"；与之配合的队友一般体型相对较小，称为"上面人"。

思考题：

　　1. 技巧运动共有几种类型的动作组合？分别是什么？

　　2. 技巧运动双人项目中的搭档是如何分工的？

文章 2

阅读下面这篇关于国际技巧运动联合会的文章，讨论文后的思考题。

国际技巧运动联合会

　　国际技巧联合会于 1973 年成立，现任主席是保加利亚人索蒂罗夫，工作用语为俄语和英语。国际技巧联合会的最高立法和执行机构是代表大会，每四年举行一次。各会员国可派不超过三名代表出席，但只有 1 票表决权。代表大会闭会期间，国际技巧联合会的领导机构为执行委员会。执委会由主席、副主席、秘书长和委员组成，由代表大会选举产生，任期四年。

　　国际技巧联合会主办的比赛主要包括：世界技巧锦标赛，第一届于 1974 年在苏联举行，此后，每逢双数年举行一次；技巧世界杯，每逢单数年举行一次。

　　1979 年 12 月，国际技巧联合会接纳中国技巧协会为会员。我国此后成功举办的世界技巧比赛主要有：第五届技巧世界杯、第二届世界技巧青年锦标赛、第二届亚洲技巧锦标赛和第十一届世界技巧锦标赛。中国技巧运动员的精湛表演享誉海内外。

思考题：

1. 国际技巧联合会执行委员会由哪些职能部门组成？
2. 国际技巧联合会主办过哪些体育赛事？
3. 中国曾举办过哪些技巧比赛？

第三部分 练习

请完成以下练习。

1. 技巧运动是否适合在中小学体育教学中展开？谈谈你的观点。
2. 查阅资料，以技巧运动在中国的发展为题，撰写一篇不少于 250 字的短文。

第四部分 规则与概念

1. 技巧比赛项目共五项：女子双人、男子双人、混合双人、女子团体、男子团体。
2. 技巧比赛最高裁判组由一名项目裁判长、两名艺术裁判员、两名执行裁判员和难度裁判员组成。
3. 艺术裁判员严格按照评分规则对动作的艺术性进行评分，评分时不准相互讨论。
4. 所有成套动作的时间最长为 2 分 30 秒，没有最短时间限制。
5. 双人或集体项目平衡动作最少保持 3 秒。
6. 必须要有至少 6 个双人 / 集体动作，其中 3 个静态平衡动作，3 个动力性动作（包括 1 个抛接动作）。每个动作难度值至少为 1。
7. 动力性平衡动作要保持 1 秒，以计算难度值。
8. 动作完成情况评分标准：动作开始和结束的合理性与有效性，完成动作技术的有效性，身体姿势和线条的准确性，动作的幅度，平衡动作的伸展性，腾空动作的最大高度，静力性动作的稳定性，抛接的效果和稳定性，以及落地控制。

9. 静力性动作要表现出力量、平衡、柔韧和灵巧性。

10. 在动力性动作中，运动员必须运用变向、旋转、扭转、变换造型和跳跃等来控制自己和同伴的空中姿态。

第五部分 拓展阅读

阿瑟·戴维斯

阿瑟·戴维斯是一位退役的美国技巧运动员，他曾携手顶级技巧运动员希娜·布思（已退役）两次获得技巧比赛混双世界冠军。

2002 年德国里萨世界技巧锦标赛上，戴维斯和布思成为美国第一组赢得混双全能金牌的选手。同年，他们在俄罗斯的克拉斯诺达尔 Machuga 杯比赛中获得全能第二名。

在 2002 年、2003 年和 2004 年美国国家体育技巧锦标赛上，戴维斯和布思连续三年获得全能金牌。他们还获得了国家级表演奖、技巧奖和编排奖。

第 11 课 蹦床

第一部分 听和说

活动 1

🎧 听下面的对话，然后两人一组将其表演出来。

（在学校蹦床课上，爱德华向老师询问蹦床动作的组成，以及这项运动的特征和比赛规则。）

A: 老师，您能讲讲一套蹦床动作的组成吗？

B: 可以呀，挺简单的。一套完整的蹦床动作由各种向前或向后的转体空翻或非转体空翻动作组成。

A: 听起来挺简单的。那蹦床动作有什么特点呢？

B: 特点挺多的，如动作的高飘，极具观赏性，动作之间富有节奏的连接和变换，特别是双脚起跳、背弹、腹弹和坐弹动作等。

A: 还有个问题，蹦床比赛时能否出现空中停顿呢？

B: 不可以。

A: 真的吗？为什么呢？

B: 规则规定运动员在全套动作中间不能有空中停顿。

A: 哦，我清楚了。谢谢老师。

活动 2

👥 两人一组，回答下列问题。

> 问题 1：你在游乐园玩过蹦床吗？你能做出哪些动作？
>
> 问题 2：你认为蹦床运动员必备的身体素质有哪些？

第二部分 阅读

文章 1

阅读下面这篇关于蹦床运动的文章，讨论文后的思考题。

蹦床运动（一）

蹦床运动，又称回弹技巧运动，是运动员利用从蹦床反弹过程中表现杂技技巧的竞技项目，属于体操运动的一种。它将运动和艺术完美结合，素有"空中芭蕾"之称。

蹦床动作包括翻转与筋斗动作的十种基本技巧。运动员需完成各种特技动作，包括自由弹跳、抱膝跳、屈体跳、前后空翻或更为复杂的动作组合。蹦床动作的特点主要有：高度很高，跳跃连续且富有节奏感，动作没有停顿和中间跳等。一套动作中一般不会出现重复，如果出现重复，其难度不计入成绩。

1947 年美国得克萨斯州举行了首届全国蹦床表演赛；1948 年起蹦床运动被列入正式比赛，后传入欧洲。1964 年首届世界蹦床锦标赛在英国举行。2000 年奥运会上，蹦床项目比赛首次列为正式项目。

自蹦床运动成为奥运会比赛项目后，中国成功涌现了一批世界一流的蹦床运动员。2007 年世界男子锦标赛上，中国蹦床队首次取得成功；之后在 2008 年奥运会上，中国蹦床运动员夺得了男、女个人项目的两枚金牌。

思考题：

1. 蹦床运动有哪些特点？
2. 蹦床运动何时成为奥运会的比赛项目？

文章 2

阅读下面这篇关于蹦床运动的文章，讨论文后的思考题。

蹦床运动（二）

世界上第一张蹦床最早由乔治·尼森设计。20 世纪 30 年代早期，乔治·尼森观察到杂技演员们从安全网弹起时会表演各种戏法，于是，他在自己的车库里复制出了一个小型安全网，以训练跳水、翻筋斗等动作。这就是第一张现代蹦床。后来，尼森创立公司专门生产蹦床，并以此为营销手段，通过蹦床运动吸引大众观赏并鼓励人们参与其中。由此，蹦床运动诞生了。

在美国，蹦床运动很快被引入学校体育课程以及私人娱乐会所。在世界其他地区，蹦床运动在欧洲和苏联迅速流行开来。自蹦床运动于 2000 年进入奥运会以后，越来越多的国家开始大力发展这项运动。

思考题：

1. 第一张蹦床是由谁设计的?
2. 蹦床运动是如何产生的?

第三部分　练习

请完成以下练习。

1. 2008 年北京奥运会上，何雯娜、陆春龙分别摘取了蹦床项目的金牌。请自拟题目，撰写一篇 250 字的新闻稿。
2. 撰写一篇文章，描述儿童在公园玩蹦床的场景，字数不少于 250 字。

第四部分　规则与概念

1. 蹦床比赛包括三套动作，每套由十个动作组成。
2. 决赛中运动员的出场顺序按预赛成绩的相反顺序，即得分低者先出场。
3. 预赛第一套动作包括自由动作和规定动作。成套动作编排的顺序由运动员自行决定。
4. 在预赛和决赛中，每个运动员上网比赛前有 30 秒准备活动时间，如果超过限制时间，裁判长可指示技术裁判员扣该运动员 0.3 分。
5. 除了两腿交叉跳跃动作外，选手的所有动作必须双脚双腿并拢，脚和脚趾伸直。
6. 空翻周数相同，但采用团身、屈体和直体三种不同姿势，视为不同的动作，不算动作重复。团身和半团身的姿势视为同一种姿势。
7. 整套动作必须以双脚落在网上、身体直立的姿势结束，否则按规定扣分。
8. 最后落在网上后，运动员应直立站好且至少停留 3 秒钟，否则，按动作不稳定扣分。

第五部分 拓展阅读

何雯娜

何雯娜，中国女子蹦床运动员。在 2008 年北京夏季奥运会上，她以总分 37.80 分的好成绩摘得金牌，这也是中国蹦床队的首枚金牌。

在 2007 年和 2009 年两届蹦床世锦赛上，她摘得两枚团体金牌。2009 年，她获得了个人银牌。在 2011 年蹦床世界锦标赛中，她赢得了团体和个人两枚金牌，巩固了中国在奥运会蹦床项目上的地位。

在 2012 年夏季奥运会上，她在预赛中名列前茅，但在决赛动作即将结束时出现失误，位列第三。2016 年里约奥运会上，何雯娜排名第四位。不久后，她宣布退役。

球类运动

第12课 足球

第一部分 听和说

任务 1

🎧 听下面的对话，然后两人一组将其表演出来。

（足球比赛中，一名运动员正在和裁判员争论自己是否应该被罚黄牌警告。）

A: 裁判，我有疑问。为什么给我黄牌？我犯规了吗？

B: 是的，我已经鸣哨终止了比赛，但你依然继续踢球。

A: 为什么鸣哨？

B: 你越位了，助理裁判员已经举旗示意。

A: 赛场太吵，我没有听到哨音。能不能取消黄牌？

B: 那不行，我必须公平执法。

A: 我知道了。

任务 2

👥 两人一组，根据以下所给情景设计对话。

> 情景 1: 足球比赛中一名队员摔倒受伤，裁判员问："你是否能继续比赛？
> 如果坚持不了，请换人，下场治疗后再上场。"
>
> 情景 2: 裁判员鸣哨终止比赛并跑到犯规队员近前向其出示黄牌。

第二部分 阅读

文章 1

阅读下面这篇关于足球的文章，讨论文后的思考题。

足球

足球是一项主要用脚控制球的球类运动。现代足球运动是世界上最受欢迎、影响最大的运动项目之一，被称为"世界第一运动"和"运动之王"。

1848 年，《剑桥规则》诞生，确定了足球比赛的一些基本规则。1857 年，英国成立了第一个足球俱乐部——谢菲尔德足球俱乐部。1863 年 10 月 26 日，英国 11 个足球俱乐部在伦敦成立了世界上第一个足球运动组织——英格兰足球协会，统一了足球运动的基本规则。大家把这一天视为现代足球运动的诞生日。同年 12 月 8 日，剑桥大学修改了世界上第一部文字形式的足球规则——《剑桥规则》，规定足球比赛只能用脚踢球，不得用手触球，并把 football 称为 association football，在学校则称之为 soccer。

英格兰足协成立后，现代足球运动开始在全英流行，并通过海员、士兵、商人、工程师、牧师等传播到欧洲大陆和世界各地。1904 年国际足联成立后，开始举办世界杯足球赛，四年一次。足球比赛规则随之不断完善，足球技术不断创新。1974 年，荷兰人创造了全攻全守的整体型打法，使足球运动进入了"全面型"时代。从此，世界足球运动迎来了崭新的开端，现代足球运动日益发展。

思考题：

    1. 世界上最受欢迎的运动是什么？

    2. 什么是《剑桥规则》？

    3. 国际足联是如何推动足球运动发展的？

文章 2

阅读下面这篇关于国际足联的文章，讨论文后的思考题。

国际足联

国际足球联合会，简称国际足联，是一个国际性体育组织，由世界各国的足球协会组成。总部设于瑞士苏黎世，目前共有 209 个会员协会。国际足联于

1904 年在巴黎成立，现任主席为瑞士人约瑟夫·布拉特。国际足联组织举办世界性足球赛事，负责制定球员转会的规则，评选每年的世界足球先生等奖项，每月公布一次世界排名。足球比赛的规则由国际足球联合理事会制定。

国际足联组织的赛事主要有：世界杯足球赛（1930 年开始，四年一届）、奥运会足球赛（1912 年被正式列为奥运会项目，四年一届）、世界青年足球锦标赛（20 岁以下）（即可口可乐杯赛，1977 年开始，两年一届）、世界少年足球锦标赛（17 岁以下）（1985 年开始，两年一届）、五人足球世界杯等。

世界杯是国际足联的主要营销手段，有庞大的观众群，通过门票、电视转播权、赞助、交易而获得巨额经济收益。此外，部分经费来自会费和参赛报名费。

中国于 20 世纪 30 年代加入国际足联，1958 年中国足协宣布退出。1979 年，中国足协恢复在国际足联的合法席位。

思考题：

1. 国际足联于何时在何地成立？
2. 国际足联的主要职责有哪些？
3. 你能列举出国际足联主办的体育赛事吗？

第三部分 练习

请完成以下练习。

1. 观看一场中超足球比赛，谈一谈你对我国足球现状的看法。
2. 如果某一替补队员使用无礼的、侮辱的或辱骂性的语言，或做下流动作，裁判员是否可以向其出示红牌将其罚下场？

第四部分 规则与概念

1. 足球比赛是在长方形的草地或人造草皮的球场上进行，场地长 105 米，宽 70 米。在国际比赛中，球场长度最短 100 米，最长 110 米；宽度最短 64 米，最长 75 米。
2. 队员不得使用或佩戴可能危及自己或其他队员的装备或任何物件。队员必备的基本装备是：套衫或运动衬衣、短裤、长袜、护胫与鞋。

3. 每场比赛由一名主裁判掌握，全权执行与比赛有关的竞赛规则。裁判员需穿着明显区别于两队队服颜色的制服。

4. 掷硬币获胜方有权先选择开球或场地。开球前所有队员必须待在本方半场。

5. 当球完全从球门柱间及横梁下越过球门线，即为进球得分。

6. 球在界内并且裁判没有终止比赛时称为活球；球整个出了边线、底线或球门线，或裁判停止比赛时称为死球。

7. 进攻队员进攻，比球或对方球员先接近对方球门线时，则该球员处于越位位置。

8. 防守方在己方禁区严重犯规时判给对方点球。

9. 在犯规或违反规则时，判罚任意球。当执行任意球时，犯规方的所有队员必须离球 10 码（9 米）。任意球可以是直接任意球，也可以是间接任意球。

10. 罚直接任意球时，可将球直接射入犯规队球门得分；罚间接任意球时，只有球在进入球门前曾触及过其他队员，才能得分。

第五部分 拓展阅读

罗纳尔多

罗纳尔多·路易斯·纳扎里奥·利马，即罗纳尔多，巴西足球运动员，已退役。他是公认的"奇才"，被专家和球迷认为是有史以来最伟大的足球运动员之一。罗纳尔多是三届世界足球先生和两届金球奖得主，被列入国际足联 2004 年所编的百位最伟大球星名册。他还入驻了巴西足球博物馆名人堂和意大利足球名人堂。

罗纳尔多效力于巴西队，参加了 98 场比赛，攻入 62 球，是巴西国家队进球第二多的选手。17 岁时，他已经是巴西国家队的一员，并赢得了 1994 年的世界杯足球赛冠军。1998 年世界杯，他因助力巴西晋级决赛而获得联赛金球奖，然而后来他腿部痉挛了数小时，巴西队最终输给了法国队。2002 年世界杯，他在决赛中两度进球，赢得了第二个世界杯冠军，并获得金靴奖的最佳射手。2006 年世界杯期间，罗纳尔多实现了他的第 15 次世界杯进球，创造了当时的世界杯纪录。

第 13 课 篮球

第一部分 听和说

活动 1

🎧 听下面的对话，然后两人一组将其表演出来。

（篮球比赛中，教练让 15 号队员替换 10 号队员上场。此时他正在叮嘱 15 号队员上场后的注意事项。）

A: 15 号队员准备上场，换下 10 号。

B: 是，教练。

A: 上场之后，告诉 8 号，盯紧对方的右后卫。

B: 好的，请放心。

A: 你清楚上场后的位置吗？

B: 知道，站在 4 号大前锋位置，协助 8 号为中锋做策应。

A: 很好。上场后注意防守，移动速度要快。

B: 明白，教练。现在就去换人吗？

A: 是的，去记录台吧。

活动 2

👤 两人一组，根据以下所给情景设计对话。

> 情景 1： 请组织队员进行赛前准备活动。由队长负责组织队员做准备活动，进行跑步、徒手操、投篮和跑动上篮练习。
>
> 情景 2： 现在是暂停时间，教练和队员正在讨论改变联防为人盯人战术，因此队员需要紧跟防守队员，注意协防。

第二部分 阅读

文章 1

阅读下面这篇关于篮球的文章，讨论文后的思考题。

篮球

篮球运动起源于 1891 年，由美国马萨诸塞州斯普林菲尔德市（春田市）基督教青年会国际训练学校（现春田学院）的体育教师詹姆士·奈史密斯博士发明。最初，奈史密斯想要寻找一种让学生们充满活力的合适的室内运动，使他们在新英格兰漫长的冬季仍能保持健康。他起初设想了一些活动，但是它们或是过于激烈，或是不适合室内运动场馆。后来，他受果农采摘桃子然后将其扔进篮子活动的启发，在 3 米高的架子上钉了一个篮筐，让学生投球。篮球就这样诞生了。

经过初创、试行、改进、传播、普及、创新和全面发展等阶段之后，现代篮球运动逐步形成了。在篮球赛中，运动员需要协作、对抗、进攻、防守并快速移动。篮球运动具有综合性、职业性和商业性的特征，因而深受大众喜爱。

篮球的运球技术主要包括：投球、传球、控球和篮板球。篮球队员通常负责不同的位置：身材最高最壮的被称为中锋或大前锋，体格稍矮但更为敏捷的是小前锋，身高最矮或运球技术最好的球员为得分后卫。得分后卫负责指挥全队的场上行动，实施教练的战术，控制进攻或防守的执行（指挥球员位置）。

思考题：

1. 篮球起源于何时何地？
2. 篮球的运球技术有哪些？

文章 2

阅读下面这篇关于国际篮联的文章，讨论文后的思考题。

国际篮联

国际篮球联合会，简称国际篮联，是由世界各国的篮球协会组成的国际组织，总部设于瑞士日内瓦。国际篮联于 1932 年成立，四年后篮球被国际奥委会正式承认为奥运会比赛项目。国际篮联现有会员国家 215 个，分为五个地区委员会，分别是：非洲地区委员会、美洲地区委员会、亚洲地区委员会、欧洲地区委员会和大洋洲地区委员会。各委员会专责处理该地区篮球事务。

国际篮联负责制定国际篮球球例，制定篮球运动的设施和设备规格（例如：篮球筐的高度、篮球场的长度和宽度、禁区的大小、三分线的距离等），规制不同国家之间球员的转会，任命国际篮球比赛裁判，组织举办大型篮球比赛等。

国际篮联男子篮球世界杯是世界性的篮球比赛，每四年举办一次，获胜队赢得奈史密斯杯。女子篮球世界杯赛同样每四年举办一次，与男子世界杯赛同年举办，但举办国家不同。

思考题：

1. 国际篮联在哪一年建立？
2. 你能描述一下国际篮联的主要职责吗？

第三部分 练习

请完成以下练习。

1. 针对中国篮球职业联赛总决赛最后一场比赛，请准备一些采访问题，对主教练进行赛前采访。你可以请他谈谈对比赛的看法、对对手的评价和对结果预测。
2. 请撰写一段短文，评论你校篮球队的情况。例如，你可以谈谈每位选手以及教练的特点，并提一些改进建议。

第四部分 规则与概念

1. 篮球比赛由两个队参加，每队出场 5 名队员。每队目标是将球投入对方篮筐得分，并阻止对方队得分。比赛由裁判员、记录台人员和技术代表（如到场）管理。
2. 比赛场地应是一块平坦、无障碍的硬质地面，长 28 米，宽 15 米，从分界限的内沿丈量。
3. 队长由教练员指定，在赛场上代表其所在球队。比赛期间，他可与裁判员交流以获得信息，做此举要有礼貌，但是只能在球成死球和比赛计时钟停止时进行。

4. 比赛应由 4 节组成，每节 10 分钟（国际篮联比赛）或 12 分钟（NBA 比赛）。

5. 当活球从上方进入球篮并停留在球篮内或穿过球篮则可得分。

6. 运球是指一名队员控制一个活球的一系列动作：掷、拍、在地面上滚动球或故意将球掷向篮板。

7. 当某队在前场控制活球并且比赛计时钟正在运行时，该队的队员不得停留在对方队的限制区内超过连续的 3 秒钟。

8. 根据裁判员判断，一名队员在违反规则的精神和意图的情况下直接抢球，因此发生的接触犯规是违反体育道德的犯规。

9. 撞人是持球队员或不持球队员推开或移动到对方躯干的非法身体接触。

10. 阻挡是阻碍持球或不持球对方队员行进的非法身体接触。

第五部分 拓展阅读

科比·布莱恩特

科比·布莱恩特，美国职业篮球运动员，效力于美国国家篮球协会（NBA）洛杉矶湖人队。

科比是前美国职业篮球运动员乔·布莱恩特的儿子。在宾夕法尼亚劳尔梅里恩高中，科比凭借惊人的高中篮球生涯赢得了全美国的认可，成为顶级篮球运动员。1996 年高中毕业后，他直接参加 NBA 选秀，以第一轮第 13 顺位被夏洛特黄蜂队选中，之后被交给洛杉矶湖人队。作为新人，科比赢得了 1997 年全明星赛扣篮大赛的冠军，并在第二赛季获得"全明星"称号。

科比的整个职业生涯都效力于湖人队，5 次赢得 NBA 总冠军，入选"全明星"18 次，"NBA 最佳阵容"15 次，以及"最佳防守阵容"12 次。他带领球队联盟两次得分，在联赛的历史常规赛和季后赛得分表中均居第三位。2008 年和 2012 年奥运会，他带领美国队两次获得冠军。

当开始了在湖人队的第 20 个赛季（2015—2016 赛季）后，科比宣布他将在赛季结束后退役。

第 14 课 排球

第一部分 听和说

活动 1

🎧 听下面的对话，然后两人一组将其表演出来。

（排球比赛即将开始。裁判鸣哨，让双方队长掷硬币挑边。）

A：双方队长掷硬币挑边，蓝队是图案，先挑。你要发球还是接发球？

B：我要接发球。

A：7 号的项链和 8 号的戒指太危险，必须要摘下来，否则不能比赛。

B：好的，7 号已经把项链摘下来了，但是 8 号的戒指太紧摘不下来，她上场时
已经用胶布缠起来了，请放心。

（比赛进行中。）

A：队长，自由人替换要快一点，不能在我鸣哨之后进行，否则判你们延误比赛。

B：知道了，裁判。但对方发球时总有队员故意遮挡我们。

A：我会注意的。

B：裁判，我们没有四次击球，为什么判罚？

A：我已经解释过了。你要么继续比赛，要么抗议。否则我要判你延误比赛。

B：我选择抗议，裁判员先生。

A：可以，请你比赛后再确认。另外，告诉你们的队员不要挑衅对方队员。

B：知道了，裁判。谢谢。

活动 2

👤 两人一组，回答下列问题。

> 问题 1：排球比赛中自由后卫刚从场上被替换下来。技术暂停结束后，
> 他 / 她能否继续上场比赛？
>
> 问题 2：排球比赛中如何进行换人？

第二部分 阅读

文章 1

阅读下面这篇关于排球运动的文章，讨论文后的思考题。

排球

排球运动是当今世界最成功、最流行的体育运动项目之一。它兼具竞技性和娱乐性，并极具爆发力。它是一项团队运动，每场比赛有两支球队，每队 6 人，中间用网隔开。根据相关的规则，一支球队努力将球击打到对方球队的场地，以此得分。自 1964 年以来，排球一直是夏季奥运会的比赛项目。

排球运动起源于 1895 年，由美国马萨诸塞州霍利约克市体育教练威廉·摩根先生发明，最初取名为"Mintonett"（意即"小网子"）。后来，观察家哈尔斯博士根据这一运动的截击特性为其重新取名为"排球"。1905 年排球运动传入中国。

排球运动主要形式分为两大类：一类是竞技排球，如 6 人制排球、沙滩排球；一类是娱乐排球，如软式排球、气排球、4 人排球、9 人排球和残疾人排球等。正式的 6 人制排球比赛由发球方开始。发球方后排右边队员发球过网，对方球员须在三次之内把球击回。每方最多击球三次（拦网除外），每位队员不得连续击球两次（拦网除外）。当出现以下情形时，比赛暂停：（1）球被击落到对方场地；（2）对方球员的手或手臂触球后，球被打出场；（3）有球员犯规。比赛采用每球得分制，先得 25 分并超出对方 2 分的队伍胜一局。整场比赛采用五局三胜制，决胜局（第五局）采用 15 分并领先 2 分为胜。

思考题：

1. 你能说一下排球运动的起源与发展吗？

2. 你知道排球运动有哪些种类吗？

3. 你知道排球运动的规则吗？

文章 2

阅读下面这篇关于国际排球联合会的文章，讨论文后的思考题。

国际排球联合会

国际排球联合会，简称国际排联，是国际室内排球、沙滩排球、草地排球运动的管理组织。总部位于瑞士洛桑，现任主席为阿里·格拉萨。截至 2010 年，国际排联拥有 220 个会员。

1947 年，来自五大洲的 14 个国家的代表在鲍尔·黎伯的带领下于法国巴黎成立了国际排球联合会。世界男排锦标赛于 1949 年首次举行，1952 年世界女排锦标赛开始举行。这两项赛事，加上 1964 年开始正式成为奥运会项目的排球比赛，一直都是排球领域最重大的赛事。1969 年，排球领域的新盛事——世界杯排球赛开始举行。1984 年国际排联总部迁至瑞士洛桑，制定政策并加强在世界范围内推广排球运动的力度，主要包括：创办世界排球联赛、世界排球大奖赛等赛事，将沙滩排球引入奥运会项目，以及修改排球运动规则以提高其公众关注度。

国际排联的主要职责是在全球范围内主办排球赛事，发布排球比赛的赛程赛果、公布积分排名等。

思考题：

1. 国际排联于哪一年成立？
2. 你能复述一下国际排联的历史吗？
3. 国际排联的主要职责有哪些？

第三部分 练习

请完成以下练习。

1. 撰写一篇不少于 250 字的短文，描述排球活动的场景，内容突出活动过程中队员的交流、情绪与动作表现等。
2. 观看一场排球比赛，评价球员的进攻战术。

第四部分 规则与概念

1. 排球比赛的裁判员由第一裁判员、第二裁判员、记录员和 4 名（两名）司线员组成。

2. 比赛开始由第一裁判员主持抽签，决定第一局首先发球的队和场区。进行决胜局比赛前，应再次抽签。

3. 比赛前队长在记分表上签字，并代表本队抽签。若球成为死球，只有场上队长可以和裁判员讲话。

4. 正常的比赛间断有"暂停"和"换人"。每局比赛中，每队最多可以请求两次暂停和 6 次换人。

5. 比赛中队员与球的任何接触都被视为击球。每队最多击球 3 次（拦网除外）将球击回对区，如果超过 3 次，则判为"四次击球"。

6. 球可以触及球员身体的任何部位，也可以向任何方向弹出。

7. 在不干扰对方比赛的情况下，允许队员在网下穿越进入对方场地。

8. 发球队员在击球或发球跳起时，不得踏及场区（包括端线）和发球区以外地面。

9. 在一个动作中，球可以连续（迅速而连贯地）触及 1 名或更多的拦网队员。拦网触球不计入 3 次击球内，因此拦网触球后该队还可以击球 3 次。

10. 国际排联世界性成年比赛中，队员可以超出 12 名，但超出的名额必须是后排自由防守队员，且最多两名。后排自由防守队员不能担任队长和场上队长。

第五部分 拓展阅读

郎平

郎平，中国女子排球运动员，现任中国女排主教练。

20 世纪 80 年代，郎平是中国女排的核心人物，被视为一代文化偶像，也是现代中国体育史上最受尊敬的运动员之一。她随中国队多次赢得世界排球大赛冠军，1984 年奥运会上助力中国女排实现"三连冠"。

1995 年，郎平成为中国女排主教练，带领中国女排摘得 1996 年奥运会银牌、1998 年世界排球锦标赛银牌。后由于身体原因，郎平从国家队辞职，先后去了意大利和美国。2013 年，她重新执教中国女排，带领中国女排赢得 2016 年里约奥运会冠军。

郎平是有史以来第一位以运动员和教练员两种身份夺得奥运金牌的传奇人物。

第 15 课 乒乓球

第一部分 听和说

活动 1

🎧 听下面的对话，然后两人一组将其表演出来。

（哈利打完一场乒乓球比赛后与朋友罗伯特见面，他们正在讨论比赛结果。）

A: 哈利！你面色红润，是刚打完球吗？

B: 是啊，筋疲力尽，太热了，一身的汗！

A: 打得怎么样？

B: 挺有意思的，但是打了 5 场，输了 4 场。

A: 不会吧？你这实力够强的，旋转花样多，落点那么刁，怎么输的？

B: 约翰年轻，体力好，挥拍速度那叫一个快，但这还不是根本原因。

A: 但是你的挥拍速度和力量应该不逊于年轻人啊？

B: 我呀，关键是步法有问题，没年轻人利索。

A: 估计他也使出了浑身解数才赢了你。这人颇有天分啊。

B: 确实是。今天我才真正体会到了，速度、力量、旋转、落点和步法，哪一样都缺不得。

活动 2

👥 两人一组，根据以下所给情景设计对话。

> 情景 1: 你为朋友下载个训练视频，让他在打乒乓球时专门进行步法练习。
>
> 情景 2: 听朋友说专卖店有一种打底油，刷在海绵上能提高球速，你想试一试。

第二部分 阅读

文章 1

阅读下面这篇关于乒乓球的文章，讨论文后的思考题。

乒乓球

乒乓球起源于 19 世纪的英国，曾是上层社会晚饭后消遣的一种室内游戏。据传 1860 年或 1870 年间，驻守印度的英国军官发明了这项游戏。士兵们将书摆成一排为网，拿两三本书为拍，连续不断地击打高尔夫球。现代乒乓球运动在两人或四人间进行，比赛时，球员用球拍来回击打和推送一个重量很轻的球。比赛通常在有网隔开的硬质桌面上进行。

乒乓球拍有直板和横板两种。基本技术包括握拍、发接球、推挡球、攻球、削球、弧圈球等。影响乒乓球技术的四大要素是速度、力量、旋转和落点。乒乓球战术包括发球战术、发接球战术、搓攻战术、削中反攻战术等。发球抢攻是我国直板快攻打法的"杀手锏"，是力争主动、先发制人的一种战术。各种类型打法的运动员都普遍采用这种战术抢占上风。发球战术运用的效果主要取决于发球的质量和前三板进攻的能力。

世界乒乓球锦标赛、世界杯和奥运会是乒乓球运动的三大赛事。乒乓球自 1988 年成为奥运会比赛项目，分不同类别的比赛。1988 年至 2004 年，乒乓球比赛分为男子单打、女子单打、男子双打和女子双打。2008 年后，团体赛取代了双打比赛。

思考题：

1. 乒乓球是如何产生的？

2. 你能列举一些打乒乓球的基本技术吗？

3. 2008 年后，奥运会乒乓球比赛包括哪些项目？

文章 2

阅读下面这篇关于国际乒联的文章，讨论文后的思考题。

国际乒联

国际乒乓球联合会，简称国际乒联，是国际乒乓球赛事的管理机构。1926年在德国柏林成立，总部设在瑞士洛桑。现任主席是德国人托马斯·魏克特，2014年上任。现有222个协会会员，分属六个大洲联合会，即欧洲乒联、亚洲乒联、非洲乒联、拉丁美洲乒联、北美洲乒联和大洋洲乒联。中国乒乓球协会，简称中国乒协，于1953年正式加入国际乒联。

世界乒乓球锦标赛，简称世乒赛，是国际乒联承担的主要赛事，也是国际乒联主办的最高水平的世界乒乓球大赛，具有国际影响。世乒赛共设有7个正式比赛项目，每一项目都设有专门奖杯，各项奖杯都是以捐赠者的姓名或国名命名的。

中国当之无愧是国际乒联最具实力的会员，培养出许多世界著名的运动员和教练员，如：国际乒联终身名誉主席徐寅生，中国乒乓球协会主席蔡振华，三届世乒赛冠军张德英，奥运冠军、世乒赛冠军孔令辉，北京奥运会单打冠军马琳和雅典奥运会男双冠军陈玘（与马琳搭档），以及世界冠军王皓和郭跃，等等。

思考题：

1. 国际乒联承担的最重要赛事是什么？
2. 你能向你的同学介绍几位中国著名的乒乓球运动员吗？

第三部分 练习

请完成以下练习。

1. 假设你要去采访一位著名的乒乓球教练。请拟定一个采访提纲。
2. 谈谈你对中国乒乓球运动发展的认识。

第四部分 规则与概念

1. 乒乓球比赛赛区空间应不少于14米长、7米宽、5米高。光源距离地面不得少于 5 米。

2. 发球开始时，球自然地置于不持拍的手掌上，手掌张开，保持静止。

3. 发球时，发球员须用手将球尽力垂直地向上抛起，不得使球旋转，并使球在离开不执拍的手掌之后上升不少于 16 厘米，然后下降；球被击出前不能碰到任何物体。

4. 对方发球或还击后，本方运动员必须击球，使球直接越过或绕过球网装置，或触及球网装置后，再触及对方台区。

5. 一局比赛中，先得 11 分的一方为胜方；10 平后，先多得 2 分的一方为胜方。

6. 通常一场比赛采取三局两胜制或五局三胜制。通过抽签来选择发球权或方位。

7. 运动员经常利用擦汗、系鞋带或其他方式来改变比赛的节奏。

8. 与顶级乒乓球运动员交锋时，又短又低的发球是避免遭到对手抢攻的最安全的策略。

9. 下旋过程中，球拍触球的瞬间拍面后仰且有向下摩擦乒乓球底部的动作，目的是使球速变慢，在球落台后（尽量减少反弹）赢得比分。

10. 正手扣球是选手常用的战术之一。在此过程中，击球力量重、球速快。除了增加上旋外，选手通过手腕发力击球过网可使对手难以判断球的落台位置。

第五部分 拓展阅读

张怡宁

张怡宁，中国乒乓球运动员，被认为是女子乒乓球运动史上最伟大的运动员之一。

从 2003 年至 2009 年，张怡宁在国际乒联几乎一直排名第一，曾获得 4 次奥运冠军，10 次世锦赛冠军和 4 次世界杯冠军，至今仍是女子乒坛的风云人物。

她是 2004 年夏季奥运会女子单打和双打的双料冠军。在 2008 年北京奥运会上，她获得了女子单打和女子团体两枚金牌。在女子单打决赛中，她以 8∶11，13∶11，11∶8，11∶8，11∶3 的比分击败队友王楠，成功卫冕。她经常被评论家称为"大魔王"，表明她在这项运动中的霸主地位。

2009 年 10 月，她步入婚姻殿堂，之后再未参加比赛。2011 年 3 月，张怡宁正式宣布退役。

第 16 课　网球

第一部分　听和说

活动 1

🎧 听下面的对话，然后两人一组将其表演出来。

（麦基网球打得很好，而艾伦是初学者，艾伦正在向麦基请教关于发球的问题。）

A: 麦基，听说你网球打得不错。网球的发球我看不懂，你能给我解释一下吗？

B: 当然可以。发球者站在自己场地中点一边的端线后，把球击到球网对面同自己所处位置成对角线的接发球区。

A: 那么，每场比赛的第一球应该站在哪边发球？

B: 对于每场比赛的第一球，发球者应站在中点的右边发球，第二次打球则在左边，第三次又回到右边，如此交替进行。

A: 我在电视上看网球赛时常听到 "let"，这是什么意思呢？

B: 发球时，球如果擦网，但还是落在正确的发球区内，这样的球就叫 "let"，即擦网球，意思是该发球不算，重新发球。

A: 如果第一次发球就出现 "擦网球" 呢？

B: 如果第一次发球时出现 "擦网球"，那么该发球运动员仍有两次发球机会。

A: 明白了。网球比赛怎么计分呢？我总弄不清楚。

B: 看上去确实让人费解，但实际上还是比较简单的。

A: 但我还是不太明白。

B: 别担心，我好好跟你讲讲清楚。每盘比赛开始时，双方队员都没有分，英文中叫 "love"。一方运动员赢第一球总分计为 15，赢第二球后为 30，第三球后计为 40，如果赢得第四球，且对手没有到 40 的话，那么该运动员就赢得了这盘比赛；如果双方打到 40 平，那么先赢两球的一方获胜。

A: 知道了。谢谢你的讲解！

B: 别客气。

活动 2

👤 两人一组，回答下列问题。

问题 1： 接球员可以站在场地界线以外的地方接发球吗？

问题 2： 发球方在第一次发球后，球拍从他的手中脱落，在球落地前碰到了球网。那么，这算发球失误，还是算发球员失分？

第二部分 阅读

文章 1

阅读下面这篇关于网球的文章，讨论文后的思考题。

网球

网球通常是在两个单打球员或两人组合之间进行的一种运动。球员用网球拍将网球击打过网至对方球场。网球由橡胶制成，表面裹一层毛毡，内部中空。网球比赛的目标是使对手不能有效回球；如果不能将球击回，则不得分，反方得分。

网球起源于 12 世纪法国的一种用手掌击球的庭院游戏，后来才有了球拍。这项运动在法国和英国逐渐流行起来，起先只是贵族们在玩，后来因为贵族们修建了公共球场，渐渐吸引了平民百姓的参与。1869 年，英国军官沃尔特·温菲尔德发明了"司法泰克"运动，这就是现代草地网球的前身。到了 1873 年，温菲尔德开始向大众推销这种运动以及球拍和橡胶球，迅速受到人们的欢迎。现在，网球被称为世界上第二大球类运动。

网球比赛按性别和参赛球员数量划分，主要有男子单打、女子单打和双打比赛。四大满贯比赛是网球运动的顶级赛事，按时间先后顺序每年举行一次，分别是：澳大利亚网球公开赛（硬地球场）、法国网球公开赛（红土球场）、温布尔登网球公开赛（草地球场）、美国网球公开赛（硬地球场）。

思考题:

    1. 你能描述一下网球的起源与发展吗?

    2. 网球运动员是如何得分的?

    3. 四大满贯比赛包括哪些?

文章 2

阅读下面这篇关于世界网球组织的文章,讨论文后的思考题。

世界网球组织

    国际网球联合会成立于 1913 年,是世界上最早的国际网球组织,总部设在伦敦。主要职责是:负责有关网球比赛的一切事务,制定网球规则,推动青少年网球运动的普及与发展,组织戴维斯杯、联合会杯和奥运会网球比赛,指导四大公开赛。

    世界男子职业网球协会成立于 1972 年,它是世界男子职业网球选手的自治机构。其主要任务是协调职业运动员和赛事之间的伙伴关系,负责组织和管理职业选手的积分、排名、奖金的分配,以及制定比赛规则和给予或取消选手的参赛资格。每年负责举办 ATP 世界巡回赛 1000 大师赛。

    国际女子网球协会成立于 1973 年,它是世界女子职业网球选手的自治组织。其主要任务是组织女子职业选手的各种比赛,主要负责 WTA 巡回赛年终总决赛、四大公开赛等 60 多个赛事。其主要职责是代表女子职业球员的利益,保证世界范围内的女子职业球员能够有机会参加比赛,并推动女子网球运动的发展。

思考题:

    1. 国际网球联合会是何时成立的?

    2. 世界男子职业网球协会的职责有哪些?

    3. 国际女子网球协会的职责有哪些?

第三部分　练习

请完成以下练习。

1. 假设你是一名记者，要写一篇关于李娜的文章。想一想，你的文章中会包括哪些信息？

2. 观看一场网球比赛，撰写一篇不少于 250 字的观后感。

第四部分　规则与概念

1. 在常规比赛中，报分时应首先报发球运动员的比分。计分如下：无得分——0；第一分——15；第二分 —— 30；第三分——40；第四分——局比赛结束。

2. 比赛可以采用三盘两胜制，先赢两盘的运动员 / 队赢得这场比赛；或采用五盘三胜制，先赢得三盘的运动员 / 队获胜。

3. 运动员应在每一盘的第一局、第三局和随后的每一个单数局结束后交换场地。在平局决胜局中，运动员应在每 6 分后交换场地。

4. 在准备活动开始前，通过掷币的方式，决定获得挑选场地和比赛的第一局谁作为发球员或接球员的权利。

5. 在开始发球动作前，发球员必须立即双脚站在底线后（即远离球网那一侧）中心标志的假定延长线和边线的假定延长线之内的区域里。

6. 在常规发球局中，每一局的发球员都应当从场地的右半区开始，交替站在同侧场地的两个半区后面发球。发出的球应当越过球网，在接球员回击发球之前落到对角方向的发球区内。

7. 运动员 / 队应当分别相对站于球网两侧。发球员指在开始比赛时发出第一分球的运动员，接发球员指准备回击发球员所发出球的运动员。

8. 如果球触线，则该球被认为是落在以该线作为界线的场地之内。

9. 如果运动员在某一分球的比赛中受到对手故意举动的干扰，那么这名运动员应当赢得该分。

10. 以任何方式与运动员进行交流、提出建议或指示都被认为是指导。

第五部分 拓展阅读

诺瓦克·德约科维奇

诺瓦克·德约科维奇，塞尔维亚职业网球选手，目前在职业网球协会世界男子单打排名第一。他被公认为有史以来最伟大的网球选手之一。截至 2016 年 8 月，德约科维奇的公开赛获胜率为 83%，排名第一。

德约科维奇已经赢得了 12 个大满贯单打冠军，历史排名第四，并以 214 周的比赛总数位居 ATP 排名榜首。他曾六次获得澳网公开赛冠军、三次获得温网冠军、两次获得美网冠军、一次获得法网冠军。2016 年，他首次夺得法网公开赛冠军，成为历史上第八位完成全满贯的网球运动员。

德约科维奇是第一位 ATP 排名世界第一的塞尔维亚选手，也是塞尔维亚第一位获得大满贯冠军的男子选手。他曾获得 2012 年、2015 年、2016 年劳伦斯世界体育奖年度最佳运动员奖、2011 年 BBC 年度海外体育人物等奖项，五次获得国际网联世界冠军，四次获得 ATP 年度最佳球员。

第 17 课 羽毛球

第一部分 听和说

活动 1

🎧 听下面的对话，然后两人一组将其表演出来。

（邓肯十分热爱羽毛球。他正在和教练罗伯特先生谈论羽毛球新规贯彻执行后的一些变化。）

A: 教练，羽毛球比赛的新规则有哪些大的变化呢？

B: 最大的变化是取消了发球得分制。单打比赛规定每局获胜分统一定为 21 分，并超过 2 分为胜，采取三局两胜制，同时增加了 1 分钟的技术暂停。

A: 那么双打比赛又是如何规定的？

B: 和单打比赛一样，不同的是取消了第二发球。

A: 这样比赛的速度是不是加快了？

B: 是的。

A: 是不是也节约了比赛时间？

B: 是的，这样使比赛节奏更加紧凑。

活动 2

👥 两人一组，回答下列问题。

> 问题 1: 在羽毛球单打比赛中，首局获胜一方在第二局比赛中可以率先发球吗？
>
> 问题 2: 在羽毛球单打比赛中，如果双方比分打成 20∶20 平时，率先得到第 21 分的一方是否就算获胜呢？

第二部分 阅读

文章 1

阅读下面这篇关于羽毛球的文章，讨论文后的思考题。

羽毛球

羽毛球是一种用球拍击球过网的运动。非正式羽毛球比赛多在户外进行，如院子里或沙滩上；正式比赛在长方形室内球场上进行。运动员用球拍击打羽毛球，球落在对方界内即可得分。

在球被击过球网前，双方选手只能击球一次。球落地，或裁判、发球裁判或对方球员（在裁判和发球裁判不在场的情况下）因失误叫停比赛，则该球比赛结束。羽毛球为羽毛或塑料（非正式比赛）的抛射体，与其他比赛中的球体的飞行方式有很大不同。特别是羽毛球的拖尾更高使球能更快减速。与其他球拍运动相比，羽毛球飞行的速度相当快。

羽毛球运动从早期的球拍和羽毛球游戏发展而来。丹麦是欧洲的羽毛球强国，但是这一运动在亚洲也广受欢迎，如今中国已经成为世界级的羽毛球大国。羽毛球从 1992 年起被列入奥运会比赛项目，包括男子单打、女子单打、男子双打、女子双打和混双五项比赛。顶级羽毛球比赛需要运动员具备优秀的身体素质：要有耐力、敏捷度、力量、速度和准确度。羽毛球也是一种技术运动，需要运动员有良好的运动协调能力，并不断学习复杂的挥拍动作。

思考题：

1. 羽毛球运动的基本规则是什么？
2. 奥运会羽毛球比赛包括哪些项目？
3. 你认为羽毛球是一项风靡全球的运动吗？为什么？

文章 2

阅读下面这篇关于世界羽联的文章，讨论文后的思考题。

世界羽联

世界羽毛球联合会是羽毛球运动的国际管辖机构，1934 年成立，最初名为国际羽毛球联合会。2006 年在马德里召开的特别会员大会上，国际羽联更名为世界羽毛球联合会（简称世界羽联）。世界羽联下设亚洲羽联、欧洲羽联、泛美羽联、非洲羽联和大洋洲羽联五个地区联合会，现有 176 个协会会员。中国羽毛球协会于 1981 年加入国际羽联。

世界羽联的主要任务是在全世界普及和发展羽毛球运动，加强各国羽毛球协会之间的联系，举办大型国际赛事。世界羽联负责组织羽毛球界的六大赛事：奥运会羽毛球赛、世界男子团体锦标赛（汤姆斯杯）、世界女子团体锦标赛（尤伯杯赛）、世界锦标赛、世界团体锦标赛（苏迪曼杯）和世界青年锦标赛。

思考题：

1. 世界羽毛球联合会在何时成立？
2. 世界羽联举办哪些体育赛事？

第三部分 练习

请完成以下练习。

1. 观看一场国内／外羽毛球比赛，撰写一篇不少于 250 字的观后感。
2. 与你的朋友观看一场羽毛球双打比赛，针对比赛设计一段对话。

第四部分 规则与概念

1. 羽毛球比赛中，发球员的分数为零或双数时，双方运动员均应在各自的右发球区发球或接发球。发球员的分数为单数时，双方运动员均应在各自的左发球区发球或接发球。
2. 球发出后，由发球员和接发球员交替对击直至成"死球"或"违例"。
3. 接发球员违例或因球触及接发球员场区内的地面而导致球成死球，则发球员得一分。随后，原发球员再从另一发球区发球。
4. 发球员违例或因球触及发球员场区内的地面而导致球成死球，发球员即失去发球权。接发球员成为发球员，且双方均不得分。
5. 一局比赛开始，获得发球权的一方应从右发球区发球。只有接发球员才能接发球；如果队友接球或被球触及，则发球方得一分。
6. 自发球被回击后，由发球方的任何一人击球，然后由接发球方的任何一人击球，如此往返直至成死球。

7. 自发球被回击后，运动员可以在己方球场的任何位置击球。

8. 羽毛球发球时，手臂须在肩膀的位置以下，击球过程中双脚不能离地。手臂过肩的发球方式是违规的，球拍必须在发球者的手腕以下。

第五部分 拓展阅读

李玲蔚

李玲蔚，中国羽毛球选手，20世纪80年代的风云人物，女子羽毛球历史上最伟大的选手之一。

作为优秀的全能型球员，李玲蔚的球场覆盖能力和近网攻击给人留下了极其深刻的印象。她在队友、对手，甚至有时在双打搭档韩爱平面前一直保持着整体优势。在20世纪80年代，她们二人占据了国际女子羽毛球的主导地位，分别获得世界羽毛球锦标赛（两年一次）冠军两次，并合力赢得1985年世界羽毛球锦标赛双打冠军；她们还带领中国队赢得两年一度的尤伯杯冠军。

李玲蔚1989年退役，1998年入选羽毛球名人堂。

她从未参加过奥运会，因为羽毛球运动直到1992年才成为奥运会的比赛项目。然而，她依然被选为2008年北京奥运会开幕式上护送会旗的五位退役运动员之一。2012年7月，她当选为国际奥委会委员。国际奥委会主席雅克·罗格授予其"国际奥委会金牌"。

第 18 课 棒球

第一部分 听和说

活动 1

🎧 听下面的对话，然后两人一组将其表演出来。

（乔伊是个棒球迷。今天，他邀请好朋友杰克观看棒球比赛。这是杰克第一次观看棒球比赛，因此乔伊正在向他解释有关棒球的一些问题。）

A: 一支棒球队由几名队员组成？

B: 9 名队员，实际上一个队可以有 20 多名队员，但一次只能有 9 人上场。

A: 了解。那有几名替补队员呢？

B: 替补队员没有数量限制，但是替补队员只能上场一次。

A: 每个队都有一个投手和一个击球手，对吧？他们在场上的位置是怎样的呢？

B: 是的。投手站在投手区的平台上，击球手站在本垒板旁边。

A: 怎样才能跑垒得分？

B: 一名队员跑完全部垒后返回本垒，期间未被投中出局即得分。出局三次双方交换位置。

A: 听起来挺复杂的。

B: 刚开始会觉得复杂，一旦你能看明白了，你会发现棒球比赛相当有趣。

活动 2

👥 两人一组，回答下列问题。

> 问题 1：棒球比赛的基本规则有哪些？
> 问题 2：跑垒得分的可能方式有哪些？

第二部分 阅读

文章 1

阅读下面这篇关于棒球运动的文章，讨论文后的思考题。

棒球运动

棒球比赛在两支球队之间展开，每队 9 人。比赛时，两队轮流进攻（击球和跑垒）和防守（投球和守备）。两队各攻守一次为一局。每场比赛包含九局。一队的投手将球投向另一队的击球手，击球手要努力击中球。如果球没有被击中，那么该球被称为"好球"。如果一位击球手三次击球未中，那么他就会失去回击机会并且被判出局。如果击出去的球被对方球员接住，击球手也会被判出局。但是，如果击出去的球没有被接住，那么击球手要按逆时针方向尽可能跑一个或多个垒。如果击球手把球击出了围栏或者球场，那么他就可以跑四个垒。当一名队员跑完所有的垒返回本垒而未被判出局即得分。

18 世纪中期，英国最早出现了以棒击球的运动，棒球便由此发展而来。这一运动后由移民带入北美洲，现代棒球在此得以发展。到 19 世纪后期，棒球运动已经被公认为美国的"国球"。如今，棒球在北美洲、拉丁美洲、加勒比地区和东亚各地广泛流行。

棒球项目自 1992 年开始出现在奥运赛场上，但是在 2005 年召开的国际奥委会会议上决定棒球不再是 2012 年夏季奥运会的比赛项目。

思考题：

    1. 棒球比赛中每支队伍有几名队员？

    2. 棒球比赛通常共分几局？

    3. 美国的"国球"是什么？为什么？

文章 2

阅读下面这篇关于国际棒球联合会的文章，讨论文后的思考题。

国际棒球联合会

国际棒球联合会，简称国际棒联，成立于 1938 年，曾为国际奥委会正式承认的国际性组织，负责监管、决定、执行棒球运动的相关政策。

国际棒联现为世界棒球垒球联盟下属机构之一，管理世界棒球（垒球）事务。在世界棒球垒球联盟的监管下，国际棒联的主要职责之一是组织、规范、批准棒球的 124 个国家管理机构举办国际比赛，以此决定男女棒球运动的世界冠军，并计算世界排名。在 2013 年世界棒球垒球联盟成立并取代其地位之前，国际棒联是唯一能够将"世界冠军"头衔授予某国棒球代表队的组织。国际棒联办公室设于世界棒球垒球联盟总部瑞士洛桑。国际棒联管辖的主要赛事为奥运会棒球比赛、世界锦标赛、世界杯赛和世界俱乐部杯赛。

2011 年 4 月 1 日，国际棒联与国际垒联宣布，双方将商议合并提案，以争取恢复棒球和垒球在 2020 年夏季奥运会上的比赛资格。2013 年 4 月，国际棒联与国际垒联合并为世界棒球垒球联盟，共同管理两项运动。

思考题：

1. 国际棒联主办的体育赛事都有哪些？
2. 国际棒联的职责有哪些？

第三部分 练习

请完成以下练习。

1. 简述我国棒球运动的发展状况。
2. 观看棒球比赛，撰写一篇 250 字左右的观后感。

第四部分 规则与概念

1. 若发生下列任何一种情况，则跑垒员出局：（1）跑垒员在到达下一个垒之前被封杀；（2）该跑垒员未上垒即被触杀。
2. 犯规球指的是从本垒滚入一垒线内或本垒与三垒线外的被击打球。击球手若击中犯规球则不允许第三次接球和最后击球。
3. 如果犯规球被击打两次后，击球手可继续击球。如果发球犯规的球在落地前被接住，击球手出局。
4. 界内球被击中后，击球手跑入一垒。
5. 防守队的任何选手通过手持的球或者持球的手套触碰未上垒的跑垒员，可以将对方任何跑垒员触杀出局，除非是一垒越垒跑。

6. 内野高飞球指的是被击入空中，外野手在球着地前能够接住的球。

7. 棒球比赛是击球员脚的速度和防守员甩臂的速度之间的较量。

8. 跑垒员不能触垒的时候可能会被触杀或者封杀出局。

第五部分 拓展阅读

杰基·罗宾森

杰克·罗宾森，又称杰基·罗宾森，美国职业棒球手，现代第一位进入职业棒球大联盟的非裔球员。

罗宾森的职业生涯熠熠生辉。1947年获得首届美国职业棒球大联盟最佳新人奖；1949年至1954年连续六次入选全明星赛；1949年夺得全国联赛最具价值球员奖——他是第一位获此殊荣的黑人运动员。他六次参加世界职业棒球大赛，助力道奇队在1955年获得冠军。1962年入选棒球名人堂。1997年，职业棒球大联盟所有球队将杰基的42号球衣退役。从2004年起，大联盟将每年的4月15日定为"杰基·罗宾森日"，那天所有球队的球员都要穿着42号球衣。

罗宾森的个人性格以及毋庸置疑的天赋挑战了人们传统的种族隔离偏见，对美国人的生活产生了很大影响。除了文化影响力外，他还对民权运动做出了伟大贡献。罗宾森也是职业大联盟的第一位黑人电视评论员。在20世纪60年代，他帮助建立了自由国家银行（非裔美国人所有的金融机构，位于纽约哈莱姆）。为了表彰他在球场内外的斐然成就，他死后被授予"国会金质奖章"和"总统自由奖章"。

第 19 课 垄球

第一部分 听和说

活动 1

🎧 听下面的对话，然后两人一组将其表演出来。

（丹喜欢打垄球，而马克喜欢棒球。他们正在讨论垄球与棒球之间的区别。）

A: 我知道垄球在美国很受欢迎。

B: 是的，我们之前就提到过。你还记得垄球和棒球之间的区别吗？

A: 当然了。它们在场地大小、设备和投球方式这三个方面有区别。

B: 记得不错！

A: 谢谢！但有一点补充说明。

B: 哦？

A: 垄球有三大类别：快速投球、慢速投球、变换式投球。

B: 就是这样的！

A: 你平时玩垄球吗？

B: 事实上，我棒球玩得多些。棒球挺有意思的，在中国也很受欢迎。

A: 是的，但是垄球在中国流行度不高，主要原因应该是宣传力度不够。

B: 完全同意。

A: 我们自身也许可以在垄球宣传上出一份力。

B: 嗯，听起来不错。相信孩子们一定会喜欢它，因为它真的很有趣。

活动 2

👤 *两人一组，回答下列问题。*

○ 问题 1：棒球和垒球有哪些区别？
○ 问题 2：你认为打垒球需要哪些设备？

第二部分 阅读

文章 1

阅读下面这篇关于垒球的文章，讨论文后的思考题。

垒球

垒球是棒球的一种变体，它的球更大，场地更小。1887 年在美国芝加哥地区发明了这种室内比赛，在不同时期曾被称为室内棒球、软球、游戏场球、软外滩球、软式棒球和女士棒球（参赛者为女性）。1926 年被命名为垒球。1933年在芝加哥世博会举办的垒球比赛使这项运动受到欢迎。

垒球运动主要包括慢速垒球、快速垒球和变换式垒球三种类型。慢速垒球的球比标准垒球（12 英寸）大；一支队伍有 10 名队员；禁止触击和偷球。快速垒球要求投球迅速；有 9 名球员上场；允许触击和偷球。垒球比赛与棒球比赛的规则有所不同，最主要的区别有两点：（1）垒球比赛必须采取下投球，男子离投球板 46 英尺（14 米），女子离投球板 43 英尺（13.1 米），而棒球比赛为60.5 英尺（18.4 米）；（2）垒球比赛共分 7 局，而棒球比赛则是连续比 9 局。

尽管垒球名字中有 soft "软的"，但它用的球并不很软。垒球内场场地小于棒球内场；每垒到下一垒之间为 60 英尺（18 米）长，而棒球是 90 英尺（27 米）。

思考题：

1. 垒球何时何地被发明？
2. 垒球运动包括哪几种类型？
3. 垒球和棒球的规则有哪些不同？

文章 2

阅读下面这篇关于国际垒球联合会的文章，讨论文后的思考题。

国际垒球联合会

国际垒球联合会，简称国际垒联，是世界棒球垒球联合会（国际奥林匹克委员会和国际单项体育联合会公认的棒球、垒球运动的管理机构）的下属机构。1952 年成立，总部设于美国佛罗里达州。现有 127 个国家管理机构。

2005 年 7 月，国际奥委会在新加坡举行第 117 次会议，投票决定 2012 年夏季奥运会将不举行棒球和垒球比赛。为了争取垒球回到 2020 年奥运会场，2013 年 4 月，国际垒联和国际棒联合并为世界棒球垒球联盟。

通过世界棒球垒球联盟，国际垒球联合会组织开展世界锦标赛，包括男女快速垒球、青年男女快速垒球，女子、男子及混合慢速垒球、男女变换式垒球等。国际垒球联合会还认定区域冠军，并为区域（多运动）比赛提供技术支持。国际垒球联合会为国际竞赛提供官方比赛规则，但不局限于奥运会、世界锦标赛、区域锦标赛、区域赛及其他管辖下的比赛。

思考题：

1. 国际垒球联合会成立于何时？
2. 国际垒球联合会主办哪些运动赛事？
3. 垒球比赛目前是奥运会的比赛项目吗？

第三部分 练习

请完成以下练习。

1. 撰写一篇不少于 250 字的垒球赛事介绍。
2. 观看垒球比赛，撰写一篇评论球员进攻战术的文章。

第四部分 规则与概念

1. 比赛裁判最少 1 个，最多 7 个。司球裁判员不超过 1 个，最多可以有 3 个司垒裁判和 3 个外场裁判。
2. 根据裁判制服颜色，官方裁判通常被称为"蓝色"。司球裁判通常使用一个指示器（有时称为遥控器或计数器）跟踪比赛进程。

3. 决策通常使用手势和口令来表示。"安全"口令，手掌放平，手心向下，双手舞动，并发出口令"安全"。"出局"口令，右手握拳向上举起，并发出口令"出局"。

4. 击球指示由司球裁判发出，手势与"出局"口令一样，同时发出"击球"口令。得分只有口令，没有手势。裁判也可以选择不发口令。

5. 犯规球通过扩展双臂的手势和口令"界外球"来指示，而"界内球"只需指向界内区域，不须做口头指示。接近但没压线的球没有口令给出，而只有手势信号。

6. 裁判所做判决即最终判决。不允许抗议"判决口令"，如得分、击球、犯规等。

7. 垒球比赛可以持续 3—9 局，根据联赛、规则、比赛类型而定。不过 7 局比赛是最常见的。

8. 在一局比赛中，每个球队击球直到三个击球手出局。两队轮流击球。除了某些比赛和冠军赛，在出现平局的情况下，通常会有加时赛，直到分出胜负。

第五部分 拓展阅读

詹妮·林恩·芬奇

詹妮·林恩·芬奇，美国垒球投手、棒球一垒手，曾效力于亚利桑那野猫队、美国国家垒球队和芝加哥匪徒队。

2001 年，芬奇赢得了大学女垒世界职业赛冠军。此后，她带领美国队摘得了 2004 年奥运会金牌和 2008 年奥运会银牌。《时代》杂志曾评选她为史上最伟大的垒球运动员。2010 年芬奇退役，将生活重心转移到家庭上。她留下了完美的个人声誉，同时激励了那些热爱垒球运动的女孩们。

第 20 课 高尔夫球

第一部分 听和说

活动 1

🎧 听下面的对话，然后两人一组将其表演出来。

（帕特里克邀请朋友小李去打迷你高尔夫。但是当小李到了之后，他觉得有些失望，认为这不是真正的高尔夫球场。因此，帕特里克向他解释了什么是迷你高尔夫。）

A: 我们到了！

B: 帕特里克，你确定这真是高尔夫球场？

A: 这不是真正的高尔夫球场，这叫 putt-putt golf，跟游乐场有点像。

B: Putt-putt golf？

A: 就是迷你高尔夫球场。

B: 哦，迷你高尔夫。所以，这不是那种用来比赛的正式高尔夫球场。

A: 要是去那样的球场，我们肯定是最糟糕的球员。现在，握好球杆，准备 Tee off。

B: Tea？喝茶？我不渴呀！

A: 不是 T-E-A，是 T-E-E，是固定高尔夫球的小木桩。Tee off 就是开球。在日常生活中，你要是开始做什么事的话也可以用这个词。比如，昨天我们老板在员工会议上做了一个精彩的开场白。

B: 明白了。准备开球吧！

活动 2

👥 *两人一组，回答下列问题。*

> 问题 1： "golf" 这个词的含义是什么？
>
> 问题 2： 对于高尔夫球的起源，众说纷纭，你怎么看？

第二部分 阅读

文章 1

阅读下面这篇关于高尔夫球的文章，讨论文后的思考题。

高尔夫球

现代高尔夫球起源于 15 世纪的苏格兰，但其古代起源尚不清楚，众说纷纭。关于高尔夫球的文字记录最早出现在 1457 年，当时詹姆斯二世禁止人们进行这一运动，以专心学习箭术。1502 年，詹姆斯四世废除这一法令，因为他自己就是高尔夫爱好者。1860 年 10 月 17 日，在苏格兰埃尔郡普雷斯特威克高尔夫俱乐部举办了公开锦标赛，这是世界上最早的高尔夫比赛，也是第一次高尔夫大赛，苏格兰选手获得了冠军。

高尔夫球运动是一种以棒击球入穴的球类运动，球员在球场上用尽可能少的杆数将球击入洞内。它不需要规则的比赛场地，这在球类运动中并不多见。比赛通常在有 9 个或 18 个球洞的场地上进行，球洞按序排开。场上的每个球洞都要有开球台和果岭区，且每个球洞形状各异，大小不一。

高尔夫球比赛分为比杆赛和比洞赛两种。比杆赛为一一对抗，在数个球洞内取得的总杆数最低者获得优胜。比洞赛为一一对抗或两组对抗，每一洞杆数低者得分，最后根据选手赢得的球洞数决定胜负。大多数高尔夫球赛选用比杆赛规则。

1904 年，高尔夫球第一次进入奥运赛场。时隔 112 年，高尔夫球运动在 2016 年里约奥运会上回归。

思考题:

　　1. 第一次高尔夫比赛于何时在何地举办?

　　2. 高尔夫球比赛有哪些赛制?

文章 2

阅读下面这篇关于高尔夫球组织的文章,讨论文后的思考题。

高尔夫球组织

　　高尔夫球比赛,一般可以被划分成专业比赛和非职业比赛:从级别上,可分为国际比赛、省赛和俱乐部赛;从形式上,可分为公开赛、冠军赛、邀请赛、高尔夫巡回赛和大师赛。

　　影响最大的高尔夫四大赛事也称为四大满贯赛,它们是美国名人赛、美国公开赛、英国公开赛和美巡赛。所有高尔夫运动员都把能够获取高尔夫四大赛事的冠军看作至高无上的荣誉。

　　圣安德鲁斯皇家古老高尔夫俱乐部,简称 R&A,位于苏格兰圣安德鲁斯,名字来源于皇家古典高尔夫俱乐部,专职于制定高尔夫规则、运行公开锦标赛和其他重要赛事,以及推广高尔夫运动。

　　皇家古老高尔夫俱乐部是除美国和墨西哥外的世界高尔夫球主管机构,美国和墨西哥高尔夫由美国高尔夫球协会主管。美国高尔夫球协会成立于1894年,总部位于美国新泽西州远山镇。它是美国和墨西哥高尔夫运动的管理机构,也是一个由高尔夫球员管理并为高尔夫球员服务的非营利性组织。

思考题:

　　1. 最具影响力的高尔夫球赛有哪些?

　　2. 高尔夫球赛的比赛规则由谁制定?

　　3. 美国和墨西哥的高尔夫球运动由哪个机构管理?

第三部分 练习

请完成以下练习。

1. 高尔夫球在 2016 年回归奥运会赛场，对此你怎么看？

2. 搜索一条关于高尔夫球的最新消息，谈谈高尔夫运动在中国发展的前景。

第四部分 规则与概念

1. 在比赛中，高尔夫球员最多可携带 14 支球杆。在一个球洞的比赛过程中，球员不得练习击球。

2. 如果球员在发球区外发球：在比洞赛中，该球员不受处罚，但是其对手可以立即要求他重新击球；而在比杆赛中，该球员被罚 2 杆，并且必须在正确的区域内再打一球。

3. 在球洞区击球时，球员应当确保旗杆已被移走或被照管。即使球在球洞区外，也同样可以移走或照管旗杆。

4. 如果某球员的静止球被球员本人、其同伴或球童以外的任何人移动，该球员不受处罚，但要把球放置回原位。

5. 如果静止球被风吹动，或者因自身原因而移动，球员不受处罚，只要在球现处位置继续击打即可。

6. 如果球员击出的球因本人、其同伴、球童或者装备而变向或停止，该球员被罚 1 杆，然后在球现处位置继续击打。

7. 如果球员击出的球撞到其他静止球而变向或停止，该球员不会受到处罚，只要在该球现处位置继续击打即可。

8. 球员可以移动任何地方的可移动妨碍物（即人造的可移动妨碍物，如沙耙、饮料罐等）而不用受罚。如果球因此而移动，必须把球放回原位，但该球员不受罚。

9. 如果球被击出水障碍区外或者出界后丢失，该球员被罚 1 杆，即在上一杆打球的地方再打一球，也就是"一杆加距离"。

10. 球员有 5 分钟的时间来找球；5 分钟内未能找到该球，该球即为遗失。

第五部分 拓展阅读

泰格・伍兹

艾德瑞克・泰格・伍兹，美国职业高尔夫球运动员，是有史以来最成功的高尔夫球员之一，曾连续数年列为世界上收入最高的运动员之一。

伍兹曾多次打破高尔夫球纪录。他曾 11 次获得 PGA 年度最佳球员，8 次获得拜伦－尼尔森奖平均最低调整杆数奖，并在 10 个不同赛季的奖金榜排名首位。他曾 14 次获得职业高尔夫球锦标赛冠军，该纪录在所有高尔夫球员中居于第二位（第一位是杰克・尼克劳斯，18 次获得该赛冠军），并且获得 79 场美巡赛冠军（仅次于萨姆・斯尼德，赢得 82 场）。

伍兹是完成高尔夫职业生涯大满贯最年轻的球员，在赢得过 50 场巡回锦标赛冠军的球员中，他也是最年轻、用时最短的。此外，他曾 3 次完成职业大满贯（仅次于杰克・尼克劳斯）。自 1999 年开创世界高尔夫球锦标赛以来，伍兹共获得 18 次冠军。

第四章 舞蹈

第21课 体育舞蹈

第一部分 听和说

活动 1

🎧 听下面的对话，然后两人一组将其表演出来。

（丽莎正在练习体育舞蹈中的旋转动作。但是她发现自己转得不稳，速度也不够快。因此，她向教练请教这一问题。）

A: 教练，为什么我转动时总是站不稳？

B: 因为你身体的中心轴没有垂直于地板，你得把背挺直。

A: 我知道了，那我怎样能转得快一些呢？

B: 转动时身体一定要先扭紧，这样才能发上力。

A: 您看这次我做得好些了吗？

B: 好多了，但是如果轴心腿再伸直一些会更好。

A: 啊，我知道了，感觉稳多了。

B: 很好，现在注意头部。转动时方向要清晰，注意力要集中。

A: 谢谢您的帮助，我会更加努力练习的。

活动 2

👥 两人一组，根据以下所给情景设计对话。

情景 1: 解释转圈时如何保持平衡。

情景 2: 拉丁舞决赛马上要开始了，请参赛选手尽快更换服装，准备比赛。

第二部分 阅读

文章 1

阅读下面这篇关于体育舞蹈的文章，讨论文后的思考题。

体育舞蹈

体育舞蹈也称国际标准舞，起源于英国伦敦。1924 年由英国发起，欧美舞蹈界人士在广泛研究传统宫廷舞、交谊舞及拉美国家的各式士风舞的基础上对此进行了规范和完善。1925 年正式规定了华尔兹、探戈、狐步、快步四种舞蹈形式，总称摩登舞。这种舞蹈最先在西欧进行了一些比赛，之后推广到世界各国，受到许多国家的欢迎和喜爱。

体育舞蹈按舞蹈的风格和技术结构分为摩登舞和拉丁舞两大类，十个舞种。摩登舞包括华尔兹、探戈、狐步、快步和维也纳华尔兹，除了探戈外，都起源于欧洲大陆，以端庄、含蓄、稳重、典雅的风格著称。拉丁舞包括桑巴、恰恰、伦巴、斗牛舞和牛仔舞，除斗牛舞外，都起源于拉丁美洲，以热情、奔放、浪漫的风格著称。

体育舞蹈按竞赛项目分为摩登舞、拉丁舞和集体舞三类。集体舞是摩登舞和拉丁舞的混合舞，音乐、舞姿、队形和选手们的和谐配合达到完美统一。每个舞种均有各自的舞曲、舞步及风格。根据各舞种的乐曲和动作要求组编成不同的成套动作。

思考题：

1. 体育舞蹈是如何产生的？
2. 摩登舞包括哪些不同的舞蹈类型？
3. 拉丁舞包括哪些不同的舞蹈类型？

文章 2

阅读下面这篇关于黑池舞蹈节的文章，讨论文后的思考题。

黑池舞蹈节

黑池被称为欧洲的游艺之都、英国的拉斯维加斯。黑池舞蹈节创办于1920年，于每年的 5 月份在英国黑池冬季花园的皇后舞厅举行，历时一个多星期，是英国历史最悠久的舞蹈节。黑池舞蹈节被誉为国际舞的奥运会，是舞者心中的圣殿，更是展现各国国标舞发展水平的重要舞台，是世界上第一个也是最著名的国际性交谊舞比赛。

黑池舞蹈节举办的比赛有：交谊舞大赛、拉丁舞大赛和英国公开锦标赛（包括业余双人赛、职业双人赛、业余团体赛和职业团体赛）。2005 年起增加了英国新星业余交谊舞和拉丁舞大赛。此外，舞蹈节还举办职业团体赛和表演赛两场邀请赛，最吸引观众眼球。一年一次的少年舞蹈节、黑池序列舞舞蹈节（包括英国序列舞锦标赛）和英国国家舞蹈节也在黑池举办。

2004 年，我国的栾江和张茹获得了职业拉丁新星组第一名，取得了亚洲选手参加黑池公开赛以来的最佳成绩。

思考题：

1. 黑池舞蹈节每年于何时在何地举办？
2. 黑池舞蹈节的重要性体现在哪里？
3. 黑池舞蹈节包括哪些比赛？

第三部分 练习

请完成以下练习。

1. 你最喜欢哪种舞蹈风格？谈谈你的看法。
2. 提高舞蹈技能的关键是什么？

第四部分 规则与概念

1. 世界体育舞蹈锦标赛赛事分两类：一类为标准舞，或称摩登舞，包括华尔兹、探戈、维也纳华尔兹、狐步舞和快步舞；一类为拉丁舞，包括桑巴、恰恰、伦巴、斗牛舞和牛仔舞。
2. 表演曲目中至少要包括规定的五支舞蹈中的三支，且其比重要占到整支舞蹈编排的 75%。其他舞蹈元素或者舞蹈形式必须限制在整支舞蹈编排的 25% 以内。
3. 选手必须向组委会提供以下材料：所选音乐 CD 盘的两个备份；所选音乐的

完整、准确的最新曲目列表，包括曲目名称、作曲者、编曲者、出版者以及 CD 或者记录号。

4. 一场比赛最多包括一轮预赛和一轮决赛。选手们在每一轮比赛中必须按照同样的顺序使用相同的音乐表演相同的编排曲目。

5. 每支舞蹈编排中最多允许有三次托举动作。每次托举持续时间不得超过 15 秒。

6. 舞蹈表演中不允许使用任何小道具。

7. 世界体育舞蹈联合会的服装规则适用于其管辖的所有比赛。双人比赛服装可以表现或者提示舞蹈编排或表演的主题，但是必须是拉丁舞或摩登舞风格的。

8. 选手们的表演顺序应由裁判长或裁判长批准的人进行抽签决定。所有选手或者其代表必须出席抽签仪式。

第五部分 拓展阅读

汉娜·卡汀娜

汉娜·卡汀娜，芬兰职业拉丁舞蹈家。她从孩童时期起便热爱舞蹈，曾学习芭蕾舞。

作为专业的拉丁舞者，她与保罗·基利一起代表英国赢得了英国公开赛冠军、国际冠军、世界系列赛冠军、世界大师赛冠军，四次获得英国国家舞蹈大赛冠军。除此之外，他们还一起获得了主要职业比赛的亚军，如世界锦标赛和欧洲锦标赛。在 2002 年英国公开赛上，他们在五种舞种中的两项——伦巴和斗牛舞比赛都名列前茅，距离冠军之位仅一步之遥。

第22课 体育舞蹈欣赏

第一部分 摩登舞

华尔兹：华尔兹的风格特点是庄重典雅，华丽多彩。舞蹈时男伴似王子气宇轩昂，女伴似公主温文尔雅，雍容大方。其动作流畅起伏，婉转多变；舞姿飘逸优美，文静柔和，动作如流水般顺畅，像云霞般光辉。潇洒自如、典雅大方，如波浪起伏接连不断地潇洒旋转，享有"舞中皇后"的美称。跳舞时舞者做圆形运动，身体流畅地小幅度旋转，舞步优雅迷人。舞曲为 3/4 节拍；每小节有 1、2、3 拍，第一拍为重音，第二、三拍为弱音；速度为每分钟 28—30 小节。

探戈：探戈舞步独树一帜，风格动静交织、潇洒豪放，斜行横进，步步为营，俗称"蟹行猫步"。探戈动作刚劲锐利，棱角分明，动静快慢，错落有致，沉稳中见奔放，闪烁中显顿挫。舞曲为 2/4 节拍，每分钟 30—34 小节。舞步分 S（慢步）和 Q（快步），其中 S 占一拍，Q 占半拍。探戈音乐柔和，气氛肃穆，振奋精神。

狐步舞：狐步舞的风格特点是舞步轻柔、多变。在动作衔接中呈现出降中有升、升中有降的线行流动状。前进时，脚步与地面轻轻地摩擦移动，后退时不能将鞋跟重重地在地板上做拖曳。舞步不能间断，要连续流畅，且富于变化。连续进退上身采用反身动作位置，反身不能过大。前进或后退时要始终用上半身的力量引导。狐步舞音乐节奏为 4/4 拍，每分钟约 30 小节，有快有慢，快占一拍，慢占两拍。

快步舞：快步舞的风格特点是轻快活泼，富于激情。舞步自由，饱含力量和表现力。快步舞节奏为 4/4 拍，每分钟 50—52 小节，音乐欢快，节奏感强。基本节奏为慢快快慢、慢慢快快。升降形态通常为：第一步结尾时开始上升，二、三步继续上升，第四步保持上升，结尾下降。不同的舞步有不同的升降方式，但是升降大都是依狐步舞的形式，也有的舞步是依华尔兹的升降形式，因此要掌握好升降的运用和各种舞蹈技巧。

维也纳华尔兹：维也纳华尔兹的风格特点是舒展大方，旋律动人，动作优美，舞步轻快流畅，旋转性强。基本动作是左右快速旋转步，完成反身、倾斜、摆荡、升降等动作。舞步平稳轻快，翩跹回旋，热烈奔放。舞姿高雅庄重。舞曲节奏轻松明快，为 3/4 拍节奏，每分钟 56—60 小节；每小节为三拍，第一拍为重拍，第四拍为次重拍。基本步伐是六拍走六步，两小节为一循环，第一小节为一次起伏。

第二部分 拉丁舞

桑巴：动作粗犷，起伏强烈，舞步奔放、敏捷，富于强烈的感染力。音乐节奏为 2/4 拍，每分钟 48—56 小节。

恰恰舞：音乐有趣，动作诙谐花俏。恰恰舞编排不要求男女舞者动作一致，多半是男子随后；步法利落紧凑。它的舞步源于爵士，有强大的生命力、爆发力、感染力。音乐节奏为 4/4 拍，速度为每分钟 29—32 小节，其节奏为 1、2、3、4 和 1，每一拍的 1、2、3 各走一步，第四拍两步。因此，恰恰舞每小节由 5 步构成。

伦巴舞：音乐缠绵浪漫，舞态柔美。古巴人习惯头顶东西行走，以胯步向两侧的扭动来调节步伐，保持身体平衡。伦巴的舞步秉承了这一特点。原始的舞蹈风格融进现代的情调，动作上表现为髋部富有魅力地扭摆，上体自由舒展，能充分展示女性婀娜多姿的美态。舞姿缠绵妩媚，浪漫优美，以表达情侣之间的爱情这一主题。配上缠绵委婉的音乐，使舞蹈充满浪漫情调。音乐节奏为 4/4 拍，每分钟 27 小节左右。第一拍为重拍，基本舞步为 4 拍走 3 步。

斗牛舞：舞姿挺拔，无胯部动作及过分膝盖屈伸，用踝关节和脚掌平踏地面完成舞步。动静鲜明，力度感强，发力迅速，收步敏捷顿挫。舞蹈风格阳刚味十足。音乐雄壮威武，为旋律高昂雄壮、鲜明有力的西班牙进行曲。音乐节奏为 2/4 拍，每分钟 60—62 小节。基本舞步为一拍一步，八拍一循环。

牛仔舞：风格特点是音乐热烈，舞态豪放。舞步敏捷、跳跃，舞姿轻松、热情、欢快。基本舞步包括踏步、并合步、跳跃、旋转等，要求脚掌踏地，腰和胯部做钟摆式摆动，保持美国西部牛仔刚健、浪漫、豪爽的气派。音乐旋律欢快，强烈跳跃，节奏为 4/4 拍，第二拍为重拍。每分钟 42—44 小节，六拍跳八步。

第23课 民间舞

第一部分 听和说

活动 1

🎧 听下面的对话，然后两人一组将其表演出来。

（皮特正在上舞蹈课，其中有一些舞蹈术语他不太明白，因此便向老师请教。）

A: 老师，我不明白舞台方位是什么意思，您能给我讲讲吗?

B: 好的。舞台方位是指舞蹈的八个方位，即 1—8 点，是规范舞者面向和走向的专业术语。

A: 哦，那 1—8 点是指什么呢?

B: 场地正前为第一方位，即"1 点"；右前、右旁、右后为第二、三、四方位，即"2、3、4 点"；正后为第五方位，即"5 点"；左后、左旁、左前为第六、七、八方位，即"6、7、8 点"。

A: 明白了。但我还有一个问题，怎么区分"面向"和"视向"呢?

B: 面向是指身体正面所朝的方向，视向指视线。比如"眼看 8 点"，即脸和视线均朝向 8 点。

A: 谢谢您。还有一个问题，"留头"和"甩头"的区别是什么呢?

B: "留头"指身体开始转动而头仍留向原方位不动；"甩头"指头从一方位迅速转向另一方位，是亮相时的常用动作。

A: 知道了，谢谢老师。

活动 2

👤 两人一组，回答下列问题。

> 问题 1: 中国民间舞蹈的一个显著特点是舞蹈与歌唱的紧密结合。你如何理解?
>
> 问题 2: 古典舞包含哪些舞蹈类型?

第二部分 阅读

文章 1

阅读下面这篇关于民间舞的文章，讨论文后的思考题。

民间舞

民间舞产生并流传于民间，受民俗文化制约，即兴表演但风格相对稳定，以自娱为主要功能。由于受生存环境、风俗习惯、生活方式、民族性格、文化传统、宗教信仰等因素影响，以及受表演者的年龄性别等生理条件所限，不同地区、国家的民间舞蹈在表演技巧和风格上有着显著差异。民间舞具有朴实无华、形式多样、内容丰富、形象生动等特点，是古典舞、宫廷舞和专业舞蹈创作不可或缺的素材来源。

我国幅员辽阔、人口众多、历史悠久、文化遗产丰富，在人文、地貌、语言、习俗、文化、宗教信仰等方面都独具特色。中国民族众多，不同的民族因生产方式和宗教文化等方面的差异，形成了内容、形式、韵律、风格各显异彩、斑斓夺目的民间舞蹈，大体可分为祭祀（宗教）性舞蹈、娱乐性舞蹈、礼仪舞蹈、历史（劳动）舞蹈等，对促进我国舞蹈事业的发展产生了重要影响。

思考题：

1. 什么是民间舞？
2. 民间舞有哪些特点？
3. 中国的民间舞有哪些种类？

文章 2

阅读下面这篇关于桃李杯、荷花奖和 CCTV 电视舞蹈大赛的文章，讨论文后的思考题。

桃李杯、荷花奖和 CCTV 电视舞蹈大赛

"桃李杯"舞蹈比赛是国内规格最高的青少年舞蹈大赛，是中国文化艺术政府奖（即专业艺术"文华奖"）的子类奖项文化艺术院校奖的重要奖项之一。1985 年由北京舞蹈学院发起，每三年举行一届，有"中国舞蹈奥斯卡"的美誉。

"荷花奖"舞蹈大赛是 1996 年经批准的全国性专业舞蹈评奖活动。原则上

每两年举办一次，芭蕾比赛每三年举办一次。

　　"CCTV电视舞蹈大赛"是面向全国专业团体和广大舞蹈爱好者的舞蹈大赛，由中国中央电视台主办，遵循"公平、公正、公开"的宗旨和充分鼓励群众参与的原则，每两年举办一次。作为唯一的全国性电视舞蹈大赛，以其权威性、丰富性而闻名。凭借其舞蹈的电视化呈现优势获得了很多舞蹈演员和编导的青睐，在舞蹈界和观众中颇受好评。

思考题：

　　1. 什么是"桃李杯"舞蹈比赛？

　　2. 什么是"荷花奖"舞蹈大赛？

　　3. 什么是"CCTV电视舞蹈大赛"？

第三部分 练习

请完成以下练习。

1.　观看一场民族舞表演，试着学习一些舞蹈动作。

2.　钢管舞利用钢管为支撑进行攀爬、旋转、倒立等舞蹈动作，是世界十大民间舞蹈之一。请谈谈钢管舞的健身和娱乐价值。

第四部分 规则与概念

1.　舞蹈比赛主要以舞蹈的编排、整齐度、动作的表现、参赛服装的搭配、音乐的选用为评分标准。

2.　评分细则一般包括六个方面。

3.　舞蹈编排应合理、连贯、完整、有创意。

4.　表演者对舞曲音乐应理解准确，舞蹈动作应吻合音乐旋律，轻松流畅，有节奏感和表现力，技巧性强。

5.　舞蹈表演应具有时代感，抒发健康情怀，能够展示风采。

6.　服装造型应符合舞蹈表演形式。

7.　表演者应精神饱满、台风端正，表现出良好的艺术气质。

8.　表演者应与观众互动，活跃气氛，如遇突发情况需处理得当。

9. 舞蹈评分总分 10 分。最终得分精确到 0.01 分，去掉最高分和最低分后，计平均分。

10. 民间舞在很大程度上受到传统文化的制约，源起的时代显现了大众舞蹈和高雅舞蹈之间的差异。

第五部分 拓展阅读

杨丽萍

杨丽萍，导演、编导，歌舞剧《云南印象》主演，在中国的演出可谓座无虚席。2004 年至 2008 年间，杨丽萍导演和编导了大型舞蹈"三部曲"——《云南印象》《香格里拉的回声》《西藏神话》。2004 年，《云南印象》获全国"荷花奖"五大奖项，包括舞蹈金奖、最佳编导和最佳女演员。为了创作具有异域风情的歌曲，编排《云南印象》恢宏壮观的舞蹈，杨丽萍前往云南 26 个少数民族部落的边远村庄，历时数年，挑选了 60 多个具有音乐和舞蹈天赋的农民，从他们身上吸取灵感，创作了这场视听盛宴。

第 24 课 民族民间舞欣赏

第一部分　藏族舞蹈

　　藏族人民主要居住在西藏、青海、甘肃、四川、云南等地。藏族民间舞蹈由农牧文化与宗教文化融合而成，种类极其丰富，分为自娱性舞蹈和宗教舞蹈，两大类舞蹈都有各自丰富的文化内涵、优美而潇洒的翻跹舞姿和独具特色的舞蹈风格及形式。

　　表演形式：藏族自娱性舞蹈分为"谐"和"卓"两大类，主要表演形式是热巴、踢踏舞、勒谐、堆谐、果谐、弦子、锅庄等。

　　风格特点：在膝部上分别有连续不断的、小而快的、有弹性的颤动，或连绵柔韧的屈伸，呈现出速度、力度和幅度的不同。步伐上形成的重心移动，带动了松弛的上肢运动。节奏由慢至快、由小至大、由轻至重，不断变化。

　　代表作品：最具代表性的是锅庄，舞时男女分站、拉手或搭肩，轮流唱歌或共舞，不时加入呼号。锅庄是古代人们围篝火、锅台而舞的圆圈形自娱性歌舞，其中包括"拟兽"和其他表示爱情的词汇。俗称"跳神"舞蹈的羌姆，则属于宗教舞蹈类别中最为重要的寺院祭祀性舞蹈。

第二部分　蒙古族舞蹈

　　蒙古族主要聚居于我国北方，从事游牧和狩猎劳动，由此创造了灿烂的草原文化。蒙古族民间舞蹈是草原文化中特有的一枝奇葩。

　　表演形式：动作多以抖肩、翻腕来表现蒙古族姑娘开朗热情的性格。男子的舞姿造型挺拔豪迈，步伐轻捷洒脱，表现出蒙古族男性剽悍英武、刚劲有力之美。

　　风格特点：节奏明快，音乐热情，歌词新颖，风格独特。

　　代表作品：筷子舞、马刀舞、驯马舞、盅碗舞、挤奶员舞、鹰舞等。筷子舞自娱性很强，由坐式表演，逐步发展为边蹲、边站、边走、边巧妙自如地击打自己的身体来表演，视觉形式变化多样，从而真切地抒发了牧民热爱生活、乐观积极的性格和感情。

第三部分　维吾尔族舞蹈

新疆维吾尔族地区素有"歌舞之乡"的美誉，历史上"丝绸之路"带来商业贸易和农业的繁荣，使新疆歌舞呈现出独特的传统和风格。

表演形式：现流传于新疆各地的民间舞蹈形式主要有：赛乃姆、多朗舞、萨玛舞、夏地亚纳、纳孜尔库姆、盘子舞、手鼓舞以及其他表演性舞蹈。

风格特点：身体各部位的动作同眼神配合以传情达意，从头、肩、腰、臂到脚趾都有动作。昂首、挺胸、直腰是基本的体态特征。通过动、静的结合和大、小动作的对比以及移颈、翻腕等装饰性动作的点缀，形成热情、豪放、稳重、细腻的风格韵味。

代表作品：手鼓舞《摘葡萄》、歌舞《喀什赛乃姆》、大型舞蹈《多朗麦西来甫》《拉克》《鼓舞》《天山女工》等。

第 25 课 现代舞

第一部分 听和说

活动 1

🎧 听下面的对话，然后两人一组将其表演出来。

（吉姆刚开始学习现代舞，对于现代舞的分类，他还有很多不明白的地方。因此，他正向老师请教。）

A: 老师，我想了解一下现代舞都有哪些类型呢？

B: 现代舞种类很多。按舞蹈特征来划分，一般分为专业舞蹈、国际标准交谊舞和时尚舞蹈三大类。

A: 那么，专业舞蹈指哪些舞蹈呢？

B: 专业舞蹈包括古典舞、民族舞、民间舞、现代舞、踢踏舞和爵士舞。

A: 知道了。那国际标准交谊舞呢？

B: 国际标准舞，也可叫国标舞，包括拉丁舞，像伦巴、桑巴、恰恰、斗牛舞和牛仔舞，还有摩登舞，像华尔兹、维也纳华尔兹、探戈、快步和狐步舞。

A: 时尚舞蹈又是指的哪些舞蹈呢？

B: 时尚舞蹈一般指的是迪斯科、锐舞、街舞、芭啦芭啦、啦啦队舞和热舞。

A: 哇！没想到竟然有这么多种！我知道了，谢谢老师。

B: 不客气！

活动 2

👤 两人一组，回答下列问题。

> 问题 1: 现代舞的与众不同之处在于"没有既定规则，每一个艺术家都在创造自己的法则。"谈谈你对这句话的认识。
>
> 问题 2: 金星，中国现代舞第一人，杰出的现代舞舞蹈家，获得过无数荣誉。你知道她的著名作品有哪些吗？

第二部分 阅读

文章 1

阅读下面这篇关于现代舞的文章，讨论文后的思考题。

现代舞

现代舞，19 世纪末 20 世纪初在德国和美国最先兴起，又称"当代舞蹈""新兴舞蹈""现代派舞蹈"。现代舞是一种与古典芭蕾相对立的舞蹈派别。它摆脱了古典芭蕾的程式和束缚，打破了既定的舞步和芭蕾的叙事性结构，以自然的舞蹈动作自由地表现思想情感和生活理念，反映了现代西方社会的矛盾和人们的心理特征。

近百年来，随着邓肯、拉班、丹尼斯、肖恩、韩芙莉、格莱姆、坎宁汉等几代人的探索实践，现代舞已发展成为遍布全球的世界性舞蹈艺术。

中国现代舞的崛起依托着广阔的文化背景，从中国国情出发，表现着新时代的风貌、时代意识和人民大众的思想情感。

思考题：

1. 现代舞兴起于何时何地？
2. 现代舞和古典芭蕾的区别是什么？
3. 现代舞的特点有哪些？

文章 2

阅读下面这篇关于美国现代舞先驱的文章，讨论文后的思考题。

美国现代舞先驱

泰德·肖恩是美国著名的男性现代舞先驱之一。除了与前妻露丝·圣·丹尼斯一起创立丹尼肖恩舞蹈学校外，他还建立了著名的男子舞蹈学校——泰德·肖恩与他的男性舞者。男性舞蹈的创新思想使得肖恩成为当时最具影响力的编舞和舞蹈家。此外，他还创建了马萨诸塞州的"雅格布之枕舞蹈节"。

1915 年，露丝·圣·丹尼斯和泰德·肖恩在加利福尼亚洛杉矶建立丹尼肖恩舞蹈学校，帮助舞者们完善舞蹈技能。该校的著名学生包括：玛莎·格莱姆、多丽斯·韩芙丽、莉莲·鲍威尔、查尔斯·韦德曼、杰克·科尔，以及无声电影明星露易丝·布鲁克斯。这所学校对芭蕾和现代舞蹈的发展影响巨大。

由于丹尼斯和肖恩的婚姻问题和财政困难，丹尼肖恩舞蹈学校于 1929 年关闭。因此，肖恩从其执教的马萨诸塞州春田学院挑选运动员为学生，建立了一所男性舞蹈学校。主要任务是为美国男性舞者的地位而斗争，从男性角度解读舞蹈这一艺术形式。

思考题：

1. 美国现代舞先驱是谁？
2. 你知道丹尼肖恩舞蹈学校有哪些著名校友？
3. 肖恩建立男性舞蹈学校的目的是什么？

第三部分 练习

请完成以下练习。

1. 以大学生练习现代舞为素材，撰写一篇 250 字左右的短文。
2. 谈谈中国现代舞的发展。

第四部分 规则与概念

1. 现代舞主要包括黑人舞、韩国舞、迪厅舞等类型。
2. 从表演形式上来看，现代舞有霹雳舞、机械舞、锁舞、爵士舞等。
3. 霹雳舞：手脚触地，着重个人的独特性及力量的表现，为最早的嘻哈舞种。
4. 机械舞：模仿机器人的动作和形态，注重肌肉的张弛及收缩，加以关节的撞击。
5. 锁舞：最初称为 Campbellocking，带有明显的街舞风格。锁舞依赖快速的手脚运动，搭配比较放松的臀部和腿部运动。舞者以微笑或高举双手击掌来与观众互动。
6. 爵士舞：源于欧洲的古典芭蕾舞，具体分为以下三类：街头爵士舞、现代爵士舞和流行爵士舞。
7. 街头爵士舞，混合了嘻哈元素，在流行音乐中十分常见。现代爵士舞，糅合了芭蕾舞及现代舞的特色，富有艺术性，极具技巧性，舞者随柔和的音乐舒展身体。流行爵士舞，以流行曲作引，讲求力量与形态相结合，舞步多变，较具商业性，以舞台表演为主要目的。

8. House 舞：起源于 19 世纪 80 年代，糅合了非洲土著舞、拉丁舞和欧洲踢踏舞而成。该舞蹈特色体现在脚部快速而流畅地踏踢，讲究身体的律动。

第五部分 拓展阅读

金星

金星，中国芭蕾舞女演员、现代舞蹈家、编导、演员，一手创建了当代舞团"上海金星舞蹈团"。金星是中国第一个得到政府认可做了变性手术的女人，她也是为数不多的几个变性人中第一个被中国政府正式承认的。

金星十分热爱舞蹈表演。9 岁时，她加入了中国人民解放军，接受舞蹈和军事训练。1987 年，金星赴纽约学习了四年的现代舞，后游学欧洲。1991 年至 1993 年期间，金星在罗马教舞蹈，随后进行了世界巡演，并在 26 岁时返回中国。1996 年，她进行了变性手术。手术后，她的左腿瘫痪了一段时间。恢复健康后，她到了上海，从事舞蹈编排并教授学生。

武术及其他传统体育项目

第 26 课 中国武术

第一部分 听和说

活动 1

🎧 听下面的对话，然后两人一组将其表演出来。

（约翰是个武术迷。他正向教练请教关于武术的问题。）

A: 教练，您好，向您请教个问题，可以吗？

B: 当然可以，请说。

A: 我想知道武术比赛都有哪些项目？

B: 主要项目包括刀、枪、剑、棍、徒手、对练和集体项目。

A: 嗯，那徒手项目有哪些？

B: 有长拳、南拳、太极拳，等等。

A: 我知道了。太极拳挺有意思的，您可以教我吗？

B: 当然可以。

A: 太谢谢您了！

活动 2

👥 两人一组，回答下列问题。

> 问题 1: 你学过太极拳吗？你是如何理解武术中的搏斗及武德的？
>
> 问题 2: 一运动员在武术训练时左腿受伤，摔倒在地，现在不能活动。
>   应如何处理？

第二部分 阅读

文章 1

阅读下面这篇关于中国武术的文章，讨论文后的思考题。

中国武术

中国武术，或称中国功夫，是在中国几千年历史长河中发展起来的成百上千种武术风格的总称。这些武术风格按共同特征可分为"家""派""门"。武术是以技击动作为主要内容，以套路和搏斗为运动形式，注重内外兼修的中国传统体育项目。

中国武术内容丰富，分类方式很多。如传统的分类方法中，有以是否"主搏于人"而分为内家与外家；有按山川、地域分为少林、武当、峨眉等门派；此外，还有"南拳北腿"之说。目前依领域不同，还可将武术分为竞技武术、学校武术、民间传统武术和军事武术等。

中国武术最大的特点是：既有相击形式的搏斗运动，也有舞练形式的套路运动。在武术动作中，一般都具有攻防含义和技击内容，如踢、打、摔、拿、劈、刺等动作，各具有不同的特点和技击方法。

"冬练三九，夏练三伏。"练武不仅能培养人们坚忍不拔的意志，也是修身养性的良好手段。"未曾学艺先学礼，未曾习武先习德"，通过练拳习德，可以培养青少年尊师重道、讲理守信、见义勇为、不恃强凌弱等良好品质。

思考题：

1. 中国武术的主要内容和运动形式是什么？
2. 中国武术的分类形式有哪些？
3. 中国武术最显著的特点是什么？

文章 2

阅读下面这篇关于国际武联的文章，讨论文后的思考题。

国际武联

国际武术联合会，简称国际武联，成立于 1990 年 10 月 3 日，总部设在中国北京。国际武联的正式工作语言为中文和英文。目前共有来自五大洲的 146

个协会成员。国际武术联合会下设执行委员会、技术委员会、传统武术委员会、医务委员会、营销和发展委员会。历任主席是李梦华、伍绍祖、李志坚，现任主席是于再清。

1985年8月，中国武协在中国西安举办了第一届国际武术邀请赛，并成立了国际武术联合会筹备委员会。1994年10月22日，在摩纳哥举行的国际单项体育联合会第28届代表大会上，国际武联被接纳为该组织的正式成员。1999年6月20日，在韩国首尔召开的国际奥委会第109次全会上，国际武联通过国际奥委会的决议而得到承认。2001年10月10日，国际武联与世界反兴奋剂机构签订协议。

国际武联管辖及举办的主要比赛有：世界武术锦标赛（两年一届）、世界青年武术锦标赛（两年一届）、世界传统武术锦标赛暨世界传统武术节（两年一届）、世界杯武术散打比赛（两年一届）、世界太极拳健康大会（两年一届）等。

思考题：

1. 国际武术联合会成立于何时何地？
2. 国际武联负责举办哪些赛事？

第三部分 练习

请完成以下练习。

1. 翻译下列武术术语：手形中的掌、拳、勾；拳法中的冲拳、贯拳、上钩拳；腿法中的弹、踹、扫腿；以及步形、步法、平衡、跳跃、跌扑翻滚。

2. 如何理解下列武术谚语："文以评心，武以观德"；"师父领进门，修行在个人"；"冬练三九，夏练三伏"；"内练一口气，外练筋骨皮"；"坐如钟，立如松，行如风，卧如弓"。

第四部分 规则与概念

1. 武术竞赛项目包括长拳、南拳、太极拳、剑术、刀术、枪术、棍术、太极剑、南刀、南棍等。

2. 对练分为徒手对练、兵械类对练、徒手和兵械类对练，以及团体对练。

3. 参赛运动员根据竞赛规则和规程要求选择难度和必选动作。

4. 比赛分为个人赛、团体赛、个人及团体赛。

5. 套路完成时间：成年不少于 1 分 20 秒；青少年（含儿童）不得少于 1 分 10 秒。

6. 个人项目比赛场地 14 米长、8 米宽，四周设定 2 米宽的安全区域。

7. 裁判人员由一名总裁判长和一到两名副总裁判长组成。

8. 裁判长从运动员的应得分中减去"裁判长的扣分"，加上创新动作的加分，即为运动员最后得分。

第五部分 拓展阅读

李小龙

李小龙，美籍华人，武术大师，动作电影演员，武术教练，哲学家，电影制片人及截拳道的创始人。李小龙被评论家、批评家、媒体等公认为有史以来最有影响力的武术家之一，是 20 世纪的流行文化偶像，还被赞誉为"改变了亚洲人在美国电影中的形象"。

李小龙于 1940 年 11 月 27 日在旧金山的唐人街出生，后在香港九龙长大。在身为粤剧明星的父亲的引导下，李小龙进入电影行业，以童星身份出演了几部电影。18 岁时，李小龙前往美国接受高等教育。也正是在这期间，他开始了武术教练生涯。李小龙修习咏春拳，后将多种武术精髓融入自己的武术哲学精神，自创"截拳道"。

李小龙参与制作的香港和好莱坞电影大大提高了香港传统武打片的知名度和认可度，也掀起了 20 世纪 70 年代西方学习中国武术的浪潮。他指导的电影改变和影响了美国及世界其他地区的武术和武打电影。李小龙参演的五部著名的电影有《唐山大兄》（1971，导演罗维）、《精武门》（1972，导演罗维）、《猛龙过江》（1972，李小龙自编自导）、《龙争虎斗》（1973，导演高洛斯）和《死亡游戏》（1978，导演高洛斯）。

第 27 课 武术散打

第一部分 听和说

活动 1

🎧 听下面的对话，然后两人一组将其表演出来。

（约翰在散打课上肌肉拉伤了。现在他正跟医生讨论受伤情况。）

A: 您好，医生！

B: 你好，有什么可以帮你的吗？

A: 我的大腿内侧这些天一直疼，我想可能是受伤了。

B: 请坐下，不要动。你是怎么受伤的？

A: 可能是散打课上下竖叉的时候受伤的。

B: 我先给你拍个 CT，看看骨头有没有问题。

（拍完 CT 后）

B: 骨头没有问题，那就是肌肉的问题了。我觉得是你下叉过度，导致肌肉拉伤了。

A: 哦，原来是这样。

B: 回去涂一些红药水，接下来的几天要减少运动量。

A: 好的，谢谢医生。

活动 2

👥 两人一组，根据以下所给情景设计对话。

> 情景 1: 在散打训练时，一个学员的腿拉伤了，现在不能过量运动。
>
> 情景 2: 你这些天一直头晕发烧，于是决定去看医生。

第二部分 阅读

文章 1

阅读下面这篇关于武术散打的文章，讨论文后的思考题。

武术散打

　　散打，又称中国拳术、中国散打，是一种防御型武打项目，由中国军队习练传统功夫和现代武打技巧的基础上发展而来。散打将拳击（包括近距离快速连续出拳和踢腿）与摔跤、摔倒、扔掷、扫腿、踢拿等结合起来，在一些比赛中还会采用肘和膝盖攻击。

　　散打是中华武术的精华，是具有独特民族风格的体育项目，演化至今已成为华夏民族灿烂文化遗产中的瑰宝。据历史记载，中国武术徒手搏击早在一千多年前就传到日本，当时称"唐手"，后来改称"空手"。现在，散打是一种中国武术格斗项目，是在规则条件限制下，两人运用武术中的踢、打、摔和防守等技巧，进行徒手对抗。

　　1979 年，散打在我国正式成为竞技比赛项目。2000 年，首届中国武术散打王争霸赛在湖南长沙举行。这是中国武术散打发展史上的里程碑，中国武术散打自此进入了专业赛制时期。如今有许多国家的武术爱好者不仅喜爱中国套路技术，而且喜欢散打运动。通过国际的武艺交流，中国散打运动走向了世界。

思考题：

　　1. 什么是散打？
　　2. 散打技巧有哪些？

文章 2

阅读下面这篇关于世界自由搏击协会的文章，讨论文后的思考题。

世界自由搏击协会

　　世界自由搏击协会是世界上最早的、最大的职业和业余自由搏击组织，其正式名称是"世界自由搏击和空手道协会"。

　　世界自由搏击协会前身是世界空手道协会，1976 年由霍华德·汉森（空手道黑带）在美国创立。总部位于意大利马萨卡拉拉。1991 年霍华德·汉森将协会出售给戴尔·佛洛伊德。1994 年，保尔·英格卡姆接手该组织。自 2012 年 9 月 29 日起，世界自由搏击协会有了新的管理团队——米歇尔任新主席。

此协会是第一个应用独立控制评级表、第一个成立女子冠军赛、第一个吸收亚洲国家的非营利机构，是职业空手道的主要认可机构之一。早期的世界自由搏击协会明星包括"喷气机"本尼·尤奎德兹、唐"龙"·威尔逊、凯文·科斯特纳和葛拉席·贾西雅等。

世界自由搏击协会在欧洲、亚洲、大洋洲、非洲和北美洲都颇受欢迎。

思考题：

1. 世界自由搏击协会成立于何时？
2. 你能列举一些世界自由搏击协会的明星吗？

第三部分 练习

请完成以下练习。

1. 撰写一篇描述我国散打发展现状的新闻稿，字数不少于 250 字。
2. 对于跆拳道在少儿群体间广泛流行这一现象，谈谈你的观点。

第四部分 规则与概念

1. 散打比赛允许使用踢、打、摔等各种武术流派中的攻防技法。
2. 散打比赛不允许使用擒拿，不许攻击后脑、颈部、裆部等要害部位。
3. 散打比赛得分有效部位有头部、躯干和大腿。
4. 侵人犯规包括在口令"开始"前或喊"停"后进攻对手、击中对手禁击部位或以禁用方法击中对手。
5. 技术犯规包括消极搂抱对方，背向对方逃跑，处于不利状况时举手要求暂停，有意拖延比赛时间，上场不戴或有意吐落护齿、松脱护具，比赛中对裁判员有不礼貌的行为或不服从裁判。
6. 运动员故意伤人，将被取消比赛资格，所有成绩无效。
7. 运动员使用违禁药物或局间休息时输氧，将被取消比赛资格，所有成绩无效。
8. 一方被重击（侵人犯规除外）倒地不起达 10 秒，或虽能站立但知觉失常，则另一方为本局胜方。

第五部分 拓展阅读

柳海龙

柳海龙，中国散打搏击选手。在 2000 年首届武术散打王争霸赛上，柳海龙取得 75 公斤级冠军，一举成名。他不仅赢得了在散打界的重量级地位，还战胜了实力更强的对手，取得更具有挑战性的夜间公开循环赛的胜利，被称为散打"王中之王"。凭借自身独特的实力和魅力，柳海龙已然成为中国最知名的散打运动员。

2003 年，柳海龙在第一届"超级散打"推广赛中对战散打王苑玉宝，并成功战胜他，赢得"超级散打王"的称号。在 2003 年澳门散打世锦赛上，柳海龙在非职业赛中打败了萨利霍夫，夺得 80 公斤级金牌。2005 年受伤后，柳海龙暂时退役。2009 年，他重回赛场，打败日本选手伊贺弘治。

第 28 课 民间武术

第一部分 听和说

活动 1

🎧 听下面的对话，然后两人一组将其表演出来。

（约翰正在和彼得谈论太极拳。）

A: 你学过武术吗？

B: 不算学过。一个朋友曾经教过我一点儿太极拳。

A: 真的吗？我想看看你的太极拳练得如何？也许我能给你提些建议。

B: 没问题，但是你能把要领再跟我说一下吗？

A: 当然！练太极拳要抬头挺胸，不要翘臀，移动的时候要脚后跟先着地。

B: 看来你太极拳打得不错啊。有时间我跟你好好学学，怎么样？

A: 当然可以，下次我介绍我的老师给你认识。我们互相学习，共同进步。

B: 太棒了，真是太感谢你了！

A: 不客气！

活动 2

👥 两人一组，回答下列问题。

> 问题 1：练习太极拳前要做哪些准备活动，其目的是什么？
>
> 问题 2：练习太极拳时为什么要抬头挺胸？

第二部分 阅读

文章 1

阅读下面这篇关于太极拳的文章，讨论文后的思考题。

太极拳

太极拳是中国武术的一大分支，其字面意思是"最强的拳头"。

关于太极拳的起源说法众多。传说宋朝智者张三丰看到麻雀和草蛇打架后创立了太极拳，但是大部分人认为现代太极拳起源于陈氏太极拳。陈氏太极拳起源于 19 世纪清朝道光年间。

有着道家哲学渊源的太极拳运用内力，或者说"气"，遵循"以柔克刚"的原则，属于内家功法。道家是中国最古老的哲学，著名的阴阳符号是道家思想的体现。阴阳表示不断循环运转的"气"所产生的正和负两极，阴阳相互作用、相辅相成，构成万事万物。

现代最著名的太极拳有陈氏、杨氏、武氏、孙氏和吴氏，这五种太极拳都从陈氏太极拳发展而来。据历史记载，太极拳由陈家沟（现在河南境内）陈王廷所创立。在陈氏太极拳的基础上，清朝河北人杨露禅创立了如今世界最流行的杨氏太极拳。武氏太极拳是在陈氏和杨氏太极拳基础上由武禹襄创立。孙氏太极拳则是在陈氏和武氏太极拳基础上由孙禄堂结合著名的内家武术八卦、形意和太极拳而创立。吴氏太极拳是在陈氏和杨氏太极拳基础上由吴鉴泉创立。

如今，人们所说的太极拳大多是指杨氏太极拳。杨氏太极拳在世界上广泛传播，有数百万计的习练者。

思考题：

1. 你知道关于太极拳起源的传说吗？

2. 太极拳包含什么哲学思想？

3. 现代太极拳有哪些流派？

文章 2

阅读下面这篇关于河北武术协会的文章，讨论文后的思考题。

河北武术协会

　　河北武术协会是河北武术的群众组织，是河北省体育局领导下的具有法人资格的团体。协会的最高权力机构是代表大会，每五年一届。协会下设执委会、秘书处、技术委员会、教练委员会、裁判员委员会、宣传委员会、市场开发委员会。各市区设有武术协会分会。

　　河北武术协会的主要任务是：积极宣传和开展武术活动，努力推进《全民健身计划纲要》的实施，促进河北省武术事业的发展；根据国家体育总局和河北省体育行政主管部门的规定，负责协调组织举办全省、全国及国际性比赛；研究制定竞赛制度、计划和规程。

思考题：

　　1. 河北武术协会的最高机构是什么？

　　2. 河北武术协会下设哪些机构？

　　3. 河北武术协会的职责是什么？

第三部分 练习

请完成以下练习。

1. 对于如何弘扬传统武术，提出你的看法与建议。

2. 你认为在大学生中推广太极拳运动这个想法怎么样？

第四部分 规则与概念

1. 抱拳礼在中国武术界得到广泛认同，现在是武术比赛的必行礼。

2. 参赛运动员持棍、枪行礼时，要右手握器械，左掌护右拳。

3. 所有参赛队员要遵守竞赛规则，发扬武术道德风尚，尊重裁判员和竞赛工作人员。

4. 太极拳比赛结束前 30 秒会给出有声提示。

5. 太极拳等级分的评分分为三档九级，其中：8.50 分—10.00 分为优秀；7.00

分—8.49 分为良好；5.00 分—6.99 分为尚可。

6. 太极拳比赛中因忘记套路动作而重新表演将从最后得分中扣除 0.5 分。

7. 因灯光、电脑评分系统故障等不可控原因打断比赛，不扣分。

8. 运动员比赛时裁判组用两块秒表计时。当运动员违反时间规定，同时两块秒表所计时间又不相同时，以较接近规定时间的秒表所计时间为准。

9. 中国传统武术的服装最好是棉或丝质的装饰有盘扣的中式制服。

10. 咏春拳选手在各式表演中必须展现出很好的体力和耐力，任何疲倦迹象都会减分。

第五部分 拓展阅读

孙禄堂

孙禄堂，中国著名内家武学大家，孙氏太极拳创始人。精通新儒家和道家思想，曾发表多部著作，对内家武术理论的发展做出了巨大贡献。

他早年精研形意拳和八卦掌，造诣极高，无人能及。后师从郝为真修习吴（郝）氏太极拳。虽然开始时间较晚，但在形意拳和八卦掌上的成就使他在太极拳修习上有颇高悟性，功力斐然。

随后，受杨兆熊、杨澄甫等人之邀，孙禄堂前往北京体育研习所教授太极拳。从 1914 年至 1928 年，执教 14 年，这段时期正是现代杨氏、吴氏、孙氏太极拳发展的重要时期。

第 **29** 课 舞龙舞狮

第一部分 听和说

活动 1

🎧 听下面的对话，然后两人一组将其表演出来。

（约翰想要学习舞龙和舞狮，但又觉得太难而想要放弃。张老师正在鼓励他不要放弃。）

A: 老师，能占用您点时间吗？

B: 有什么问题，请说！

A: 我对舞龙舞狮运动非常感兴趣，就是学起来好难呀！

B: 别着急！舞龙舞狮运动是中华民族的传统文化，想要学会可不是一天两天的事。

A: 哦，但我真是很喜欢，很想快点学会。

B: 嗯，耐心点，别着急。要学习舞龙舞狮千万不能忽视体能训练。

A: 我知道啦，谢谢您！

B: 不客气！相信你很快就能学会的，期待你早日加入学校舞龙舞狮队。

活动 2

👥 两人一组，回答下列问题。

> 问题 1：你对舞龙舞狮运动中的"龙"与"狮"的印象是怎样的？
>
> 问题 2：你能阐述一下舞龙舞狮运动的技巧与基本训练方法吗？

第二部分 阅读

文章 1

阅读下面这篇关于舞龙和舞狮的文章，讨论文后的思考题。

舞龙和舞狮

中国是龙狮运动的发源地。舞龙舞狮自问世以来，一直深受各族人民的喜爱，历代不衰。经过了几千年的繁荣发展，这一运动已经成为弥足珍贵的文化遗产。舞龙舞狮一般在春节、庙会、联欢或庆典时表演。

舞龙的主要道具"龙"是用草、竹、布等扎制而成。龙的尺寸大小不一，节数以单数为吉利，常见九节龙、十一节龙、十三节龙，多者可达二十九节。十五节以上的龙比较笨重，不宜舞动，主要是用来观赏。有一种"火龙"，内燃蜡烛或油灯，夜间表演十分壮观。舞龙的动作千变万化，九节以内的侧重于花样技巧，较常见的动作有：蛟龙漫游、龙头钻档子、头尾齐钻、龙摆尾和蛇蜕皮等。十一节、十三节的龙，侧重于动作表演。例如，金龙追逐宝珠，时而飞腾入空，时而破浪入海；再配合龙珠及鼓乐衬托，成为一种集武术、鼓乐、戏曲与龙艺于一身的艺术样式。

舞狮的习俗起源于三国时期，南北朝时开始流行，至今已有一千多年的历史。狮子外形威武，动作刚劲，神态多变。民间有许多不同的传说，一时变作神话，一时拉上历史，为舞狮增添了不少神秘色彩。人们相信狮子是祥瑞之兽，舞狮能够带来好运。舞狮如今分为南狮和北狮两大类。北狮流行于长江以北各地，南狮则流行于长江以南。南北狮在风格，如外形、舞步、动作以及锣鼓钹的节奏等方面大有不同。

思考题：

1. 舞龙的道具"龙"是由什么制成的？
2. 舞龙动作有哪些？
3. 你知道舞狮有什么寓意吗？

文章 2

阅读下面这篇关于国际龙狮运动联合会的文章，讨论文后的思考题。

国际龙狮运动联合会

国际龙狮运动联合会于 1995 年 1 月 23 日在香港正式注册成立，其前身是国际龙狮总会。1997 年 7 月，国际龙狮运动联合会执委会秘书处迁至北京。国际龙狮运动联合会有权管辖世界范围内的龙狮竞赛，负责裁判教练培训、龙狮技术推广等活动。

中国龙狮运动协会于 1995 年成立，由各省、自治区、直辖市和行业龙狮运动协会组成，是自愿结成、非营利性、具有独立法人资格的全国群众性体育社会团体，是全国体育总会的团体会员。协会是代表中国加入国际龙狮运动联合会并参加国际龙狮活动的唯一合法组织。

思考题:

1. 国际龙狮运动联合会成立于何时？
2. 你知道中国龙狮运动协会吗？

第三部分 练习

请完成以下练习。

1. 观看舞龙舞狮比赛，撰写一篇不少于 250 字的解说词。
2. 你认为"南狮"和"北狮"的最大区别体现在哪些方面？

第四部分 规则与概念

1. 舞龙项目分四类，包括规定套路、自选套路、传统套路和技能舞龙。
2. 动作难度依次递增，分 A、B、C 三级。不同难度对应不同的量化分值。
3. 舞龙比赛在边长 20 米的正方形平整场地上举行（在特殊情况下，最小边长不得少于 18 米）。场地边线宽 5 厘米，边线内为比赛场地。边线周围至少有 1 米宽的无障碍物区。
4. 在竞赛委员会的监督下，赛前由各运动队派代表抽签决定比赛顺序。对于未参加抽签的队伍，由组委会的工作人员代替抽签。

5. 比赛时，运动员应穿具有特色的服装。要求穿戴整洁，服饰的款式与色彩需与舞龙舞狮的器材相协调。

6. 舞龙舞狮中的音乐伴奏是烘托气氛、转换节奏、激励情绪不可分割的重要部分。音乐旋律、节奏快慢等要与舞龙舞狮的动作协调一致。

7. 当裁判员评分出现明显不合理现象或有效分之间出现不允许的差数时，裁判长有权召集裁判员进行会商，或出示基准分进行调整。

8. 每队的参赛队员在比赛期间不得更换，违者取消比赛成绩。

9. 任何参赛人员不得在比赛期间对裁判人员施加影响和干扰。

10. 舞龙舞狮坚持反兴奋剂的原则，禁止使用兴奋剂。

第五部分 拓展阅读

世界龙狮锦标赛

　　世界龙狮锦标赛，每两年举办一次，由国际龙狮运动联合会会员（会友）派队参赛，必要时也可特邀非会员（会友）参赛。项目为舞龙和舞狮。

　　世界龙狮锦标赛的申办条件：交纳申办费用 1000 美元；免费提供各参赛队规定人数在规定日期内在比赛当地的食宿与交通；免费提供执委会及代表大会官员及会员（会友）代表在比赛当地的食宿、交通及会务准备；有责任通过本国（地区）政府新闻媒介对赛事及相关会议进行转播和报道；申办获胜者在交纳申办费用后享有本届比赛的广告经营权（包括电视转播）及国际龙狮运动联合会会徽标志产品的开发权等。

　　申办时间：世界龙狮锦标赛的申办必须在下一次执委会召开前一年提出。世界龙狮锦标赛的举办者在比赛结束后三个月内必须将完整的总结及相关组织、宣传资料送至国际龙狮运动联合会备案。